BONES ON THE BEACH

MAFIA, MURDER, AND THE
TRUE STORY OF AN UNDER-
COVER COP WHO WENT UNDER
THE COVERS WITH A WISEGUY

PETER DAVIDSON

BERKLEY BOOKS, NEW YORK

THE BERKLEY PUBLISHING GROUP
Published by the Penguin Group
Penguin Group (USA) Inc.
375 Hudson Street, New York, New York 10014, USA
Penguin Group (Canada), 90 Eglinton Avenue East, Suite 700, Toronto, Ontario M4P 2Y3, Canada
(a division of Pearson Penguin Canada Inc.)
Penguin Books Ltd., 80 Strand, London WC2R 0RL, England
Penguin Group Ireland, 25 St. Stephen's Green, Dublin 2, Ireland (a division of Penguin Books Ltd.)
Penguin Group (Australia), 250 Camberwell Road, Camberwell, Victoria 3124, Australia
(a division of Pearson Australia Group Pty. Ltd.)
Penguin Books India Pvt. Ltd., 11 Community Centre, Panchsheel Park, New Delhi—110 017, India
Penguin Group (NZ), 67 Apollo Drive, Rosedale, North Shore 0632, New Zealand
(a division of Pearson New Zealand Ltd.)
Penguin Books (South Africa) (Pty.) Ltd., 24 Sturdee Avenue, Rosebank, Johannesburg 2196,
South Africa

Penguin Books Ltd., Registered Offices: 80 Strand, London WC2R 0RL, England

The publisher does not have any control over and does not assume any responsibility for author or
third-party websites or their content.

BONES ON THE BEACH

A Berkley Book / published by arrangement with the author

PRINTING HISTORY
Berkley mass-market edition / June 2010

Copyright © 2010 by Peter Davidson.
Cover photos: "Skulls" © by Robert Harding Travel/Photolibrary; "Miami" © by Terry Why/
Photolibrary.
Cover design by MNStudios.
Interior text design by Laura K. Corless.

ISBN: 978-0-425-23512-6

BERKLEY®
Berkley Books are published by The Berkley Publishing Group,
a division of Penguin Group (USA) Inc.,
375 Hudson Street, New York, New York 10014.
BERKLEY® is a registered trademark of Penguin Group (USA) Inc.
The "B" design is a trademark of Penguin Group (USA) Inc.

PRINTED IN THE UNITED STATES OF AMERICA

10 9 8 7 6 5 4 3 2 1

Most Berkley Books are available at special quantity discounts for bulk purchases for sales,
promotions, premiums, fund-raising, or educational use. Special books, or book excerpts, can also
be created to fit specific needs.

For details, write: Special Markets, The Berkley Publishing Group, 375 Hudson Street, New York,
New York 10014.

Praise for the true crime reporting of Peter Davidson

HOMICIDE MIAMI

"A first-rate true crime book necessarily requires two elements—a powerful and intriguing story, and a writer who can capture its soul. *Homicide Miami* has both. I highly recommend this story of murder and greed at their worst."

—Vincent Bugliosi, bestselling author of
Helter Skelter and *Reclaiming History*

"Torture-murder for sex has, unfortunately, become yesterday's news. It is what serial killers are all about. Torture-murder for money is rare. This is what gives Peter Davidson's new book its punch. The two main characters in this sordid drama of predatory psychopaths are the embodiment of what we mean by 'evil.' Lugo and especially Dorbal are poster children for the death penalty. But they are as fantastical for stupidity as they are for depravity. First a bungled murder, then a bungled theft, and a bungled dismemberment, foiled when a woman's hair jams the killers' electric saw . . . Davidson said his book is not for the squeamish. True. But once you start it you can't put it down."

—Dr. Michael H. Stone, Professor of Clinical Psychiatry:
Columbia College of Physicians and Surgeons,
host of *Most Evil* on Investigation Discovery

MURDER AT HOLY CROSS

"Fans of true crime, with strong mental constitutions, will find this to be a treasure."　　　　　　—*Huntress Review*

Berkley titles by Peter Davidson

DEATH BY CANNIBAL
MURDER AT HOLY CROSS
HOMICIDE MIAMI
BONES ON THE BEACH

For Terry Feisthammel,
father, husband, and crime fighter,
1957–1999

MAIN CHARACTERS

THE VICTIMS

FRANK ABBANDANDO JR.—Gunned down on December 22, 1995, in North Miami.

VINCENT D'ANGOLA—Murdered by the Mob, October 1995.

JOHN DAVIDSON—Associated with Neil Napolitano, missing since December 1994.

ANIELLO (NEIL) NAPOLITANO—Presumed murdered by the Mob, he disappeared on September 13, 1995. His body parts were found fourteen days later.

JOHN PORCARO—Gambino crime family nonmember associate, missing since June 1998.

ALVINO REYES—Associated with Neil Napolitano, missing since December 1994.

MARK RIZZUTO—Murdered by the Mob, October 1995.

JAMI SCHNEIDER—Murdered by the Mob, October 1995.

JEANETTE ANNE SMITH—Murdered by the Mob, March 1999.

THE CRIME FIGHTERS

JEROME "JERRY" BROWN—Detective, North Miami Police Department.

MARK DEFUSCO—Organized crime detective, Miami Beach Police Department.

TERRENCE "TERRY" FEISTHAMMEL—FBI Special Agent in Miami assigned to the Organized Crime Squad.

GEORGE GABRIEL—FBI Special Agent assigned to gather evidence on John Gotti.

BARBARA GENTILE—Metro-Dade Police sergeant, Organized Crime Bureau.

JOSEPH GROSS—Metro-Dade Police officer assigned to Internal Affairs.

HOWE GROVER—FBI Special Agent in Miami assigned to the Organized Crime Squad.

FRANK ILARAZZA—Homicide detective, Broward Sheriff's Office.

MICHAEL LEVEROCK—FBI Special Agent in Miami assigned to the Organized Crime Squad.

MARK LINER—Metro-Dade Police organized crime detective.

JOSEPH MACMAHON—Metro-Dade Police detective, an expert on Italian organized crime.

TOMMY MORAN—Organized crime detective, Miami Beach Police Department.

GARY PORTERFIELD—Metro-Dade Police organized crime detective.

GARY SCHIAFFO—Homicide detective, Miami Beach Police Department.

BOBBY TRUJILLO—Metro-Dade Police narcotics detective.

CYNTHIA TRUNCALE—Metro-Dade Police sergeant assigned to Internal Affairs.

JULIO VARGAS—Metro-Dade Police officer, husband of Roslyn Vargas.

ROSLYN "ROZ" VARGAS—Metro-Dade Police detective who went undercover to gather evidence against the Mob.

THE MEDICAL EXAMINERS

DR. LISA FLANNAGAN—Broward County.

DR. SAM GUILINO—Miami-Dade County.

DR. BRUCE HYMA—Miami-Dade County.

DR. RICHARD SOUVIRON—Miami-Dade County.

THE CRIMINALS

FRANK ABBANDANDO JR.—Gambino crime family gangster.

ANTHONY RAYMOND BANKS—Associate of Frederick J. Massaro.

PAUL "BIG PAULIE" CASTELLANO—Gambino crime family boss until December 16, 1985.

JULIUS BRUCE CHIUSANO—Associate of Frederick J. Massaro.

JOSEPH "JOJO" COROZZO—A Gambino capo.

NICHOLAS "THE LITTLE GUY" COROZZO—Gambino capo who succeeded John Gotti as boss of the Gambinos.

NEIL DELLACROCE—Paul Castellano's underboss and mentor to John Gotti.

CARLO GAMBINO—Boss of the Gambino crime family from 1967 to 1976.

CARLOS GARCIA—Associate of Frederick J. Massaro.

JOHN GOTTI—Gambino crime family boss who succeeded Paul Castellano.

SALVATORE "SAMMY THE BULL" GRAVANO—John Gotti's underboss.

ARIEL ARMANDO HERNANDEZ—Associate of Frederick J. Massaro.

LOUIS MAIONE—Gambino crime family nonmember associate.

FREDERICK J. "TEN PERCENT FREDDIE" MASSARO—Gambino crime family nonmember associate.

CHARLES PATRICK MONICO—Associate of Frederick J. Massaro.

ANIELLO "NEIL" NAPOLITANO—Aspiring mobster suspected of drug trafficking and loan-sharking.

ROCCO NAPOLITANO—Younger brother of Neil Napolitano.

JOHN PORCARO—Gambino crime family nonmember associate.

ANTHONY "FAT ANDY" RUGGIANO—Gambino crime family captain.

FRANCIS RUGGIERO—Associate of Gambino nonmember associate Frederick J. Massaro.

ADAM SILVERMAN—Associate of Frederick J. Massaro.

JOE STRACCI—Career criminal, associate of Neil Napolitano, police informant.

ANTHONY "TONY PEP" TRENTACOSTA—Gambino crime family capo.

THE PROSECUTORS

MARY CAGLE—Assistant State Attorney, Miami-Dade County.

LAWRENCE LAVECCHIO—Assistant U.S. Attorney, Southern District of Florida.

FLORA SEFF—Assistant State Attorney, Miami-Dade County.

JEFFREY SLOMAN—Assistant U.S. Attorney, Southern District of Florida.

MICHAEL VON ZAMFT—Assistant State Attorney, Miami-Dade County.

THE DEFENSE ATTORNEYS

FRED HADDAD—Represented Frederick J. Massaro.

DOUGLAS HARTMAN—Represented Roslyn Vargas.

JOEL KAPLAN—Represented Roslyn Vargas.

STEVEN H. ROSEN—Represented Anthony Trentacosta.

JEFFREY D. WEINKLE—Represented Ariel Hernandez.

THE JUDGES

RONALD DRESNICK—Florida Circuit Court Judge who presided at the trial of Roslyn Vargas.

PAUL C. HUCK—U.S. District Court Judge who presided at the trial of Trentacosta, Massaro, and Hernandez.

SIGNIFICANT OTHERS

VELMA BYRNE—Mother of Neil and Rocco Napolitano and of Monica Byrne-Henry.

MONICA BYRNE-HENRY—Older sister of Neil and Rocco Napolitano.

GLEN CORBITT—Orlando store clerk who testified at the Vargas trial.

JOE DEFURIA—Friend of Neil Napolitano who testified at the Vargas trial.

REYNALDO GISPERT—Foster brother of Neil and Rocco Napolitano.

JEFFREY KAMLET—Miami Beach medical doctor, witness at the Vargas and Trentacosta trials.

MILDRED RIVERA—Mother of Roslyn "Roz" Vargas.

CARMEN SANCHEZ—Longtime girlfriend of Neil Napolitano.

JOANN WALTER—Bartender, confidant of Neil Napolitano, witness at Vargas trial.

INTRODUCTION

MIAMI BEACH
September 27, 1995

After two days of torrential rain and dark skies, early morning beachgoers were out in force, assured by the weatherman of a mostly blue-sky day with temperatures near ninety. The mercury had already passed eighty at seven o'clock when the cleaning crew from the Parks Department hit the beach to remove debris, mostly seaweed and driftwood that the rough seas had left on the sand. Dressed in shorts and wearing safari hats for protection from the blazing South Florida sun, the crew was busily cleaning the wide strip of pristine Miami Beach at 42nd Street when one of them made a gruesome discovery near the water's edge—bones. They appeared to be leg bones. Human leg bones. The beach cleaner alerted his supervisor, who immediately notified the Miami Beach Police Department. A uniformed cop in short pants was on the scene within minutes. He verified the grisly find and radioed the detective bureau.

September 27, 1995, would prove to be a very busy Wednesday for lawmen, and a disturbing one for swimmers.

Bones would be found at two more locations along this celebrated stretch of Miami Beach. South Florida's early evening newscasts reported the ghastly finds, just as they had reported the death of a tourist in the waters off Miami Beach the previous Sunday. The tourist, a law student from Washington, D.C., was piloting a WaveRunner through the aquamarine waters off South Beach when it collided with a boat carrying singing star Gloria Estefan and her husband, Emilio, who was reportedly at the helm of their family's twin-engine motorboat at about 4 P.M. The Estefans were not hurt, and the Florida Marine Patrol would clear them of any responsibility for the tragedy, finding that the tourist had been jumping waves at the time of the collision and did not see the Estefans' boat.

As for the bones on the beach, newscasters reported what the medical examiner's office revealed: they had not been in the water very long, and a preliminary examination found no indications of a deliberate dismemberment or a shark attack. While the medical examiner's staff continued studying the remains, lawmen went to work to find out whose bones they were and how they came to be washed up on the beach. The investigation would lead lawmen to a brutal band of criminals responsible for murders and mayhem in Miami, and to one of their own, a vivacious woman detective who went undercover but wound up under the covers with the wiseguy she had been assigned to investigate.

This is a true story of mobsters and murders. Love and lust. Loyalty and betrayal. And how bones that washed up from the sea one sunny September day led to the demise of the Gambino crime family in South Florida.

1

A DAY AT THE BEACH

Detective Gary Schiaffo had just reported for work when the report of bones on the beach came in to Miami Beach police headquarters. He sped to the scene. By the time the veteran detective arrived, other uniformed cops had responded, too, and they had the bones cordoned off with yellow crime scene tape.

To Schiaffo's experienced eye, the remains—what appeared to be a right leg from the pelvic bone to the ankle, with tissue attached to the knee and hip areas—did look to be human, but that determination would have to be made by a pathologist from the medical examiner's office. As a small crowd looked on, a police photographer snapped photos of the bones from every angle, while an investigator from the crime scene unit drew a detailed diagram.

As he waited for the medical examiner to arrive, Schiaffo made small talk with the cops and eyeballed the crowd of civilian onlookers who gathered to watch the lawmen process the scene. He recalls spotting football legend Jimmy

Johnson, then the former head coach of the University of
Miami football team, among the curious bystanders.

"Hey Jimmy, could this be one of your players?" the
detective shouted.

"No way," Coach Johnson shouted back.

Minutes later Dr. Bruce Hyma, the county's associate
medical examiner, was on the scene. The forensic pathologist knelt down to examine the remains.

"Definitely human, part of a right leg," the medic
announced, looking up at Schiaffo. The bones were collected and taken to the medical examiner's office.

Four hours later and three miles to the south, Officer
Kevin Graham was patrolling the beach when he learned
that a swimmer had encountered a pair of blue jeans floating just offshore with what appeared to be a thigh inside
the left pants leg. Aware of the earlier find to the north,
Graham asked a lifeguard to swim out to retrieve the drift-
ing denims.

Back on shore, the cop carefully examined the pants.
They were size thirty-four and bore an Italian designer
label—Sergio Tacchini—and a small flag of Italy on the
right front pocket. The loops held a black leather belt with
a metal buckle. Inside the left pants leg was what looked
like a human thigh. There was hair on it—light in color,
indicating that the deceased would have had blond, light
brown, or reddish hair. A few hours later, a beachgoer
made yet another grisly find, this time at the water's edge
behind the famed Fontainebleau Hotel at 45th Street—a
collar bone and a left shoulder with chunks of pale flesh
still attached.

Lawmen would have still another batch of human
remains to retrieve that day. At a few minutes past six, a
lower jawbone with five teeth washed up behind a high-
rise condominium on Collins Avenue at 54th Street. The
teeth were in excellent shape—no fillings or caps. It didn't
take long for the county's medical examiner to conclude

that all the body parts that rolled in with the tide that day belonged to the same person. Dr. Hyma informed Schiaffo that the bones appeared to be those of an adult white male in his midtwenties to early thirties, five feet ten to six feet two inches tall, with a thirty-four-inch waist. He weighed between one hundred and sixty and two hundred pounds. Schiaffo's first goal at the outset of the investigation was to determine whose remains they were.

———————

A twenty-five-year veteran of the Miami Beach Police Department, the Bronx-born lawman was named the county's Officer of the Year in 1991 for leading the investigation into the Baby Lollipops murder case the year before. In that sad case, a toddler's emaciated and battered body was found behind a hedge. The little boy was nicknamed Baby Lollipops because of the design on his pajamas, and Schiaffo led a massive, monthlong investigation to identify the child and bring his killer to justice.

As he had done in the Baby Lollipops case, Gary Schiaffo sent out a statewide bulletin requesting any missing-person report that matched the medical examiner's description, and he culled through dozens of missing-persons reports from around South Florida. After eliminating all the females, black and Asian males, and everyone over age forty, he was left with two possible victims—a thirty-eight-year-old who was missing from a boat off Delray Beach and a twenty-five-year-old who had been missing for three days, was last seen wearing blue jeans, and was known to go swimming while drunk.

The detective was about to phone relatives of the missing men to request dental records when he was interrupted by a call from another Miami Beach detective, Tommy Moran, a twenty-seven-year veteran who was assigned to the department's organized crime unit. The two lawmen were very close, "closer than brothers," Schiaffo says. Moran became a Miami Beach cop in 1970, after a hitch in the U.S. Navy, while Schiaffo joined the force two years later. They became partners in 1975, and they rode together for many years. Their partnership continued after they both became detectives. In 1987, they were named Officers of the Year.

In addition to working as a Miami Beach cop, Tommy Moran was a celebrity, known around South Florida as the "Doo-Wop Cop" for his appearances with 1950s rock-and-roll groups. An Irish tenor with twinkling blue eyes, he grew up singing on street corners in the Bronx. In 1988 he used his accumulated vacation time to tour with rock-and-roll legend Dion DiMucci, of Dion and the Belmonts, singing backup at Radio City Music Hall in New York and other venues from Georgia to California. In the weeks leading up to his debut as a Belmont, Moran practiced for his appearance while he and Schiaffo prowled the streets of Miami Beach looking for bad guys, singing his backup parts to "The Wanderer," "Runaround Sue," and other Dion and the Belmont hits. "I never heard an entire song, only the high backups," Detective Schiaffo remembered. But Tommy Moran was not calling to serenade his former partner. Instead, he was calling about the bones on the beach.

"Did you know that Neil Napolitano is missing?" Moran asked, adding that he had gotten a tip from an FBI agent that Napolitano had not been seen since September 13. Schiaffo quickly thumbed through the missing-persons files and replied that he had no report on Neil.

Neil Napolitano was no stranger to South Florida lawmen, especially those in Miami Beach. They were interested in his activities long before he'd gone missing. As a teen he had been a Police Explorer, but before he turned twenty, he was earning his living as a criminal—arrested in 1991 for possession of cocaine and placed on probation for two and one-half years; two more arrests, for loitering and obstructing a police officer, resulted in fines.

The lawmen suspected the handsome and brawny twenty-four-year-old of trafficking in steroids and of being an associate of a Mafia crew that was involved in loan-sharking, extortion, counterfeiting, drug dealing, and other criminal enterprises. Moreover, he was the prime suspect in the unsolved disappearance of two men who went missing the year before. The men had been arrested for receiving a shipment of illegal steroids. Under questioning, they pointed the finger at Napolitano, naming him as the man for whom they worked.

On Friday, September 29, Gary Schiaffo took a phone call from Neil's younger brother, Rocco. Only eleven months apart, the brothers were very close, and Rocco was frantic, convinced that something dreadful had happened to his older brother. Neil, Rocco said, would never go away without telling him or their mother where he was going.

"He felt that the remains could very well be his brother's," Schiaffo remembered.

When the detective mentioned that the jeans bore the Sergio Tachinni label, Rocco became distraught. He told Schiaffo that his brother had recently been in Orlando, where "he bought a lot of Sergio Tachinni items."

"Are you sure about this?" the lawman asked.

"Yes," Rocco replied.

Schiaffo put in a call to cops in the central Florida city to ask if they knew of a store in their area that sold Sergio Tachinni clothing. He was told they would check and get back to him, which they did about an hour later, advising the Miami Beach detective that the Sergio Tachinni store was located in an outlet mall on International Drive in Orlando, eighteen miles from Disney World. The lawman phoned the store and spoke with Glenn Corbitt, an employee. The detective described Neil.

Corbitt had no trouble remembering him. Neil, Corbitt

said, had been there three weeks before, and he made an indelible impression. Corbitt told Schiaffo that Neil purchased four hundred and fifty dollars' worth of clothing, which he paid for with cash, and that one of the items was a pair of jeans, waist size thirty-four. But that wasn't all the young store clerk recalled. Neil, he said, told him he was in the Mafia, that the woman he was with was his girlfriend, and that she was a cop in Miami.

"Do you think you would be able to identify the couple from photographs?" Schiaffo wanted to know. Corbitt said he would, and the lawman promised he would get back to him to set up an appointment to show him photos of the couple. Later, the detective received another call from Rocco Napolitano. He said he was certain that it was his brother's bones that had washed up on the beach.

———————

A strapping six-footer with steely blue eyes and strawberry-blond hair, Rocco Napolitano was the spitting image of his older sibling, so much so that he was often mistaken for Neil. Although they were look-alikes and extremely close, the brothers' personalities were polar opposites. Rocco liked to surf and cook, stay home and watch videos, and play Pac-Man, while Neil preferred carousing and staying out until the wee hours of the morning.

"Neil was the tough one, but Rocco was not like that," said Carmen Sanchez, who began dating Neil when she was sixteen and he was nineteen. She lived with Neil until July 1995, about two months before he went missing, when she moved out of the high-rise apartment they shared. Neil, Carmen said, was a carouser and a womanizer. "He would go out to clubs and do things, or come home at four in the morning." In the weeks before she moved out, Carmen became aware that Neil was cavorting with another woman—an older woman named Roslyn, whom Neil was introducing as a medical doctor.

In the days after his brother disappeared, Rocco Napolitano scoured South Florida. He visited his brother's hangouts—mostly strip joints and clubs in northeastern Miami-Dade County. He talked to virtually everyone who knew Neil or might have come into contact with him, including Carmen.

Rocco told Detective Schiaffo that he had also been making the rounds of law enforcement agencies in South Florida, seeking information about his missing brother. On September 23, he went to the FBI, where he demanded that the G-men help him find his brother. They referred him to local police. With his mother, Velma, and sister Monica, Rocco went to the Metro-Dade police[1] on September 24, and to the police department in Hollywood, Florida, where he filed a missing-persons report on September 25.

His mother suggested that he search the parking garages at South Florida's airports for Neil's black Lincoln Mark VIII. When a bouncer at Bermuda Triangle, a Fort Lauderdale nightclub he visited while searching for Neil, made the same suggestion, Rocco drove to Fort Lauderdale International Airport, but he did not find his brother's car. Next, he drove to Miami International Airport.

Rocco told Schiaffo that he started at the roof level and drove down toward the exit. It wasn't until he reached the lowest level that he found what he was looking for. "On my last turn going toward the exit, I found a car that was similar to my brother's, and it turned out to be my brother's." But he knew there was no chance that his brother parked his car there and boarded a flight. That's because for all his bravado, tough-guy Neil Napolitano would never board an airliner—he had a phobia about flying.

---

1 In a 1997 referendum, Dade County voters approved renaming Florida's most populous county Miami-Dade County. As a result, the Metro-Dade Police Department became the Miami-Dade Police Department. However, the initials remained the same, MDPD.

Rocco said that he last saw his brother late in the afternoon of September 13, between four and five o'clock. That was when Neil dropped him off at their mother's apartment in Hollywood and drove away. Neil wasn't alone at the time, Rocco said. He was with a woman, an older married woman. Rocco told Detective Schiaffo that he had spent most of the day with his brother and the woman. They were extremely affectionate with each other, holding hands and kissing, "acting like they were newlyweds on a honeymoon." She was in his brother's apartment when Rocco stopped there on September 11. At that time, she was lounging under the covers in Neil's bed. Her name, Rocco said, was Roslyn "Roz" Vargas—organized crime detective Roslyn Vargas, the lead detective on the investigation into the criminal activities and associations of Neil Napolitano.

―――――――――――

While Gary Schiaffo was on the phone with Rocco, thirty-six miles away in Davie, a suburban enclave of eighty thousand west of Fort Lauderdale, Metro-Dade Police Department (MDPD) detective Roslyn Vargas was in the bedroom of the sprawling house she shared with her law-man husband, their three children, and her mother and father. Her television set was tuned to WSVN's *News at Ten*.

"My husband was in the room, and I was finishing some stuff," the veteran investigator recalled. "I think I was done with his ironing because I normally iron just before I go to bed." But the report of human bones on Miami Beach grabbed her attention. She couldn't believe what she had heard.

"I thought, 'nah'," she remembered. "But when the newscaster began giving [the description]—white male between the ages and body weight, then I really became nervous." She started to shake when the Fox affiliate's reporter revealed that some of the remains were inside a pair of designer jeans, Sergio Tacchinis, the reporter said. At that moment Roz Vargas knew that the bones on the beach belonged to Neil Napolitano.

The next day, the area's newspapers, the *Miami Herald* and the *Sun Sentinel*, carried news of the still unidentified bones on the beach. Although the gruesome story made the papers, it was relegated to the "B" sections, while the front pages carried banner headlines about the O. J. Simpson murder trial in Los Angeles, along with photos of Simpson lawyer Johnnie Cochran in a black ski mask proclaiming, "The gloves didn't fit. If it doesn't fit, you must acquit." As for local news that Thursday, the ongoing search for Jimmy Rice, a ten-year-old Miami boy who disembarked from a school bus on September 11 and never arrived at his home, five blocks away, still dominated the headlines.

While Miamians read their morning newspapers, a small army of cops fanned out on the beach looking for more body parts. None were found, but a week later, on October 2, a snorkeler came across what appeared to be a spine, which he gave to a lifeguard, who alerted police. Meanwhile, with Rocco's help, Gary Schiaffo was able to contact Neil's dentist. He dispatched Miami Beach detective Lori Wander to retrieve Neil's dental records and X-rays, which she immediately took to the medical examiner's office, on Bob Hope Road in Miami.

The vast three-building facility, the Joseph H. Davis Center for Forensic Pathology, occupies eighty-nine-thousand square feet adjacent to Miami's Jackson Memorial Hospital/University of Miami Medical School Center. The state-of-the-art facility opened in 1988 at a cost to county taxpayers of $10.2 million. It's a very busy facility, one of the busiest morgues in the world. Each forensic pathologist performs more than two hundred postmortem procedures each year, while the examiner's office conducts more than three thousand autopsies annually.

Bodies brought to the morgue are stored in massive refrigerated rooms. The main morgue has four. Each one can hold one hundred and twenty bodies, while the "decomp" morgue, where bodies in advanced stages of decomposition are autopsied, can store seventy-five bodies. In all, the morgue can store five hundred and fifty-five bodies, a number that the building's designers deliberately chose. They based it on the combined passenger and crew capacity of a 747 jumbo jet.

With Detective Wander looking on, the county's chief forensic dentist, Dr. Richard Souviron, X-rayed the teeth and jawbone that had been recovered from the surf on Wednesday. By comparing those X-rays with the ones Wander brought him, Dr. Souviron would be able to determine whether they came from Neil Napolitano. That's because everyone's teeth are different. They vary in size. Fillings, chips, and missing or misaligned teeth create unique patterns. After studying the X-rays, Dr. Souviron was able to positively identify the remains as Neil's. At about quarter after seven that morning, Wander phoned Schiaffo to tell him. The detective immediately called Rocco and told him the grim news.

With the remains identified, TV newscasters reported whose they were, and they interviewed Rocco, who claimed that investigators were engaged in a massive cover-up.

But with little more than bones to work with, and no determination as to the cause of death, there was no evidence that Neil had been the victim of a homicide. Nevertheless, detectives quickly theorized that the Miami Beach bad boy had been murdered. Rocco thought so, too. Schiaffo asked him if he any ideas on how it might have happened—"Shot, then put on a boat and dumped into the ocean," Rocco said. Then the detective asked Rocco why he didn't think his brother's death had been an accident or a suicide. Neil would never take his own life, Rocco declared, and he would never go out on a boat without telling someone. Lastly, Schiaffo wanted to know about motive; who would have wanted Neil dead.

"There are two possibilities," Rocco suggested. "There's Roz and maybe her husband, maybe a conspiracy, and there's these people." He was being vague, he explained, "Because I have to watch out for me and my family." Schiaffo pressed him, but Rocco was reluctant to name names, referring to possible suspects only as "these people" and "dangerous and connected people." He wanted to talk to his sister and his mother before he would reveal anything more.

While he waited for Rocco to get back to him, Schiaffo mulled the possibilities. The Mob was one. All the signs pointed to a gangland rubout. Neil, Schiaffo knew, had connections to the Gambino crime family's South Florida crew; his car had been abandoned at the airport—a not uncommon parking lot for the cars of mobsters who go missing; and his body was tossed into the ocean to sleep with the fishes forever. Or it could have been that someone wanted it to appear that Neil Napolitano had been murdered by the Mob—a betrayed husband with a law enforcement background, perhaps. Or maybe it was a case of fatal attraction in which a scorned lover, furious over being dumped by her young paramour, did him in.

After conferring with his sister and his mother, Rocco nervously told the detective about "these people:" They were Frank Abbandando Jr. (called "Junior"), Frederick J. "Ten Percent Freddie" Massaro, and Anthony "Tony Pep" Trentacosta, and they were connected to the Gambino crime family. Rocco explained that his brother and Junior Abbandando had once been very close, but Neil had recently begun working with Massaro more. Even though the two mobsters were with the Gambinos, they were rivals, and Junior viewed Neil's growing affiliation with Massaro as a sign of disrespect. Moreover, his brother recently had dinner with Massaro and Tony Pep, a ranking Gambino soldier and acting capo, who told Neil that he liked him and assured him that he would be moving up in the Mob.

Later that day Schiaffo learned that Neil's Lincoln was at a police impound lot in Hollywood, having been towed there from the parking garage at the Miami International Airport, where it had been since September 15. Schiaffo drove to the lot to examine the vehicle. Looking inside, it seemed to the detective that the driver's side seatbelt had been stretched out and that the upholstery and headliner had been splattered and stained with what appeared to be a green-colored liquid.

Schiaffo had the car towed to Fort Lauderdale, where crime scene investigators from the Broward Sheriff's Office, the BSO, would go through it with a fine-tooth comb and report their findings to him. He would have his report two days later, but in the meantime, the lawman wanted to talk to Roz Vargas, and he wanted to search Neil's residence.

The next day, September 30, 1995, Schiaffo and other officers from the Miami Beach Police Department entered Neil's apartment. Neil Napolitano's former live-in girl-friend, Carmen Sanchez, gave the lawmen permission for the search. Even though she was no longer living there, she was named on the lease as the legal tenant. There was no furniture inside the one bedroom apartment, just a mat-tress, fishing rods, handguns, and rifles. Schiaffo learned from security guards at the building and from Carmen that just three days earlier, Rocco had entered the apartment and removed items he believed belonged to MDPD detective Roz Vargas, as well as paperwork and photos that were evi-dence of Neil's relationship with her. Left behind were an assault rifle, a twelve-gauge shotgun, a Taser, a 9 mm Cal-ico Carbine, and several handguns. All the guns were reg-istered to Neil. Also left behind were several cassette tapes and videotapes, a tape recorder, and a body transmitter like those worn by informants and cooperating witnesses when they are wired to gather evidence against suspects.

With information that Neil Napolitano had spent the days before he disappeared with Roz, and that items belonging to her may have been in Neil's apartment, on the morning of October 3, Schiaffo and another detective headed for the Vargas home in Davie. "She was a subject witness who had information that I needed for my investigation," the lawman explained. He hoped that she would provide it. As he drove, Detective Schiaffo took a cell phone call from Dr. Hyma. The medical examiner told Schiaffo that he "strongly believed" that the spine that washed up the day before belonged to Neil Napolitano, too.

Roz Vargas was no stranger to Gary Schiaffo. He had met her twice before, in 1992, when their respective departments collaborated on a wiretap, and again the previous February, at a meeting with MDPD organized crime detectives investigating Neil Napolitano's connection to the disappearance of Alvino Reyes and John Davidson.

Mildred Rivera, Roz's mother, answered the Miami Beach lawman's knock, but her daughter was not there. She was at a hospital with her son. They were waiting to see a doctor and would not be home until the afternoon. Unable to speak with Roz, the detectives drove to the MDPD's Intracoastal station, where Julio Vargas, Roz's husband, was assigned. They interviewed him in their car outside the police station. Schiaffo already knew that Roz and her family had gone to Orlando over the Labor Day weekend and that Roz stayed there while Julio returned to Miami with the children. The lawman wanted to know why.

"He advised that they had an argument, and she got out of the car and left," Schiaffo wrote in his notes. "Julio stated that he and Roz had been married for twenty years and get along that way. When asked when she returned, he advised a week later. He had no contact with her during that time, and [we] asked what did she say when she returned. Julio advised that he has not spoken to her. . . . Julio advised that after being married for so long you learn to let things be, and when she was ready to talk she would do so."

To Gary Schiaffo it seemed that Julio "may have been holding back some things." He asked whether Julio knew Neil Napolitano.

"I never met him, never spoke to him, not over the phone or anytime, and I never ran him," he replied.[2]

Wrote Schiaffo, "[I] advised Julio that people were saying that he killed Neil Napolitano. At this Julio laughed and then apologized for doing so, but [said] he found the question amusing."

While Schiaffo was speaking with Julio Vargas, FBI agents armed with a federal search warrant and accompanied by Miami Beach detectives Tommy Moran and Mark DeFusco searched Neil's apartment. They found wires hanging from the drop ceiling. The find led them to believe that a video camera had once been installed there. The lawmen also found a mini tape recorder hidden in the ceiling. At the time, lawmen didn't know what to make of this. They wouldn't find out for another two years and three months.

———————

On the afternoon of Friday, October 6, Schiaffo met with Barbara Gentile at Miami Beach police headquarters. In his notes of the meeting, Schiaffo wrote that Sergeant Gentile "advised that Roz was not doing well and she could not understand why she was not cooperating with us. Interview with Sgt. Gentile lasted about one hour and information was received that Roz had taken her two sons out to dinner

———————

2   He was referring to conducting a criminal background check through the FBI's National Criminal Information Center (NCIC), a computerized database available to federal, state, and local law enforcement agencies.

with Neil on Tuesday, Sept. 11. Also it was ascertained that Roz's mother had gone to pick Roz up and Neil was with her at that time. It was determined from this that both of Roz's sons needed to be interviewed and also her mother."

On October 11, Gary Schiaffo was back at the Vargas home, but he wasn't there to speak to Roz. The Police Benevolent Association had provided her with an attorney, and she was advised not to talk to the Miami Beach lawman. Instead, he went there to serve subpoenas on her two sons and her mother. This time, however, it was Roz who opened the door.

"She began to cry and shake when she saw me," Schiaffo recalled. The lawman handed her the subpoenas and left. One week later, Mildred Rivera and her grandsons reported to the state attorney's office to tell under oath what they knew about Roz's relationship with Neil Napolitano.

2

COPS AND MOBSTERS

There were thirty-five incorporated cities, towns, and villages in Metro-Dade County in 1995. The larger ones, like the cities of Miami and Miami Beach, have their own police departments and crime scene investigation units. Many of the rest, as well as the 1.4 million residents who live in the unincorporated areas of the county, rely on the three thousand officers of the MDPD for either all or most of the services related to law enforcement. When they join the MDPD, officers take an oath:

> *I do solemnly swear that I will protect and defend the Constitution of the United States and the State of Florida; that I am duly qualified to hold office under the Constitution of the State, and that I will well and faithfully perform the duties of the office of Metropolitan Deputy Sheriff and Metro-Dade police officer.*

Roz Vargas joined the MDPD in February 1984. She was born Roslyn Rivera in a predominantly Puerto Rican neighborhood in the Bronx, New York, on April 19, 1955. She grew up in the borough's Throgs Neck section, where she attended Public School 39. For high school, Roz enrolled at Cathedral High, a strict Catholic school for girls founded in 1905 by the Sisters of Charity. After graduating in 1973, Roz enrolled at the State University of New York at New Paltz, but she didn't stay there long. Two years later, on November 16, 1975, twenty-year-old Roslyn Rivera married twenty-four-year-old Julio Vargas. Their first child, a daughter they named Vera, was born the following May. One year later, Roz gave birth to their second child, Julio Jr. By 1976, Roz, Julio, and their two children were living in South Florida. The couple's third child, Nicholas, arrived in 1979, after which Roz had her tubes tied, according to the paperwork she filled out when she applied to the MDPD in August 1983.

Roz and Julio, an MDPD cop, too, were highly regarded by their fellow officers and supervisors. After Roz spent eleven years on the force, during which she served as a patrol officer and then as a detective in the MDPD's Northeast District, Roz Vargas was looking for a new career challenge. With her strong sense of right and wrong, the chance to put mobsters behind bars seemed exciting, and Roz applied for a transfer to the MDPD's elite Strategic Investigations Bureau, the SIB, which worked major investigations including public corruption, murder conspiracies, and organized crime. She was exceptionally well qualified. Moreover, she had proved herself on the street, too.

Because of the highly sensitive nature of their investigations, the squad members worked out of a secret location two miles from the MDPD's sprawling headquarters on NW 25th Street. Its offices were on the third floor of a nondescript office building whose other tenants included law offices, real estate companies, accountants, and the Florida College of Natural Health. The SIB's operations were so cloak-and-dagger, its presence was not listed on the building's directory.

Roz interviewed with the bureau's commanding officer and, after a thorough background check and review of her work history, was notified that her application to join the SIB had been approved. Detective Roslyn Vargas, MDPD badge number 4030, officially joined the unit on Monday, October 31, 1994. She brought with her a personnel file brimming with commendations for her investigative skills, dedication to duty, and professionalism stemming from her previous work as a detective and a patrol officer. She was assigned to Sergeant Barbara Gentile's squad, Organized Crime Bureau Squad Two.

According to Gentile, "She came to my squad with high credentials. Roz was an experienced investigator, somebody I could rely on, depend on. She was able to document everything and do a thorough job on the case she was working."

As her boss, Barbara Gentile appreciated Vargas' work ethic and motivation. On a personal level, the two women had much in common: they were the same age, they lived in the same neighborhood, and they were the mothers of teenagers. Not only that, but both women were married to lawmen. It wasn't long before they became friends. "She had been to my house for parties, and I had been to her house for parties," Sergeant Gentile said.

With long dark hair, large brown eyes, high cheekbones, a firm jaw, and flawless olive skin, the five-foot-four-inch organized crime detective could easily have passed for thirty. Petite and athletic, Roz Vargas appeared even younger in shorts and a skimpy top. Despite twenty years of marriage and three kids, she had stayed in good shape. Roz still had a body to die for.

And she was an experienced investigator. Moreover, she was street-smart and assertive. She carried herself with a swagger and an air of confidence that comes from wearing a badge and carrying a .38-caliber Smith and Wesson Police Special, which is why her bosses were confident that she would get the evidence they needed to arrest Neil

Napolitano. An arrest, they hoped, would lead to charges against his higher-ups in the Gambino crew he was connected to.

Gentile's squad already had Neil Napolitano under surveillance when Roz Vargas reported for her first day of work at the SIB. Detectives from the MDPD's Criminal Intelligence Bureau, the CIB, had met with the FBI and detectives from Miami Beach on August 29 to discuss Neil. They learned that the Beach cops and the FBI had been watching Neil for more than a year. He was suspected of trafficking in illegal steroids, crack cocaine, and prescription drugs, and of working with a Mafia crew that included Fred Massaro and Frank Abbandando Jr. Neil, they said, was dealing from a Denny's restaurant on Collins Avenue and 62nd Street in Miami Beach, but he had expanded into unincorporated areas of the county, selling illegal steroids to bodybuilders in areas under the jurisdiction of the MDPD.

By all accounts, his business was booming. That's because gyms and health clubs are everywhere in South Florida, where looking good and showing off a well-chiseled body are as much a part of the lifestyle as sun, sand, and palm trees. The CIB detectives passed the information along to the SIB, and one week later, Gentile's squad members and their counterparts from Miami Beach were jointly surveilling Neil.

Neil Napolitano was born in Jersey City, New Jersey, on March 17, 1971, the third child and first son of Aniello Napolitano and Velma Jean Nawrocki Byrne. Rocco, the youngest child, was born one year later. Neil was still a toddler when the family moved to Miami Beach. When their parents' marriage ended in divorce in 1973—Rocco described their relationship as "love-hate," complicated by abuse, alcoholism, and financial woes—the boys were placed in a foster home. They lived with their foster family, the Gisperts, for many years. Neil and Rocco played baseball, surfed, and fished with the Gispert children. They attended church services with them every Sunday, rushing home afterward during football season to root for their favorite gridiron team, the Miami Dolphins. They listened to heavy-metal music from groups like Metallica, Judas Priest, and Guns N' Roses, and they were especially close to their foster brother Reynaldo. As teens, the Napolitano brothers went to live with their mother in Miami Beach, but they never severed their ties to the Gisperts.

Neil grew up surrounded by wealth and conspicuous consumption at a time when billions of dollars in drug money poured into South Florida, making the region the cocaine capital of the world and fueling an orgy of materialism. It also brought about an explosion in violent crime that sent Miami Beach into a three-decades-long downward spiral that began in the late 1960s, with the rise of competition from resorts in Las Vegas, Hawaii, Mexico, and the Caribbean.

Once-glittering flagship hotels like the Eden Roc and the Fontainebleau deteriorated, their owners more interested in taking profits out of them instead of putting money into needed renovations. Then, in 1971, Disney World opened in Orlando, 240 miles away, siphoning off much of Miami Beach's convention business as well as vacationing families. South Beach, which would not undergo its renaissance until the mid-1990s, faded into blight, becoming Miami Beach's skid row, its streets littered with sleazy hotels, winos, and drug addicts.

In 1980 Fidel Castro announced that anyone who wanted to could leave Cuba. The Mariel boatlift brought an influx of more than 125,000 refugees to South Florida. Many settled in Miami Beach. Among them were criminals who were freed from the island nation's prisons and mentally ill men and women who were released from its mental hospitals. As a result, law enforcement resources in the Miami area were stretched to the limit. Nevertheless, Miami Beach became the backdrop for one of the most popular television cop shows ever—*Miami Vice*.

Neil was an impressionable thirteen-year-old when the program debuted in 1984. He became a devotee of the popular police drama that defined South Florida. It starred Don Johnson as Sonny Crockett, a former University of Florida football star who served two combat tours in Vietnam before becoming a Metro-Dade cop and taking up residence on a sailboat with Elvis, his pet alligator. Crockett and his partner, Rico Tubbs (played by Philip Michael Thomas), portrayed a pair of undercover detectives assigned to the vice unit. The crime-fighting duo battled the forces of evil—cocaine cowboys, foreign agents, and corrupt officials. They raced around town in Ferraris and piloted speedboats on Biscayne Bay. The popular television show launched new styles in men's fashions. Thanks to *Miami Vice*, three-day-old facial stubble became fashionable for Miami's men, as did loafers without socks, Ray-Ban sunglasses, and suits and sport jackets worn over T-shirts.

And it inspired Neil to want to become a Police Explorer with the Miami Beach Police Department. He planned on becoming a cop. Neil joined the Explorer program when he was still a student at Miami Beach High School, but by age eighteen, he was showing a brazen rebelliousness and a reluctance to follow orders.

"My brother didn't like being told what to do," Rocco recalled. So it came as no surprise when he was bounced out of the program for insubordination stemming from an incident that occurred on April 26, 1989, during a visit to Miami Beach by the president of the United States.

President George H. W. Bush was in town that day to deliver a speech to the International Drug Enforcement Conference at the Biscayne Bay Marriott. The president was staying at the Doral Hotel on Miami Beach, and the

Explorers were assigned to assist police with traffic and crowd control, but during a morning briefing, there was an altercation.

"Neil Napolitano was extremely disrespectful during our meeting and the presidential detail," wrote Captain Maldonado, his supervisor. He wrote:

> *While at an inspection, Sgt. P. Socarracas was doing the inspection which was supervised by Major [Chaves] and myself. Explorer Napolitano was correcting every word the sergeant said. I then investigated the problem. Napolitano told me that the sergeant was supposed to perform as if he was in the military. Napolitano's complaints and concerns were that Sgt. Socarracas was not performing in a military manner. I then spoke to this explorer in regards to not being a part of the armed services. After speaking with the explorer I found him to be [in]subordinate and with very little regards [sic] to an authoritative figure. Major Chaves intervened and spoke with Napolitano on a one to one basis.*

Later that day, Neil's insolence played out in public during a meal break.

> *During our detail Sgt. Martin assigned everyone a post. Major Chaves gave everyone permission to eat at Burger King. Patrolman Napolitano's actions in and out of the restaurant were inexcusable. He was speaking loudly and was asked to lower his tone of voice. The major repeatedly asked him. He refused to lower his voice.*

Despite a stern warning that he would lose his badge, Neil remained defiant.

I warned him that I would take his badge and request suspension. His response, "I'll give you my badge now" in a high tone voice. I then took his badge and told him he can go home whenever he wanted to go. He refused and said, "I'll stay." Then after ten minutes, before the president's arrival, he left his post. At the time, his behavior was unacceptable and inappropriate. I am requesting that Neil Napolitano be terminated from Police Explorers.

According to Rocco, Neil became disillusioned with the Explorers and the police long before the Burger King incident, when he suspected that funds earmarked for the Explorer program were finding their way into the pockets of the program's leaders. In addition to leaving the Explorers, Neil dropped out of Miami Beach High School. By age eighteen, he abandoned his plans to pursue a career as a crime fighter, choosing to become a lawbreaker instead.

He and some pals from the neighborhood became smash-and-grab thieves, breaking into cars to steal cell phones, luggage, and anything else of value. They vandalized vending machines and post office stamp machines, draining them of nickels, dimes, and quarters, and they mugged shoppers in supermarket parking lots, targeting Rolex wearers for their expensive timepieces. And that wasn't all.

"My brother sold cocaine, marijuana, anabolic steroids," Rocco Napolitano admitted, adding that Neil was also involved in credit card fraud and loan-sharking.

"He stole when he was younger. As he got older, it went more to drugs and lending money out, racketeering." And his experience as a Police Explorer came in handy—he had learned the ins and outs of the Miami Beach Police Department. He knew most of its officers by sight, if not by name, and he was familiar with many of its procedures.

By the time he turned twenty, Neil had developed a fiery

temper, a tough-guy persona, and a powerful build. A solid six feet one, a fitness enthusiast who didn't drink or smoke, he had become an accomplished kickboxer and tae kwon do enthusiast. If anyone asked, he would say he worked as a bodyguard, but whose body he guarded was a mystery. His usual attire was Fila athletic wear, either jogging suits or sweats. He became enamored with gangster movies, especially the three *Godfather* films. He even began calling himself Sonny, after Sonny Corleone, the mercurial gangster played by James Caan. Other film favorites were *Goodfellas*, *A Bronx Tale,* and *The Untouchables*. He'd view them again and again, acting out scenes in front of a mirror and reciting lines from the films verbatim.

But there was also a kinder, gentler side to Neil Napolitano. He rescued stray dogs and paid for their care if they were sick. He gave generously to down-and-out panhandlers, and he was protective of his troubled mother, watching over her and giving her money. He was Velma's favorite child, a loving son who never fought with her and stayed in Miami while his three siblings left the Sunshine State; Rocco to New York, Monica to Hawaii and later to California, and another sister, Teresa, to New Jersey. To the cops, however, Neil Napolitano was an ambitious young thug.

"In his mind, Neil believed that he was a big-time Mob figure, and he played the role," Gary Schiaffo said.

And he made no secret about his budding relationship with the Mob. "Some criminals are very quiet about their behavior, and they conduct themselves in a way not to bring attention," said Rocco Napolitano. "My brother didn't do that. Instead, he attracted attention." To bolster the perception that he was an Italian gangster, Neil hung a flag of Italy license plate on the front of his car and tattooed the green, white, and red Italian flag on his left arm. Among those whose attention he attracted was the FBI's organized crime unit in Miami. "We knew who he was and the people

he hung out with," declared former agent John L. Barrett
Jr., who at one time was in charge of organized crime and
drug investigations in South Florida.

Neil hung out with mobster Frank Abbandando Jr.,
whose headquarters was Party Girls, a sleazy nude bar he
owned on Biscayne Boulevard in North Miami. Abbandando, whom everyone called Junior, saw Neil as an eager
new recruit, someone he could groom for a life of crime.
They were introduced in 1992 by Joe Stracci, a drug addict
and petty thief Neil met three years before, when they
both worked at a beachfront hotel on Collins Avenue. Neil
was employed there as a security guard, while Stracci, an
aging and mostly down-and-out small-time hoodlum and
drug dealer known around town as "Poppa Crack," worked
there, too, as a handyman.

———————

Violence was in Junior Abbandando's DNA. His father and
namesake, Frank "The Dasher" Abbandando, was a feared
killer for Murder Inc. The band of coldblooded killers
from Brooklyn's Brownsville and East New York neigh-
borhoods carried out dozens of contract murders for the
Mob bosses. The Murder Inc. killers had various murder
scenarios that depended on the reason for the rubout. For
example, informers would turn up with a dead rat stuffed
into their mouths; civilian witnesses who talked to the
police or prosecutors would have their eyes gouged out;
men who molested or seduced women related or married
to mobsters would be castrated and then murdered, their
genitals stuffed into their mouths. And sometimes victims
just disappeared, their bodies buried under tons of garbage
in a landfill, crushed inside a scrapped automobile in a
junkyard, or dumped at sea to sleep with the fishes.

The carnage began in the 1930s, and it lasted well into
the 1940s. The Dasher was the suspected hit man in more
than forty slayings. Junior was six years old in February

1942, when his thirty-two-year-old father went to the electric chair at New York's Sing Sing prison for the brutal ice-pick murder of Brooklyn loan shark George "Whitey" Rudnick. Although Junior was heir to his father's penchant for violence, he did not inherit The Dasher's good looks, nor did he inherit his father's flair for fashion.

"Junior always looked like he just crawled out of a sewer," said John Bonino, an FBI agent who investigated him in the 1980s. Abbandando, the G-man said, "was a dangerous little guy."

The Brooklyn-born gangster arrived in South Florida in the late 1970s after a string of arrests in New York. His first, at age sixteen, was for possession of a loaded gun. More arrests followed for extortion, grand larceny, and assault. Setting up shop in the Miami area, Junior wasted no time getting into loan-sharking and drug trafficking. Convicted in 1983 of racketeering and selling bootlegged quaaludes, an unrepentant Abbandando resumed his life of crime with Gambino's South Florida crew after he was released from prison in 1989.

At first Neil admired and trusted the gangster, who stood just five feet four, weighed one hundred and fifty pounds, and had receding gray hair and dark brown eyes. He dressed in nylon jogging suits, which he wore unzipped nearly to his navel, revealing ample chest hair and heavy gold chains that dangled from his neck. A heavy smoker, he had a heart condition, a raspy voice, and a thick New York accent that added to his Italian gangster persona, as did the tattoo of an eagle with the number "1954." It occupied a prominent position on his left arm. Junior, who operated several secondhand stores in South Florida as cover for his criminal activities, was missing the upper part of his left middle finger. It had been sliced off by another gangster in a dispute over a marijuana deal.

Neil saw Junior Abbandando as his ticket into the Mafia, and the diminutive mobster appreciated Neil's timely warning about a drug sting that could have sent a high-ranking Gambino mobster to prison. Lawmen in Florida had set a trap for the mobster, Joseph "JoJo" Corozzo, a Gambino capo from New York, but Neil tipped him off to the setup. As a reward, Junior Abbandando introduced Neil and Rocco to JoJo, an honor not usually bestowed upon low-rung wiseguys. But Neil was seen as an up-and-coming mobster, and the meeting took place at one of Junior's secondhand stores in Broward County.

Said Rocco: "It went like this: we drove to the store. My brother asked me to stay in the car and he would come back outside, and at that time he would say it was okay for me to come in. He left. He went inside. They discussed what they discussed. Sometime later, my brother came outside and said, 'You can get out of the car now.' I went inside and I was introduced to Joseph Corozzo as JoJo."

"This is my boss," Rocco remembered Junior telling him.

"If you ever need anything, Junior will tell you where I am in New York," Rocco recalls JoJo—the brother of five-foot-five-inch Nicholas "The Little Guy" Corozzo, one of the most powerful gangsters in the Gambino family—saying to him. The meeting was brief. "They were thankful that my brother helped them out."

While the gangsters were grateful that Neil had tipped them off, the lawmen were furious. "Neil was a thorn in their side," says Rocco, adding that Neil "liked to outsmart the cops; to him it was a game."

Tommy Moran agreed. "Neil loved to make us look foolish," the detective said.

===

Italian gangsters and their associates are as much a part of South Florida's recent history as the Spanish Conquistadors are of its more distant past. In 1928 Al Capone bought a walled-in waterfront retreat for his wife, Mae, on Miami Beach's Palm Island. The two-story Spanish-style home at 93 Palm Avenue had fourteen rooms, a dock and a swimming pool, and a two-bedroom gatehouse that housed Capone's ever-present entourage of bodyguards and hoodlums.

The mansion had originally been built for Clarence Busch of the Anheuser-Busch beer family in 1922, but while Prohibition enabled Capone to make a fortune, the nationwide shutdown of legal beer brewing brought hard times to the Busch family. From his winter retreat, the Chicago crime king directed his criminal empire, which included extensive gambling and bootlegging interests in the Miami area.

Local residents didn't exactly roll out the welcome mat for the notorious mobster, who was named "the greatest gang leader in history" by the *New Yorker* magazine. Local newspapers launched a campaign to drive him out of the Sunshine State. The City of Miami Beach sued Capone, calling his Palm Island estate a threat to "the safety and well being of residents." Florida governor John Martin even ordered the states' sheriffs to arrest the gangster on sight.

Despite the constant surveillance and several arrests, Capone would not be driven out of Florida. He was being questioned by lawmen in Miami when his henchmen in Chicago, dressed as cops, lined up seven members of rival Bugs Moran's North Side Gang against a garage wall and mowed them down with Thompson machine guns. The St. Valentine's Day Massacre, on February 14, 1929, made headlines across the country, and it is still considered the bloodiest slaughter in Mob history. Jailed for income tax evasion in 1932, Capone returned to his Miami Beach estate after his release from Alcatraz in 1939. He died there from syphilis on January 25, 1947.

At one time the Sunshine State had its own Mafia god-father. Through the 1950s and into the 1960s, the cunning

Santo Trafficante Jr. of Tampa was the uncontested boss of Florida's Gulf Coast, and mobsters from elsewhere knew better than to encroach on Trafficante's rackets. It was in Miami Beach in 1961, at the posh Fontainebleau Hotel, that the Tampa crime boss allegedly had a sit-down with a CIA agent. It's said that the G-man handed the gangster ten thousand dollars to poison Fidel Castro. The meeting had been set up by another South Florida mobster, Johnny Roselli. He mysteriously disappeared in August 1976. Days later, Roselli's car was found in a parking garage at Miami International Airport, while his dismembered body turned up floating in a barrel in Biscayne Bay.

Another mobster who called South Florida home was the legendary Meyer Lansky. For more than three decades, the crafty gangster made Miami Beach the financial-planning headquarters for the Mob's business ventures, both legal and illegal. A gifted money man, Lansky was reputedly able to commit complex financial transactions to memory, avoiding the necessity to keep written records, which could fall into the hands of law enforcement. Lansky, who was Jewish, forged alliances with the Italian godfathers and helped them create secret syndicates to funnel their enormous illicit profits into legitimate businesses—nightclubs, restaurants, Las Vegas and Caribbean casinos, and Swiss bank accounts.

Both before and after World War II, Lansky and his younger brother Jake operated illegal gambling joints and betting parlors in Broward and Dade counties. In his later years, he routinely met with his underworld associates over matzo-ball soup and pastrami sandwiches at a booth inside Wolfie's, a Miami Beach delicatessen on Collins Avenue and 21st Street. Living in New York in the 1930s, Lansky was closely allied with Charles "Lucky" Lucciano, the underworld strongman who in 1931 established La Cosa Nostra's ruling body, the secret board of directors that became known as the Commission. It organized crime in the United States, setting rules and keeping a tenuous peace among the five warring New York *borgatas*, or gangs, that would eventually become known as the Bonanno, Lucchese, Colombo, Genovese, and Gambino crime families.

The commission's tentacles spread nationwide, eventually bringing twenty-four Italian borgatas from Chicago, Detroit, Philadelphia, Cleveland, Boston, and elsewhere under its authority. Each had its own boss, its own territory, and its own rackets. They thrived for years thanks to the stubbornness of J. Edgar Hoover, the longtime director of the FBI. He denied the very existence of organized crime, preferring to have his agents hunt down bank robbers and communists instead. But that would begin to change in November 1957, when Mafia leaders from across the country convened in Apalachin, a tiny town in upstate New York.

An alert state trooper noticed an unusually large number of black limousines. He decided to investigate. More than sixty gangsters were rounded up and identified, and among them were commission members Joe Bonanno and Vito Genovese. It would be another three years before the forces of law and order would start marshaling their resources against organized crime. Eventually, investigators would learn that one of the rules the commission put in place was the directive that no La Cosa Nostra family could claim Las Vegas or Florida as their own.

"No single family exercised exclusive territorial rights in Florida, and the Miami area has always been wide open to Mafia entrepreneurs," says *New York Times* organized crime reporter Selwyn Raab, author of *Five Families: The Rise, Decline, and Resurgence of America's Most Powerful Mafia Empires*.

Free to set up outposts in the Sunshine State, by 1980 South Florida was crawling with mobsters from the northeast. Dozens of them with colorful nicknames like "Jimmy Blue Eyes" and "Joey the Scooch" set up shop in the area, living in what lawmen referred to as "the Mob belt," a swath of palm trees and sand stretching from Miami Beach north to Pompano and Boca Raton. Their crimes included loan-sharking, extortion, credit card fraud, bank fraud, boiler-room scams, sports betting, drug trafficking, and murder.

3

MOB RULES

"When you're a wiseguy, you can steal, you can cheat, you can lie, you can kill people—and it's all legitimate." That's what Benjamin "Lefty Guns" Ruggiero told the man he knew as Donnie Brasco. At the time, the two men were sipping drinks at a hotel bar in Miami Beach. Lefty didn't know it then, but Brasco was really Joe Pistone, the intrepid FBI agent who spent six years undercover, posing as a gangster to infiltrate the Mob. His exploits were made into the 1997 film *Donnie Brasco*, starring Johnny Depp and Al Pacino.

Pistone had just asked the gangster to explain the benefits of becoming a wiseguy, a word that includes both Mob associates as well as "made" members of the Mafia, a term that refers only to those who have been formally inducted into La Cosa Nostra in an elaborate ritual.

"They take an oath where they prick their finger with blood, and they take a vow of omertà—a vow of silence never to discuss anything that happens in the family," said Joseph McMahon, the MDPD's longtime expert on Italian organized crime. He was able to listen to a 1989 FBI recording of a Mafia induction.

Said McMahon: "They swear that they will put the family, the individuals within the family, above their own family, God, and themselves, meaning that all of the individuals up to the rank of soldier put the La Cosa Nostra crime family ahead of anything else. Nothing can come in front of it. It's blind allegiance, total loyalty."

Wiseguys live every day of their lives knowing that they can be whacked. "Mistakes mean death," Pistone wrote in *The Way of the Wiseguy*. "In life, you break the social contract, such as speeding in your car, and you get a fine. In business, you make a mistake you get demoted or fired." But that's not the way of the wiseguys. Pistone says they "wake up every day, aware that this may be the day they get killed, at any moment, for lots of different reasons," like cheating other wiseguys out of money; murdering or even hitting another wiseguy without the blessing of the bosses; screwing a wiseguy's wife, daughter, or girlfriend; testifying before a grand jury or in a courtroom; and talking to a cop.

"Anything more than 'Nice day, officer,' is grounds for execution," says Pistone.

Testifying in federal court in New York, turncoat soldier Michael "Mickey Scars" De Leonardo described in intimate detail his 1988 induction into the Mafia, which was presided over by Gambino consigliere Salvatore "Sammy the Bull" Gravano:

> *[Sammy] asked me if I knew why I was there, which I acknowledged no. He then says, "Do you know these men?" I says, "Yes." He says, "Do you respect these men?" I said, "Yes." He says, "We have been watching you for a long time. This is not a club. This is a secret society. There is one way in this society, the way you would come in today, and one way out, on a slab."*

He says, "Do you want to be a part of us?" I acknowledged yes. He says, "Which finger do you shoot with?" I put up my index finger. There was a saint, a picture of a saint on a table, which was crumbled up and placed in my hand. Jackie D'Amico pinches my finger, pricks it, drops some blood on to the saint, whereas then Gravano says, "I'm going to light it on fire, and roll it around in your hands, and repeat after me." And, he did so. He says, "If I betray the oath of omerta, may my soul burn in hell like the saint."

He congratulated me and says, "This is your new family, we come first before your blood family. If we call you, you come in when we call you. Even if you have to kill your own brother, this is what it is. Jackie is now your new father." He told me to go around and kiss all of the captains. That is what I did. I went around the table and came back to the head of the table.

We were locked in, a procedure called locking in. Everybody stands up, we all hold hands, some words are spoken in Italian to the effect whatever is done here today or discussed here today, stays here. That was supposed to be locking in, keeping the secret.

Then they started to tell us about the hierarchy of our family—our boss, John Gotti, underboss Frank Locasio, consigliere was Sammy. Captains, roles of captains, roles of soldiers and associates, and how we should treat each other.

Then they gave us the hierarchies of the other families in our areas. The captains were then telling us about the don'ts—what not to do, things you could get killed for, such as, sleeping with another member's wife, you would be killed for that. If you were married and you slept with another member's family, you would be killed for that. If you murdered

without permission, you could be killed for that.
If you dealt drugs, you would be killed for that. If
you dealt in stocks and bonds, you would be killed
for that. Raise your hands to another member, you
would be killed for that. If you robbed from the fam-
ily, you would be killed for that. And there are a few
other ones.

Sammy the Bull became a "made man" in 1976 at an induction ceremony in the basement of a house not far from where he grew up, in the Bensonhurst section of Brooklyn. It was "the biggest day of my life," Gravano told author Peter Maas in *Underboss: Sammy the Bull Gravano's Story of Life in the Mafia*, recalling the day he became a member of the Gambino crime family. At the time, Gravano said, he sincerely believed that he was on his way to becoming a "man of honor," that he was joining a secret society that had its origins centuries before in Sicily, among peasants who had banded together to defeat occupation and oppression by invaders who occupied their island, the largest in the Mediterranean Sea. The Sicilian Mafia became a secret government, protecting citizens from their foreign oppressors. In America, newly arrived immigrants from Sicily kept up the traditions of the old country, maintaining the rituals and secrecy that bonded them together against the outsiders. The American Mafia, Gravano believed, would do the same for all Italians in the United States.

Gravano recalled the chilling words of Gambino boss Paul "Big Paulie" Castellano, who administered the oath of *omerta* and afterward lectured Sammy and another newly made man:

You are born as of today. Any grievances you have,
anybody you have disliked from before, don't bring
it up. As of today, it's over with. There is no God. We

don't have allegiance to any country. Our immediate family, like our wives and our children, is secondary. Our Thing—this thing of ours—is the only thing in your life above everything. You want to believe in God? You want to believe in your country? You want to believe in your own family? That all comes way after this.

Any time you are sent for by the boss of your family, you must come in. If your child is dying and has only twenty minutes to live, and your boss sends for you, you must leave that kid and come. If you refuse, you will be killed. When the boss sends for you, it precedes everything else. This is the one time you don't check with your captain. The reason is your immediate superior, your captain, may be the target. Maybe I want you to kill him . . . I'm the boss. I'm the father of the family. I am your God.

After Castellano finished, they all ate and celebrated. Gravano admitted that he "bought all this 100 percent." He felt that he had become part of "a brotherhood that had honor and respect." Years later, Sammy the Bull would become disillusioned: "I got to learn that the whole thing was bullshit. We broke every rule."

Gravano wasn't the first Mob turncoat to break the Mafia's code of *omerta*. Joe Valachi, a soldier with the Genovese crime family, was. In 1962, Valachi learned that his boss, Mob chieftain Vito Genovese, wanted him whacked. At the time, Valachi was serving time in the federal penitentiary in Atlanta for drug trafficking, and Genovese feared that Valachi had become an informer, a charge Valachi vehemently denied. Convinced that the Mob would stop at nothing to kill him, Valachi became an informer. In 1963, the gravelly voiced killer revealed Mob secrets to a congressional committee investigating organized crime. Robert Kennedy, the

U.S. attorney general at the time, proclaimed his testimony "the biggest intelligence breakthrough yet in combating organized crime."

Valachi's testimony was broadcast on national television. Americans heard him identify more than three hundred Mafia members, including the leaders of the crime families. He also revealed the term *Cosa Nostra*, Italian for "Our Thing," explaining that they were the words Italian mobsters used among themselves when referring to their criminal syndicate.

Valachi revealed that newly made men begin their climb up the Mafia ladder as *soldati*, or soldiers, and induction into La Cosa Nostra is referred to as "getting your button." But before a soldier can be made, he has to prove that he has what it takes to be a Mafia soldier, either by carrying out a sanctioned killing or by being a big earner. Unlike made men, associates are not *in* the Mafia. They can be from any nationality or walk of life, but only Italians can get their buttons.[3] Non-Italian associates will never go any further, says Detective McMahon. "They will continue to be at the street level, conducting narcotics activities, credit card fraud, illegal gambling, stock fraud, bookmaking, counterfeiting—whatever they can do."

Soldiers and associates work in crews and are responsible to their capos, or captains, who oversee the criminal activities of their soldiers and associates, providing them with protection from rival gangs and crime families. In return the capos receive tribute, a cut of each crew member's earnings. It comes to them in cash inside paper bags, suitcases, or envelopes. It can also be paid in goods or services. The most powerful capos have been known to

---

3   Originally, only full-blooded Italians could be inducted into La Cosa Nostra, but the Gambinos relaxed the rule, requiring only that the member's father be of Italian heritage.

have one hundred or more associates and soldiers working under them.

At the Mafia's highest level is "the administration," which is comprised of the head of the family—the boss. The top deputies are the underboss and the consigliere (counselor), whose role is to advise the boss on internal family matters as well as on relations with other Mafia families. The boss sets policy, appoints the capos, settles disputes within his own family and other families, and is supposed to sanction all significant actions taken by members of his family, including murder. In return for his supervision and protection, the boss receives tribute from the capos.

The money always flows up, says Joe Pistone. "No Mafia boss is out there earning money and distributing it downward to his loyal subordinates." The system, he says, "keeps the hands of the higher-ups as clean as possible."

In 1985, John Gotti Jr. became the Gambino family boss after engineering the assassination of Paul "Big Paulie" Castellano outside a Manhattan steak house. At that time, according to federal prosecutors, the Gambino family's twenty-one crews operated in New York, Florida, Connecticut, New Jersey, and Nevada. They grossed a mind-boggling five hundred million dollars annually.

The New York papers dubbed Gotti "The Dapper Don" for his two-thousand-dollar custom-tailored suits, hand-painted silk ties, and perfectly coiffed, blow-dried hair, but there was nothing dapper or stylish about John Joseph Gotti Jr.'s early life. He was born in the South Bronx in 1940, the fifth of thirteen children. His father, John, a construction worker and factory hand, was frequently out of work, and the family moved often. The Gottis eventually settled in the East New York section of Brooklyn, where young John organized the Fulton-Rockaway Boys, a street gang named for the intersection where they hung out.

At the time, the Mob was flourishing in East New York, and Gotti's exploits as a fearless gang leader did not go

unnoticed by the local underworld. He and his pals fought
rival street gangs, stole cars, and broke into homes and
stores. By the time he turned twenty, John Gotti, five feet
ten, with square shoulders, fast fists, and a hair-trigger
temper, had become an enforcer for a crew run by Carmine Fatico, a Gambino captain. The crew's headquarters
relocated from Brooklyn to the South Ozone Park section
in Queens, where they hung out at a storefront social club
they incorporated as the Bergin Hunt and Fish Club. It was
named for Bergen Street in Brooklyn, but it was misspelled
on the incorporation documents.

Brazen and ambitious, Gotti became involved in typical Mob rackets—loan-sharking, bookmaking, and truck
hijackings at nearby Kennedy Airport. Nabbed in an FBI
sting in 1968, Gotti pleaded guilty and was sentenced to the
big house—three years in the maximum-security prison in
Lewisburg, Pennsylvania. Released in 1971, the following
year Gotti was promoted to acting crew chief at Bergin
when Fatico was indicted for loan-sharking. As a crew
chief, he was required to report to Gambino underboss
Neil Dellacroce. The two men hit it off, and the underboss
became Gotti's mentor. The promotion marked the beginning of Gotti's climb to the top. The following year he was
chosen for an assignment that he couldn't refuse.

A nephew of Carlo Gambino, the family's godfather,
had been kidnapped and murdered even though the aging
crime boss had paid a one hundred thousand dollar ransom.
The Gambinos quickly identified thirty-year-old Jimmy
McBratney, a Staten Island man with ties to the notorious
Westies, an Irish gang whose roots were in midtown Manhattan, as the kidnap mastermind. Don Carlo wanted him
dead, and the assignment went to Gotti.

On the night of May 22, 1973, Gotti and two other
Bergin crew members, Angelo Ruggiero and Ralph "Ral-
phie Wiggs" Galione, walked into Snoope's Bar and
Grill on Staten Island. Galione pumped three bullets into

McBratney. Witnesses identified the mobsters from mug shots, but before they were arrested, Galione was murdered. Gotti and Ruggiero pleaded guilty to manslaughter. They were sentenced to four years in prison; they were out in little more than two.

In 1976, while John Gotti was still behind bars, Carlo Gambino died of a heart attack at age seventy-four. Under the Mafia's rules of succession, the new godfather should have been Neil Dellacroce, the underboss, but a year before he died, Don Carlo named Paul "Big Paulie" Castellano, his cousin and brother-in-law, as his successor instead. It was a slap in the face to Dellacroce, who was more popular within the family than Big Paulie. But in a gesture of peace, Castellano extended an olive branch—he offered to keep Dellacroce as his underboss with absolute control over ten crews. Dellacroce was agreeable, but although the peace offering avoided an all-out war between the factions, it did create a serious split in the family. And the violation of Mafia protocol and tradition embittered John Gotti. In 1977 Dellacroce named his recently paroled protégé John Gotti acting capo of the Bergin crew, and it wasn't too long before the new capo began plotting against Big Paulie.

While Castellano hated Gotti, his neighbors regarded him as a pillar of his Howard Beach community, even though it was no secret that that he was in the Mafia and that he had served time in prison for gunning down a man in a bar.

John and Victoria Gotti lived in a modest house with their five children. On March 18, 1980, their twelve-year-old son, Frankie, was riding a minibike when he darted out from behind a Dumpster and was struck and killed by a car driven by John Favara, the Gottis' next-door neighbor. Traffic investigators ruled the death an accident. Favara, they found, was temporarily blinded by the setting sun. Ten days later, the young father of two tried to express his sorrow to the Gottis, but he was attacked by a distraught Victoria, who came at him with a baseball bat. On July 28, witnesses reported seeing six men force Favara into a van as he walked through a parking lot near his workplace, a Castro Convertible warehouse on Long Island.

Investigators believe the abductors were soldiers from Gotti's Bergin Hunt and Fish Club crew, and they were acting under Gotti's orders. Favara, lawmen say, was shot in the van and taken to another location where his body was stuffed into a fifty-five-gallon, acid-filled drum, which was then dumped into Jamaica Bay. John Gotti had an iron-clad alibi. At the time, he was reportedly aboard a pleasure boat off Miami Beach. Onboard with him that day were two Gambino family South Florida crew associates—John Porcaro, the boat's owner, and Fred Massaro.

The death of his young son didn't put a damper on John Gotti's ambition or his boldness. He openly expressed his resentment of, and hostility to, Paul Castellano. By 1985, Big Paulie and the brash and ambitious Gotti were at loggerheads because the Bergin Hunt and Fish Club crew was heavily invested in narcotics in defiance of Castellano's anti-drug edict.

"You deal drugs, you die," Big Paulie repeatedly told his underlings, according to Sammy Gravano. At the time, the Gambino godfather believed that the FBI had him in their crosshairs, so he ordered the family to lie low for awhile. Although the other crews complied, the Bergin crew was defiant, and Big Paulie continued to take his cut of the crew's profits from drug trafficking. The godfather's command also generated mountains of resentment among the crews that followed his orders because it took money out of their pockets.

Castellano's style added to the animosity. He reigned over the crime family from the "White House," his three-million-dollar hilltop mansion on Todt Hill, the highest point on Staten Island. It had stately columns, an Olympic-sized indoor swimming pool and commanding views of the Verrazano-Narrows Bridge and New York Harbor.

Before building his mansion, Castellano lived humbly in Brooklyn's Sheepshead Bay neighborhood, but once named godfather of the Gambinos, Castellano hardly ever mingled with his troops, and he never visited the social clubs like the Bergin Fish and Hunt Club in Queens or the Ravenite in Manhattan that served as headquarters for the crime family's crews. His isolation won him a nickname, "The Pope," because whenever he wanted to meet with his lieutenants, he would summon them to his mansion as if he was the pontiff in Rome summoning his bishops to the Vatican.

Lawmen say August 1983 marked the beginning of the end of Big Paulie's reign, and it came about because eleven men from the Bergin crew, including Neil Dellacroce's nephew Angelo Ruggiero and John Gotti's brother Gene, were arrested for heroin trafficking and racketeering. According to the charges, Ruggiero, with help from his codefendants, was running his brother Salvatore's multimillion-dollar drug operation, which he took over after Salvatore and his wife died in a plane crash in 1982. The evidence came from tape recordings made from an electronic eavesdropping device placed by the FBI inside Ruggiero's Long Island home.

While two subsequent trials ended in mistrials, a third would end in convictions of everyone except Ruggiero. Dying of cancer, he was severed from the third trial, but evidence gleaned from the tapes enabled lawmen to obtain a court order to install a bug inside Castellano's Staten Island mansion.

Despite the Bergin crew's drug dealing, John Gotti and the rest of his crew were protected as long as underboss Neil Dellacroce was alive. When Dellacroce succumbed to cancer on December 2, 1985, Gotti assumed that he would be demoted to soldier or worse—marked for death. Instead of waiting to find out, Gotti decided to strike first. His plan had been in the works for months as he lined up support from other disgruntled Gambino capos to assassinate

Big Paulie, convincing them to rally behind his effort to become the boss of the family.

Former FBI Special Agent Joe Pistone: "It is generally regarded as one of the ballsiest and best organized hits in the history of the Mob. Ballsy because Gotti acted without the support of all the other bosses. No meeting with the Commission, no election, no nothing."

At the time, Paul Castellano and the bosses of the four other New York crime families were facing federal racketeering charges based in part on evidence lawmen gleaned from bugging Big Paulie's mansion. The indictments, part of an all-out assault on the Mafia, were handed down in February. Released on bail—two million dollars in cash, which Castellano posted himself—the Gambino godfather spent the afternoon of December 16 conferring with his lawyers before leaving for a dinner meeting at Sparks Steak House on East Forty-sixth Street in midtown Manhattan.

It was snowing lightly and the sidewalks were crowded with holiday shoppers when four armed men, dressed identically in white trench coats and black Russian fur hats, took up positions on the sidewalk outside the restaurant. They were waiting for Castellano. Meanwhile, Gotti and Sammy Gravano were parked nearby, directing the men on the street with walkie-talkies. It was just before six o'clock when Castellano's black Lincoln came to a stop in front of the steak house, and the godfather of the largest and most powerful Mafia family opened the door on the passenger side.

He was barely out of the vehicle when two of the hit men opened fire. The shooters pumped six bullets into the sixty-nine-year-old mobster's body and head. At the same time, the other two hit men walked to the driver's side of the car and pumped six bullets into forty-five-year-old Tommy Billotti, Castellano's newly appointed underboss. Both men fell mortally wounded and died in the street. The four shooters calmly walked to the corner, where a getaway car waited for them. A few days later, John Gotti was officially declared boss of the Gambinos. From then on, Godfather Gotti was in the media spotlight. Unlike his predecessors, who were more low-key and hid from the glare of publicity, Gotti relished it. Despite the change at the top, the Gambino crew in South Florida was busy. It was being run by a capo named Anthony "Fat Andy" Ruggiano, a man of enormous girth and tremendous power and influence within the Gambino family.

Fat Andy was born in 1926 and hailed from the Ozone Park section of Queens. Drafted into the U.S. Army during World War II, Ruggiano faced an army court-martial for going AWOL in time of war. Convicted and sentenced to five years in prison, Ruggiano became involved with the Mafia after his release. In 1948 he was convicted of burglary in New York.

Mindful of omertà, the code of silence, in 1970 Fat Andy served thirty days in jail for contempt rather than testify before a grand jury investigating bookmaking, narcotics, and infiltration of labor unions by organized crime in the New York area. In 1977, he was convicted of criminal contempt and sentenced to one year in jail after refusing to testify yet again, this time before another grand jury investigating organized crime's attempts to acquire police protection for illegal gambling operations in the New York area. Indicted in New York in 1980 for loan sharking, Ruggiano fled to Florida, where he continued his racketeering ways in Palm Beach County.

In 1981, Fat Andy recruited Mob associate Joseph "Joe Dogs" Iannuzzi to operate the bar at Suite 100, an illegal gambling club he was planning to open in Riviera Beach in Palm Beach County. Unknown to the portly capo, Iannuzzi had turned against his Mafia pals, the result of having been beaten to a pulp with a baseball bat by a Gambino loan shark to whom he owed money. Unconscious for two days, Iannuzzi awoke with a vengeance. To get even, he went to the FBI. He consented to cooperate in a sting dubbed "Operation Home Run." To nail Fat Andy, Iannuzzi wore a wire, and he worked with John Bonino, a courageous agent the FBI brought in from Chicago. Iannuzzi introduced Bonino to Fat Andy as his business partner.

Over mussels and linguine, Ruggiano confidently showed Iannuzzi and Bonino the blueprint for the club. With Ruggiano that night was Junior Abbandando, who sat nearby as Fat Andy's bodyguard. The FBI wire Iannuzzi wore recorded the gangster talking about installing blackjack tables and how he would staff the gambling club with dealers from New York. Fat Andy boasted that he was a captain in the Gambino organized crime family. At a subsequent meeting, Iannuzzi and Bonino told the capo that they needed twenty-five thousand dollars to complete construction of the bar. Ruggiano agreed to lend them the money at two points per week, or 104 percent interest per year.

Using Fat Andy's secretly taped words against him, federal prosecutors indicted him along with eight other wiseguys, including Junior Abbandando. Among the charges were racketeering, extortion, loan-sharking, interference with commerce by threats of violence, and interstate travel in aid of racketeering. Rather than take his chances in court, Ruggiano fled. He grew a beard and hid out with a biker gang, but the corpulent capo couldn't hide from the law forever. The FBI caught up with him two years later hiding out in Miami, where he stood trial. Convicted and sentenced to seventeen years in federal prison, he served ten before being released on parole in May 1997. While he was away, Gambino boss John Gotti put the South Florida crew in the hands of Tony Pep Trentacosta, a soldier from the Bergin Fish and Hunt Club.

As a Mob associate, Tony Pep racked up convictions for felony assault with a gun, theft from an interstate shipment, obstruction, criminal contempt, gambling, and parole violations. In the 1980s, Tony Pep, his jet-black hair combed in 1950s doo-wop style, became a rising star in the Gambino crime family when he glommed on to the gasoline tax scam, filling the family's coffers and his own pockets with millions of dollars in stolen gasoline excise taxes.

The scam involved siphoning off tax revenues that gasoline wholesalers should have remitted to federal, state, and local governments. In November 1991, Sammy the Bull Gravano revealed to the FBI agents who were debriefing him that Tony Pep was rewarded with induction into La Cosa Nostra in 1986, becoming a made man at age forty-eight. He would be rewarded again when Fat Andy Ruggiano went on the lam to avoid federal charges in Florida.

But lawmen say that Trentacosta wasn't very popular among the upper echelons of the Gambino administration, especially with Nicholas Corozzo. That's because Trentacosta was thought of as a tightwad, and the bosses had to lean on him to pay what they thought they were entitled to from his earnings. Fed up with Trentacosta's penny-pinching ways, Corozzo ran Trentacosta out of New York. Banished to Georgia, by the midnineties Tony Pep was living in a palatial estate in Cumming, an enclave north of Atlanta, where he was a silent partner in a moving company and a nightclub, two legitimate businesses that provided cover for his underworld ventures.

4

A FATAL ATTRACTION

Roz Vargas knew nothing about Fat Andy, Tony Pep, or Junior Abbandando when she reported to the Strategic Investigations Bureau for her first day of work. And she knew little about Mafia rules and protocol.

"For about the first two weeks, I did absolutely nothing but sit in the office and read manuals, the SOP [Standard Operating Procedure] for the SIB [Strategic Investigations Bureau]," Vargas recalled. Among the procedures she would have read about was the requirement to document everything, especially calls and contacts with informants and targets.

For detectives accustomed to solving individual crimes, the transition to working organized crime can be difficult. A lot of police work is immediate: a crime occurs; investigators take action that may result in an arrest. Perhaps the arrest takes a week or a month, but an organized crime investigation is long term. It may take years to build a case.

Cases begin quietly, with lawmen operating in stealth mode, spending much of their working hours in the shadows gathering intelligence, watching, listening, and playing cat and mouse with their targets. In the meantime, they are required to file precise written records of everything, which means there is a huge amount of paperwork for them to do. There are work sheets to be filled out accounting for their time and confidential reports to be written specifying what they observed while conducting surveillance.

"The reports documented everything in detail," Sergeant Gentile explained. "They weren't actual police reports that the public could get ahold of. They're what are called 'red lines,' confidential reports that are discoverable if we make an arrest. They're in great detail for court at a later date."

The reports were usually handwritten and placed in a box at the front of the office for typing by one of the bureau's secretaries. As for the work sheets, detectives would indicate where they were at various times of the day, indicating "office," or "on location," or "surveillance."

Because it can take years to build a case, working organized crime can be very frustrating, and oftentimes investigative efforts bear no fruit. Nevertheless, Roz Vargas seemed to handle the transition easily, becoming the squad's go-to person for computer issues. "I was about the most computer-literate person on the squad," she said.

Barbara Gentile's detectives had been surveilling Neil Napolitano since the spring of 1994, six months before Roz Vargas joined them. When the MDPD's Criminal Intelligence Unit learned that Neil was suspected of dealing steroids in areas of the county under their jurisdiction, it was decided to assign the squad to surveil him. Before then, MDPD lawmen had been keeping a close watch on Junior Abbandando, hoping to build a case against the Gambino soldier and others in his crew, but the cagey career criminal had investigators stymied. While watching him, however, the detectives noticed that he was spending a great deal of time with Neil Napolitano.

Abbandando wasn't the only Gambino gangster with whom Neil associated. Freddie Massaro was another, and he had been an MDPD target, too, so the organized crime investigators decided to zero in on Neil. They hoped that he would lead them to Abbandando and Massaro, and beyond.

Targeting the little fish in hopes it will lead them to the bigger fish is a tried-and-true strategy law enforcement employs to penetrate the underworld. By gathering evidence against those at the lower levels of a crime family, investigators hope to gain leverage that they can use to induce the junior wiseguys to reveal secrets about those higher up. But Neil Napolitano proved to be an extremely difficult target, so two agencies, the Miami Beach police and the MDPD, began working together to build a case against the young Mafia wannabe.

"He was a very tough person to follow," Tommy Moran recalled. "He was very surveillance conscious. He drove erratically, employing evasive driving techniques."

For one thing, Neil rarely took a direct route to his destination, zigzagging his way to wherever he was going instead, frequently making sudden turns, especially U-turns. If a traffic signal was turning yellow as he approached it, Neil would speed up and race through the intersection.

To help them keep up, investigators obtained a court order that permitted them to secretly install a Teletrack, the precursor to today's more sophisticated Global Positioning System devices, on Neil Napolitano's car. On the night of October 21, 1994, Moran watched nervously as a technician from the MDPD slipped underneath Neil's Lincoln to install the device. With it, lawmen were able to track, through a computer, the location of his vehicle 24/7, and it helped them learn and document his daily routines.

He was a chronic night owl who stayed awake until well past dawn. He would sleep until the early afternoon, then drive around the region, stopping at various locations

where lawmen suspected he would meet with his growing network of drug dealers. By nightfall, he'd make the
rounds of South Florida's topless bars and nightclubs. On
the night of September 27, 1994, lawmen followed Neil as
he drove his Lincoln through Miami Beach and into Sunny
Isles, a city north of Miami Beach. They noticed that he
was leading a red pickup truck, which they learned later
was being driven by his brother, Rocco.

Detective Moran: "We noticed that Neil seemed to be
directing the red pickup to an empty lot. After a short time,
the driver of the pickup threw some packages and some
boxes out of the window." When the Napolitano brothers
drove off, the lawmen retrieved the discarded packages.
Back at the lab, analysis revealed steroid residue on the
wrappers, and when the packages were checked for fingerprints, Neil Napolitano's prints were found on some of
them.

Despite the intense surveillance, organized crime investigators were unable to gather enough evidence to charge
him. What made it even more difficult was the fact Neil
left no paper trail. Neil Napolitano owned nothing. He had
no bank account or credit card, and he paid for everything
with cash. The apartment he lived in was leased to his girlfriend, Carmen, while the car he drove was registered to
his sister Monica, even though she lived in San Diego,
California. He didn't even have a telephone of his own.
Instead, he would borrow friends' cell phones or use pay
phones whenever he needed to make a call. Neil did have
a pager, though, and if anyone needed to get in touch with
him, all they had to do was beep him.

By the time Roz Vargas was ready to hit the streets
in mid-November, organized crime detectives had been
surveilling Neil for six months. Her primary assignment:
follow Neil Napolitano. Observe his activities. Identify
and run background checks on his associates, and detail
everything in written reports. But his wasn't the only case

Barbara Gentile's investigators were working. They also handled murder-for-hire cases, and they assisted other organized crime squads, too. When two men associated with Neil mysteriously disappeared on December 11, Roz zeroed in on Neil.

━━━━━━━

Forty-seven-year-old Alvino Reyes and thirty-year-old John Davidson were mi r players in Neil's drug-trafficking network. They were recruited by Joe Stracci, but neither man was a hardened criminal. Both were sickly and collecting disability.

Reyes was a severe diabetic who never strayed far from the portable oxygen tank that helped him breathe, while Davidson suffered from a variety of physical and mental ailments that required him to take more than a half-dozen prescription medications. Their involvement in Neil's drug ring only became known to lawmen when U.S. Customs agents intercepted a large package of illegal steroids that had come in from Europe. It was addressed to Reyes. The agents alerted Miami Beach police, specifically Tommy Moran's organized crime unit.

Moran: "They told us they were in receipt of a large amount of steroids that had come in from Spain aboard an Iberia Airline flight, and the steroids were to be delivered to Alvino Reyes." The lawmen set up a controlled delivery for Friday, December 1.

A driver for Iberia Express delivered the package to the Collins Park Hotel, a rundown residential hotel where Reyes and Davidson lived in adjoining fifth-floor studio apartments. After Reyes signed for the package, the two men were taken into custody and driven to Miami Beach Police Department headquarters on Washington Avenue. Roz Vargas didn't know it at the time, but she had observed Reyes and Davidson delivering a different package to Neil the night before, while he was being surveilled by her squad.

The MDPD detectives had spent most of that Thursday following Neil, keeping him in sight as he first picked up his longtime girlfriend, Carmen Sanchez, then drove to his mother's apartment in Hollywood. The detectives watched as Velma Byrne climbed into Neil's Lincoln; then they followed it to a seafood restaurant where Neil, Carmen, and Velma had dinner. Afterward, Neil dropped his mother off at her apartment, then headed south toward Miami Beach. Somewhere along the way, the cops lost sight of the Lincoln.

"We were going crazy looking for the vehicle," Roz Vargas remembered. After searching for fifteen to twenty minutes, the police radio crackled with the voice of Barbara Gentile. "I think I've got him!" the sergeant exclaimed. Roz steered her county-issued Toyota Camry to the location.

Able to resume their surveillance, the detectives followed as the Lincoln headed west on I-195, the Julian Tuttle Causeway. Named for one of Miami's most celebrated pioneers, the roadway traverses Biscayne Bay, connecting Miami Beach with the city of Miami.

The lawmen tailed the car to a parking lot adjacent to Miami Jai Alai, where it rendezvoused with a taxi. From a distance, the detectives observed as a man emerged from the cab and handed a package to the driver of the Lincoln. From their vantage point, the MDPD sleuths were unable to identify Neil as the driver, but the next night, Vargas and another MDPD detective, Detective Mark Liner, were present when Miami Beach police interrogated Reyes and Davidson. That's when Roz learned that the cab's passengers were Reyes and Davidson and that they had delivered a package of illegal drugs to Neil the night before. Separated from each other after their arrest, both men admitted their involvement in Neil's drug-trafficking network.

Reyes and Davidson were visibly nervous as they explained to investigators that they feared Neil would kill them if he knew they were cooperating with the police.

Davidson's hands shook as he admitted that he worked for Neil, and that Neil paid them to receive shipments of illegal drugs on his behalf. As for Reyes, beads of sweat rolled off his brow as he revealed his role in Neil Napolitano's drug-trafficking network. The men also implicated Joe Stracci, and they agreed to help lawmen build a case against Neil and Joe, promising to testify against them if and when the case went to trial. It was a fatal decision. Less than two weeks later, Alvin Reyes and John Davidson went missing.

They were last seen in the early hours of December 13, 1994, in front of Meyer Lansky's old hangout, Wolfie's Delicatessen, on Collins Avenue. The MDPD's computer-tracking reports revealed that on that night, Neil's Lincoln had been there, too; then it headed north, beyond the range of the tracking device lawmen had surreptitiously installed on Neil's car in October. The signal was up again a few hours later as the Lincoln returned to the area.

Investigators believed that Neil was responsible for the men's disappearance, theorizing that they were murdered to keep them from testifying about his drug trafficking. Investigators theorized that the hit was ordered by a member of the Gambino crew, and that the men's bodies were taken out to sea and dumped.

Two days after Reyes and Davidson vanished, copies of handwritten letters, ostensibly written by the missing men, were received at the Miami Beach Police Department's Internal Affairs unit. In them, the men recanted their statements to police regarding Neil and Joe Stracci's connections to the steroid packages. They claimed that their confessions had been coerced by cops who were out to frame Neil and Joe Stracci.

"I could tell they didn't like them very much. It sounded like they hated their guts," Alvino Reyes' five-page letter declared. He explained what happened after he signed for the packages: "After receiving the boxes, I stepped out for about two and a half hours. When I returned, I found five officers in my apartment with my best friend John. They told me to get the fuck inside and they flashed badges."

The letter went on to claim that Reyes told lawmen that the packages were for a man he met at the Denny's on Sixty-second Street, where Neil and Joe Stracci conducted their business. His name was Manny, and he didn't speak English very well because "he was not an American but of Latin American descent." Manny, the letter said, had asked him if he would receive a couple of boxes for him "because his mother planned on sending him clothes."

But the cops didn't buy his story, Reyes wrote. Instead they laughed at him, accusing him of lying. Reyes claimed that the cops kicked him, and they threatened to send him to jail for forty years. They offered him a deal—he could avoid prison by testifying that the steroid packages were for Neil Napolitano and Joe Stracci, and that he and Davidson worked for Neil.

Davidson's seven-page communication corroborated his friend's allegations, adding, "I felt bad that I accused two innocent people, Joe and Sonny, for my own selfishness and fear of incarceration."

Every lawman who read the letters concluded that they were most likely dictated by Neil. According to Tommy Moran, neither Reyes nor Davidson was capable of writing a complete sentence, let alone a lengthy and detailed complaint letter. Moreover, the signatures had been notarized on December 12, one day before the two men went missing, and the notary who witnessed their signatures worked for Angelo Ali, a Miami criminal defense attorney who had previously represented Neil and Joe and other South Florida mobsters, too. The letters infuriated Roz Vargas. She vowed that she would bring Neil Napolitano to justice.

"Roz truly believed that he was involved," Sergeant Gentile declared. "She even made a statement to me [that] she'll see him in jail before she retires."

Organized Crime Squad Two had been watching Neil

Napolitano for months, but they had nothing on him. Then
Roz Vargas volunteered to go undercover.

Sergeant Gentile: "We couldn't understand what he was
actually doing. He was meeting with people. We had him
involved in steroid transactions, but there was nothing we
could arrest him for at this point. We needed further information, so we attempted the undercover. We all talked
about it, and we all agreed it would be a good idea to get
closer. But Roz would need a go-between, someone Neil
trusted who could be relied upon to introduce her to the
Mafia wannabe without arousing his suspicions."

They would need a C.I.—cop talk for confidential
informant—to introduce her. They chose Neil's partner in
crime, Joseph Thomas Stracci, a sixty-six-year-old thief,
drug dealer, and longtime informer for the Miami Beach
police. Like Junior Abbandando, Stracci had the underworld in his blood. He was the son of Lucchese crime family soldier Joseph "Joe Stretch" Stracci, a midlevel gangster
whose rap sheet included arrests for robbery, grand larceny, and drug trafficking. But unlike Junior Abbandando,
who was a "made man," the son of Joe Stretch was a Mafia
disgrace.

According to lawmen, he was a drug addict who robbed
candy stores and bodegas in New York at gunpoint in the
1950s to support his drug habit. Embarrassed by his son's
addiction to heroin, Joe Stretch exiled him from New York,
commanding him to carve out a new life for himself in
South Florida, where, in 1976, he was arrested for dealing
drugs. Over the years, other arrests for loitering, theft, and
drug possession followed.

By 1994, Miami Beach police suspected that Stracci
was dealing steroids and crack cocaine with Neil. Lawmen
also believed that he had managed to reestablish his Mob
connections and had become an associate of organized
crime figures from the Gambino family—especially Junior
Abbandando and Fred Massaro. What the mobsters didn't

know, however, was that the five-foot-ten-inch Stracci, a chain smoker who coughed a lot and reeked from tobacco and was rumored to be suffering from AIDS, was a snitch. He had been a longtime confidential informant for Tommy Moran, the Miami Beach organized crime detective. In May 1995, investigators persuaded Stracci to introduce Roz Vargas to Neil. From then on, Joseph Thomas Stracci was Detective Vargas's confidential informant.

At the time, he was cooling his heels in the county jail, where he was being held on a parole violation while detectives from the MDPD's sex crimes unit investigated him after a twelve-year-old girl alleged that Stracci, a friend of her family, had raped her. Stracci also faced the lesser charge of lewd and lascivious behavior for an alleged incident with the same girl, who claimed that he had masturbated in front of her.

Roz Vargas had been surveilling Neil for months, getting to know him from a distance. To prepare her for a closer encounter with the Miami bad boy, the MDPD assembled a team of veteran organized crime and narcotics investigators. Tommy Moran was one of them, and he was very impressed with Roz Vargas.

"She was very tough," Moran remembered. "She talked tough and she was feisty, more like one of the boys." Moran warned Roz about Neil's criminal background and penchant for violence. Nevertheless, he and the other detectives were confident that Roz, who grew up on the tough streets of the Bronx, could hold her own with Neil Napolitano and that her undercover mission would provide them with a window into the activities of Junior Abbandando, Fred Massaro, and the rest of the Gambino crew. As for Roz, she wanted to nail Neil for the mysterious disappearances of Alvino Reyes and John Davidson.

"She really felt that Neil was responsible for that," Sergeant Gentile recalled. "She felt that she could uncover something so far as his involvement in these murders." As an added incentive, Roz's career would get a huge shot in the arm if she could pull it off. Success might even win her a promotion, especially if she could get Neil Napolitano to roll over on his underworld pals.

———————

While Roz Vargas prepared for her undercover assignment, eighteen-year-old Jeanette Smith was getting ready for her high school graduation. She was born on December 26, 1976, in the New York City borough of Queens, the youngest of three daughters. She was eighteen months old when her parents, Ray, a technician, and Gina, a special education teacher, decided to relocate their young family to South Florida, where they purchased a modest house on a tidy suburban street in Cooper City, a bedroom community fifteen miles southwest of Fort Lauderdale.

By all accounts, Ray was strict with Jeanette and her older sisters, Victoria and Kristina, but neighbors say that as the baby in the family, Jeanette, who seemed more outgoing and adventurous than her siblings, was the pampered child. She showed a flair for art at Pioneer Middle School, winning an award for a food mural she painted on a wall in the school cafeteria, a project she worked on for three months, and she did well at Cooper City High School, blossoming into a beautiful young woman with dark brown hair, full lips, and a body to die for.

If she had a flaw, it was her need to be in the spotlight. "She had to have all the attention," classmate Kelly Hernaez told a reporter for the *Sun Sentinel*. Another friend agreed, declaring that Jeanette's quest for attention led her to look for it in all the wrong places, which may explain why, while still in high school, she began wearing heavy makeup and tight-fitting clothes, and why she seemed to find bad boys more attractive than more wholesome types. And it may also explain why she became a stripper.

After graduation Smith enrolled in classes at Broward

Community College, worked for a time at a nursery where she sold plants and lawn furniture, then took a job at Gold-finger, a strip club in Sunrise, Florida, that billed itself as having "great food, hot girls, cold drinks" and "the greatest, hottest friction dances in Florida." From there she moved on to the more lucrative Thee Dollhouse in Sunny Isles, a beach town in northeast Miami-Dade County, where she performed under the stage name Jade. On busy nights, especially during the winter tourist season, the stripper known as Jade would leave work with two thousand dollars or more in cash, the largesse of grateful men. Among her fans were wiseguys. One in particular, a muscular six-foot-two-inch former U.S. Marine named Ariel Hernandez, was particularly fond of Jade.

Ariel Armando Hernandez was born in Miami on July 10, 1965. His parents, Armando, an accountant, and Mary, a seamstress, were Cuban refugees. As a teen, the muscular and athletic Hernandez was a gridiron star at Monsignor Edward Pace High School, where he played fullback. He joined the U.S. Marines at age nineteen and was sent to Parris Island, South Carolina, for boot camp. According to his service record, on April 6, 1986, Hernandez was found in possession of cocaine. Urine analysis indicated that he tested positive for the drug. Nevertheless, Hernandez served out the remainder of his hitch, after which he returned to South Florida, where he told everyone who would listen that the U.S. Marine Corps had trained him as a sniper and sent him on top-secret special-ops missions.

"I could shoot the testicles off a fly," he boasted. But it was bullshit. Investigators who examined his military records found no indication that he had ever been on top-secret missions or that he had been trained as a sniper. Instead, he had been assigned to an antitank company, the Eighth Tank Battalion, Fourth Marine Division.

In 1991, the former marine was convicted of credit card fraud. By the time Jeanette Smith made her first appearance on the stage of Thee Dollhouse, Ariel Hernandez had racked up twenty-two arrests for theft, battery, and forgery, and he had served ten months at a federal prison camp. He worked for longtime Gambino associate Fred Massaro, a five-foot-five-inch, three-hundred-pound gangster who used fear and intimidation to gain control of legitimate business interests in South Florida, including a restaurant, a used-car lot, and a moving and storage company. Massaro was also a secret partner in several South Florida strip clubs. His interests in the clubs were hidden because, as a convicted felon—in 1985 he was convicted of five counts of forgery in Tampa—his clubs would have been ineligible for state liquor licenses had his ownership been out in the open.

By the 1990s, the portly mobster was not a well man. He was an insulin-dependent diabetic with a serious heart condition. Despite his ailments, Massaro was a big earner for the Gambino crime family. His headquarters was the back room at Beachside Mario's, a tiny pizza joint he owned and operated on Collins Avenue in Sunny Isles. Lawmen say it was a front, its back room the command center for the crew. From it Massaro conducted his loan-sharking business, lending money to businessmen and gamblers at illegal interest rates. When borrowers failed to make their weekly payments, Massaro sent musclemen like Ariel Hernandez and, while he was still alive, Neil Napolitano, to persuade them to pay up.

Beachside Mario's was also where Ariel Hernandez produced counterfeit checks, which he and others used to purchase expensive merchandise, mostly televisions sets, computer equipment, and office supplies, which they would return for cash refunds or sell to others. But bank fraud and shylocking weren't the only activities that went on in the pizza joint's back room. Investigators say it was also where Freddie Massaro and his associates plotted murder.

5

UNDERCOVER

South Florida was in the grip of a record-setting heat wave on Wednesday, May 17, 1995, and everyone was talking about it. With temperatures in the midnineties, and with no letup in sight, the *Miami Herald* coined a new word to describe the region's sizzling weather—"smoltering," which the newspaper defined as "a blend of sweltering and smoldering."

The sizzling summerlike weather didn't bode well for the coming Atlantic hurricane season. Nineteen named storms would churn through the Atlantic and the Caribbean. Eleven would reach hurricane strength. But none of them would batter Miami, which was still recovering from Hurricane Andrew, the devastating Category Five storm that wreaked havoc in Miami-Dade County in 1992.

Despite the blistering heat and the looming hurricane season, Roz Vargas was cool and steady as she waited for a phone call from her confidential informant, Joe Stracci. He was setting up her first meeting with Neil, and he was to let her know the time and place, but neither Roz nor her colleagues at the Strategic Investigations Bureau could have imagined the consequences of her undercover assignment.

They had been preparing ever since her first meeting with Joe Stracci. In a report dated March 3, 1995, and placed in Organized Crime Squad Two's Napolitano case files, either Roz Vargas or another detective summarized what they learned from their first interview with their C.I.

INVESTIGATION INTO THE ILLEGAL ACTIVITIES OF NEAL [*sic*] NAPOLITANO

SYNOPSIS:
Narcotics information.

DETAILS:

On February 23, 1995, a source met with Detectives M. Liner and R. Vargas reference an interview concerning Aniello Napolitano. The source is now documented as a confidential informant and will now be referred to as the C.I. Some of the information received from the C.I. was verified during the interview, and other information will be verified during the course of this investigation.

According to the C.I., Aniello Napolitano uses several names. Napolitano uses the name Neal (Neil) Byrne, or Sonny. Byrne is Napolitano mother's name. Napolitano uses Sonny as a street name, or when making deals on the street. The C.I. states Napolitano began breaking into vehicles with a black male named Michael Briggs, on Miami Beach, mainly taking Cellular Phones. This all began shortly after Napolitano lost his job as a Security Guard at the Caroline Hotel. This is where the C.I. met Napolitano.

Napolitano was introduced to Frank "Junior" Abbandando (owner of The Party Girls Lounge and Junior's Thrift Store in Hollywood), by the C.I. According to the C.I., Napolitano's goal is to be a "MAFIOSO." The C.I. claims Napolitano imitates everything Abbandando does, including the way he dresses.

The C.I. stated that Napolitano would give the C.I. $50.00 just to drive around with him. The C.I. stated that Napolitano felt that he wouldn't get stopped by the Police if he had an older man in the car with him, and if he did, Napolitano would say the C.I. was his uncle.

The C.I. stated Napolitano has a brother by the name of Rocco Napolitano, which had already been verified. The C.I. stated he drove to New York with Rocco Napolitano, and that Rocco is staying in the Pelham area (The Pelham area is in the Bronx). According to the C.I., Rocco is receiving packages of steroids from his brother Neal, and Rocco is selling the steroids to an unknown source.

According to the C.I., Neal is dealing in steroids, cocaine, and a small amount of marijuana. Napolitano is receiving his steroids from a Pharmaceutical Company in Spain. The C.I. stated Napolitano had a white male by the name of Vincent (last name possibly Hovan) go to Spain sometime in June or July with a Latin male by the name of Tony (unknown last name), to place the steroid order at the Pharmaceutical Company. The C.I. claims Napolitano did not trust Tony too much, and therefore would only send Vincent to Spain alone to place the other orders. The orders are placed at the Pharmaceutical Company with an unknown female. Vincent stays in Spain approximately one week (in an unknown location), and the orders of steroids are sent to the United States by different shipping companies (UPS, Federal Express, etc.). The packages are sent to whomever Napolitano is paying to receive the packages. According to the C.I., Napolitano receives packages approximately three times a week, and six to seven packages within the same week.

Napolitano is said to get his cocaine (crack) from [someone who] lives on S.W. 3rd Street, just east of S.W. 12th Avenue. It was verified that Napolitano did go to that area during a previous surveillance. Napolitano also gets cocaine (crack) from another source, who lives at 7601 E. Treasure Drive, which is an apartment building across from Napolitano's mother's residence.

According to the C.I., [Neil's cocaine supplier] has a nephew who lives in the Lakeland area. Napolitano meets this nephew from Lakeland approximately once every two weeks. The C.I. stated that when Napolitano meets [the] nephew, they meet at a halfway point off the Florida Turnpike. The C.I. says Napolitano exits the Turnpike at Exit 133, makes a right after the exit and meets [the] nephew at any one of the four corners or at one of the Gas Stations on the corner. Previous information verifies the fact that Napolitano has driven up the Turnpike to at least Indiantown Road, and that he does have an associate who lives in the Tampa area. The C.I. states Napolitano is dealing in steroids with [the] nephew.

The C.I. states Napolitano gets his marijuana from a male by the name of Mike. Mike is said to live diagonally across from 1000 Bay Drive (The King Cole) in Miami Beach.

According to the C.I., the following [is] associated with Napolitano:

VINCENT: Travels to Spain for Napolitano to order steroids. Vincent is a dancer.

Armed with an insider's view of Neil's activities, the organized crime detectives fabricated and rehearsed what seemed like a logical cover story for Roz's undercover mission: she would masquerade as Roz Vitucci, the heiress to the Fila athletic-wear fortune, a somewhat spoiled, pampered, but tough-as-nails woman trying to strike it rich on her own by dealing in illegal steroids and other illicit drugs.

But Vargas couldn't go undercover alone. MDPD policy prohibited its officers from meeting targets by themselves, so Barbara Gentile enlisted the help of narcotics detective Bobby Trujillo, a veteran lawman with long hair and a street-person persona who "did not look like a police officer at all," she said, adding that "Neil was very alert as to what police officers looked like."

Gentile believed that no one, not even Neil Napolitano, would ever identify Trujillo as a police officer. He would pose as Roz's friend and partner Ralphie, a long-haul truck driver whose routes took him to the Northeast and the Midwest, enabling him to deliver illicit drugs to steroid users in Atlanta, New York, Chicago, and points in between.

They came up with a ploy to entice Neil. Roz drove to Party Girls, with Joe Stracci sitting next to her in the front passenger seat. The idea was to arouse Neil's curiosity enough so that he would ask Stracci about Roz. Joe would then explain that he met Roz at a bar, where they made small talk. In the course of that conversation, they began talking about narcotics. Roz, Stracci would say, revealed that she and her partner were looking to get into the illegal steroid trade.

The ploy worked, or so it seemed. In her official report, in which she referred to herself as the U.C., the undercover, Stracci as the C.I., and Neil as the target, Roz Vargas wrote:

> *On 5-16-95 the target told the C.I. he wanted to meet with the female U.C. At this time, the C.I. told the target the female U.C. broke up with her boyfriend because the boyfriend was beating the female U.C. and that the female U.C.'s father manufactured jogging suits in the Orient.*

The first face-to-face meeting was set for the evening
of May 17, between eight and half past eight at Broadway
Billiards, a pool hall on Biscayne Boulevard and NE 181st
Street. Neither Roz nor Trujillo would be armed, and neither detective would be wearing a wire. Nor would they
be carrying their police badges or their MDPD IDs. But
they would have backup. Other detectives, including Barbara Gentile, would be nearby to assist them should anything go awry. The backup units would be in direct radio
communications with each other via point-to-point fre-
quency, but while inside the pool hall, detectives Vargas
and Trujillo would be out of sight and out of touch with
their colleagues.

At a few minutes past eight, Roz and her partner were
waiting inside Broadway Billiards. Gentile and three other
MDPD detectives took up positions nearby. Twenty minutes later Neil drove up in his black Lincoln Mark VIII.
Gentile watched as he emerged from his car with two other
men, one of whom she recognized as Joe Stracci. The other
man would be introduced to the undercover detectives as
Al. In her report, in which she referred to herself and her
partner as the "U.Cs.," Detective Vargas wrote:

8:22 P.M.

*U.Cs. met with C.I. at Broadway Billiards (181
St. & Biscayne Blvd.). C.I. introduced U.Cs. to
Sonny and Al. Sonny, Al & U.C.s became involved
in a game of pool. Target immediately chose the
female U.C. as a partner. During the 1st game target engaged himself in very little small talk with the
female U.C. asking questions about an ex-boyfriend.
Target is under the impression female gets beaten
by [ex-boyfriend] and target asked male U.C. what
kind of work he did. The male U.C. replied he was a
truck driver and had his own personal rig.*

A second game of pool was played. Again the tar-
get picked the female U.C. as a partner and still only
small talk was done.

As the players circled the table, chalking their pool cues
for a third billiards game, Roz announced that she was too
tired to play. She wanted to sit down and watch the others
play instead. Immediately, Neil ordered Joe Stracci to take
his place at the pool table.

"I want to talk to Roz," he barked.

"I want you to know a little bit about me if we're going to
do business together in the future," he told her. He began by
telling her about his experience as a Police Explorer, boasting that he was the best Explorer the Miami Beach Police
Department ever had. Then he lied about why he left:

The target stated that he left the explorers because
of a confrontation with an explorer with more rank
and conflict [with an] order which a police sergeant
had given the target on a detail. The target said his
friend Eduardo was the chief of explorers (now a
P.O. for M.B.P.D.) & Eduardo didn't have the nerve
to help out the target, so the target eventually quit.

Neil confessed that he was a criminal and a pool hustler.

The target told the female U.C. how he used to break
into cars all the time and how he would go to shoot
pool in order to make money. The target continu-
ally spoke using police codes and police jargon. The
female U.C. however would stop the target and ask
what he meant regarding the numbers he used in
conversation. The target would then explain what
the code (numbers) meant. The target even told the
U.C. about his last arrest (4-7-95) which included his

*mother and sister being arrested. Note: The female
U.C. had watched the arrest taking place. The target
added and deleted some facts.*

And he proclaimed himself the Miami Beach Police
Department's public enemy number one:

*The target claims that Miami Beach P.D. started
an entire unit called SIU just to try and catch him.
The female U.C. asked what the SIU stood for and
the target replied "Strategic Investigations Unit."
The target said he had to go to court the next day
(5-18-95) regarding the arrest on 4-7-95. According
to the target he hoped not to get a conviction . . . or
the family was going to have to send him away possibly to Vegas. When the female U.C. asked what he
would do in Vegas the target said, "The family is
going to make me a pit boss in one of the casinos."
    The target also said he had to be cool for a while
because of the C.I.'s two friends. The target continued by saying, "I can't tell you too much right now
because I don't know you too well."*

After talking about himself, Neil wanted to know about
Roz:

*The target then asked the female U.C. where she was
from and what did she do. The female U.C. told the
target she was from N.Y. and did little things here
and there. The target then told the female U.C. he
had many different resources and if there was anything the female U.C. needed she should ask him
and he could probably help. The target mentioned
several times he liked the fact that the male U.C. had
his own rig and that the rig could be very useful.*

Finally, Neil steered the conversation to business:

The target began talking about a deal the C.I. mentioned to him. The C.I. told the target that the female U.C.'s father manufactured Fila jumpsuits in the Orient. The female U.C. had to cover herself by saying she and her father are not on speaking terms due to the so-called ex-boyfriend. The target asked the female U.C. to try and get on better terms with her father so the target and the female U.C. and the male U.C. can do business. The target advised the female and male U.C. there was a possibility that the police may follow or even harass both U.C.s merely because they would be around the target. The target said he felt the need to tell the U.C.s this information if they were going to do business together.

The target said he was not doing anything illegal because things were a little hot. The target used the following as an example. The target said "It's like being grounded and I have to wait until I am off groundment [sic], [and] then we can do business."

The meet lasted for ninety minutes. Neil asked Roz for a date:

The target still insisted on getting to know both U.C.s a little better. The target said he would get ahold of the female U.C. so they can get together and either go to the movies or out to dinner. The female U.C. explained to the target that she does not go anywhere w/o the male U.C. ref the ex-boyfriend. The target said that was okay because he wanted to know the male U.C. a little better also. The male and female U.C.s walked outside and moments later the C.I. walked outside and said the target would like

*our phone numbers. Both male and female U.C.s
walked back inside and gave the target beeper numbers for each U.C.*

They met again five days later. This time Neil was waiting for them at a steak house in North Miami Beach.

*The target was waiting outside the restaurant when
the female and male U.C. arrived. Upon entering
the restaurant, the target advised he already had
a table, where the informant had already been sitting. The target stated to the female U.C. "I thought
you would be alone," then chuckled and said "Oh,
that's right, you're never alone." When the female
U.C. asked if it was a problem, the target smiled and
said "No."*
    *The target engaged himself in small talk with both
the female and male U.C., asking how things were,
then began discussing the menu. Once the waiter
had taken the order, the target began to somewhat
talk about doing business. This lasted all through
dinner and sometime after the meal. The target
claimed he wanted to do business but right now had
to be careful reference drugs. However the target
several times mentioned the male U.C.'s rig and how
it could be used several ways.*

On Friday, May 26, Detective Vargas learned in a late
afternoon phone conversation with Neil that her true iden-
tity had been revealed to him by Joe Stracci. In her report,
she wrote:

*Contact made with target who says he picked up C.I.
somewhere near Fort Lauderdale airport early this
morning. Target says C.I. told him that the female
U.C.'s real name was Roslyn Vegas, or Vagas, or*

something like that. Target says C.I. told him the female U.C. works with a Det. Mark Liner and a female sergeant who's cute and has brown curly hair.

According to the target, the C.I. gave him a work phone number for the female U.C. However, when the target was saying the phone number the only numbers heard clearly were 994. During this entire conversation, there seem [sic] to be a little distortion in the target's voice as if he were trying to disguise his voice with some sort of device.

The target said he didn't know what to believe since the C.I. happened to have been high on crack cocaine. The target said he was sorry that he (C.I.) was working with the police. The target said, "If Joe is lying, he deserves an Academy Award for last night's performance."

Alluding to Reyes and Davidson, Neil hinted that Joe Stracci was responsible for their disappearance.

The target also says the C.I. told him (target) that he (C.I.) did something very bad and that it was a capital punishment crime and the C.I. felt he was going to jail. The target claims to know what the crime is. The female U.C. asked what the crime is. The female U.C. asked what it was that the C.I. did, but then the female U.C. said never mind, I don't want to know.

The target asked the female U.C. if she was a cop and the female U.C. said, "No, are you a cop?" The target said he can't do anything until Tuesday. The female U.C. told the target she couldn't believe what he was saying. The target said he was not that imaginative to think up such a story. The target also said he believed what the C.I. said, but was unsure about the information about the female U.C. The

*target said he didn't care if the female U.C. was a
cop, because he's never done anything illegal nor
talked about anything illegal with either the female
or male U.C.*

*The female U.C. asked the target, "I thought
you are very busy on Fridays and Saturdays, but
yet you have time to talk about this? What are you
doing this weekend?" The target replied by saying,
"Whatever you want, sweetheart." The female U.C.
said she was going to go away to the Bahamas or
to Orlando, reference what was going on with the
C.I., and all the nonsense. The target told the U.C.
he had a friend in the Bahamas and a rich friend in
the Orlando area. The target told the female U.C.
to relax and he (target) would call her back after or
at 8:00 P.M. The target asked about the male U.C.
and the female U.C. said she believed he was still
out of town. The target asked the female U.C. "Do
you think Ralphie (male U.C.) is a cop?" The female
U.C. said "No, not Ralphie."*

Their conversation, which Neil secretly recorded, had
been steamier than Roz's report indicated. According to an
official transcript, at one point Neil declared that he was
concerned that Roz had been wearing a wire when they
met at the pool hall and at the restaurant.

"Check my whole body," she offered.

"Maybe I'll make love to you, but I would never check
your body," he replied. He changed the subject. "There are
a lot of things going on in my mind, like why didn't you
tell me where you live? If you're an ordinary person, why
wouldn't you let me know where you live?"

In response Roz reiterated her cover story, explaining
that she was living with an abusive boyfriend, and that until
he was out of her life she could not risk having Neil call or
visit her at her residence. But Neil was unconvinced.

"The cops are out to get me," he declared, adding, "I don't give a fuck if you are a cop, Roz."

When Neil handed the phone to Joe Stracci, the informant tried to reassure Roz that he had done nothing to hurt her. Besides, he said, "I know he [Neil] likes you. He talks a lot about you. He's looking to go to bed with you."

———

Detective Vargas reported the conversation to Barbara Gentile, telling her sergeant that her cover had been blown by the informant, Joe Stracci. After consulting with her bosses, Gentile informed the squad that their investigation of Neil Napolitano was suspended. Officially, Stracci had betrayed her after her second meeting with Neil. Other investigators, especially those from Miami Beach who were familiar with Neil, believed that the young mobster knew from day one that Roz Vargas was an undercover cop, and that he was out to put one over on the police.

But it didn't matter.

Gentile: "The undercover activity was no longer effective. We had not made any criminal case against him, and too much time had been spent on it, so we decided to discontinue investigating him."

Roz didn't like the decision. "She wasn't happy about it, but she said she understood," Gentile recalled. The two policewomen agreed that the investigation would remain open, but it would remain inactive unless new developments justified resuming it. In the meantime, Organized Crime Squad Two had other cases to work, and Roz Vargas was reassigned. But if Barbara Gentile thought she was done with the young Mafia wannabe, she would be in for a very rude awakening.

6

RICO AND THE MOB

The Mafia that Neil Napolitano hoped to join as a made man was on the ropes in 1994, the result of an all-out attack on organized crime in the United States. Two weapons that authorities were able to wield against it were the Witness Protection Program and the Racketeer Influenced and Corrupt Organization Act, or RICO. It was written by Notre Dame Law School Professor G. Robert Blakey and passed by the U.S. Congress as part of the Organized Crime Control Act of 1970.

The act was aimed at the Italian Mob, but it would take more than a decade for lawmen to realize its full potential. That's because before the passage of RICO, the upper echelons of the Mafia were, for the most part, shielded from arrest. They were protected by the code of omertà and weak conspiracy laws, which meant that the Mob godfathers could order their soldiers and associates to commit illegal acts, could benefit from them, but it was virtually impossible for prosecutors to bring them to justice as long as they never committed the crimes themselves.

RICO changed that by making it illegal to participate in a criminal enterprise like a crime family. If prosecutors could prove that an individual was part of an enterprise engaged in a pattern of racketeering, they could win convictions. And the penalties are stiff—up to life in prison and forfeiture of all assets acquired as a result of racketeering activity.

But it would take a sea change in FBI procedures and strategy to successfully implement RICO. That would not happen until the early 1980s, when the bureau created separate organized crime squads, "Mob Squads," assigning more than three hundred agents to surveil, wiretap, and even infiltrate the five New York crime families. With dozens of agents assigned to the investigations, agents were able to penetrate the families' inner sanctums and link the bosses to the crimes of their underlings.

Faced with the possibility of long sentences in federal prison, dozens of wiseguys spilled their guts to investigators and agreed to testify against their bosses in exchange for reduced charges, lighter sentences, or immunity and a chance to begin life anew with their wives and children in the Witness Protection Program.

At the time of his assassination in 1985, Gambino boss Paul Castellano and the bosses of the Genovese, Lucchese, Columbo, and Bonanno crime families were defendants in what would become known as the Mafia Commission Case. They were charged in a multicount federal RICO indictment with taking part in an ongoing racketeering enterprise, "the Commission of La Cosa Nostra," the ruling body for more than one thousand soldiers and at least five thousand associates. Their crimes included extortion, loan-sharking, labor payoffs, and murder.

The heart of the case was the Commission's control of New York City's concrete industry, including bid rigging and forcing company owners to pay tribute to the crime families for every major contract they were awarded. The case was spearheaded by then U.S. Attorney for the Southern District of New York Rudy Giuliani. The lead prosecutor was Michael Chertoff, who called the godfathers "the largest and most vicious criminal business in the history of the United States."

The trial in federal court in Manhattan began on September 8, 1986. It was the first case to focus on the Cosa Nostra Commission as a criminal enterprise, but it was the culmination of more than a dozen previous RICO cases authorities brought against lower-level mobsters, like the 1981 case against South Florida mobsters Anthony "Fat Andy" Ruggiano and Junior Abbandando. Other cases were brought by federal prosecutors in Cleveland, New England, Philadelphia, Kansas City, Chicago, and elsewhere.

Success in the courtroom didn't come easily. It took years, during which investigators amassed a mountain of evidence, including FBI photographs of the underworld bosses going to and coming from a Commission meeting in New York and more than one thousand hours of electronic surveillance tapes from bugs placed inside mobsters' homes and hangouts, even inside their cars. The tapes were filled with conversations about the Commission. The godfathers could be heard discussing labor unions and construction companies they controlled, payoffs, loan-sharking, and murder. They also talked about coordinating criminal activities among the five families, settling interfamily disputes, and the induction of new soldiers into the Mafia.

If there was any doubt that the Commission members functioned as an underworld board of directors that routinely resorted to violence and murder to enforce its edict, a parade of Mob turncoats was called on to bolster the credibility of the tapes. Joe Pistone, the FBI agent who infiltrated the Bonanno crime family as Donnie Brasco, testified, too, providing an insider's view of how the Commission's rulings affected the crime families.

None of the accused mobsters took the stand to testify

in their own defense. The jury of five men and seven women convicted the defendants of seventeen racketeering acts and twenty criminal acts of extortion, labor payoffs, and loan-sharking. Genovese boss Anthony "Fat Tony" Salerno, Colombo boss Carmine "The Snake" Persico, and Lucchese boss Anthony "Tony Ducks" Corallo were each sentenced to one hundred years in prison. Five lower-ranking mobsters received long sentences, too.

The defendants appealed their convictions, but the appeals were denied. The mobsters wanted the U.S. Supreme Court to hear their cases, but the High Court declined to consider them. It seemed like the end of the Mafia was near, but the Mob was far from dead. It was seriously weakened, many of its secrets having been unraveled by lawmen. Although top Mob leaders landed in federal prison, a new generation stepped up to take over. Unschooled in the Old World values and more interested in "bling" and violence than loyalty and money, the replacements proved unable to fill the shoes of their underworld predecessors, and they were no match for RICO-armed lawmen.

It was business as usual for the Gambino family's South Florida crew, even though the boss of the family, John Gotti, had been in a federal lockup in New York since his arrest on December 11, 1990. Irked by his cocky, in-your-face style, his celebrity status, and his open defiance of them since his acquittal in a previous federal RICO case in 1987, when the press dubbed him the "Teflon Don," the feds launched a no-holds-barred effort to get Gotti and cripple the family.

Charged with murder and racketeering, the once Dapper Don faced a second federal RICO trial of his own in 1992. From informants, the FBI learned that Gotti held top-secret meetings in a tiny apartment in Little Italy, above the Ravenite. The agents bugged the apartment and captured the Gambino godfather on tape, implicating himself in three murders. Sammy Gravano rolled over on the crime boss, and his testimony supported the electronic evidence gleaned from the bugging. As a result, just two years after he was caught on tape speaking of a "Cosa Nostra for a hundred years," Gotti was sentenced to life in prison with no possibility of parole.

"The Teflon is gone," the FBI's James Foxx declared. The Federal Bureau of Prisons sent Gotti to the penitentiary at Marion, Illinois, a facility that opened in 1963 as a replacement for Alcatraz. Mafia tradition permitted a boss to retain his power while behind bars, and Gotti managed to hold on for a while, issuing orders through visitors, especially his son John Angelo Gotti, aka Junior, and his brother Peter. But when he was transferred to the Supermax prison in Colorado in 1994, the senior Gotti's power evaporated. When that happened, Nicholas "The Little Guy" Corozzo became the de facto boss of the Gambino crime family.

By then the long arm of the law was closing in on the Miami crew, too. The FBI, the Miami Beach police, and the MDPD had them in their crosshairs, and Neil Napolitano knew it. Mob activity in South Florida had been on the rise in recent years, as the vacation city's art deco district, South Beach, underwent a renaissance financed in part by wiseguy money from the Bonanno and Gambino crime families. They bought and renovated dozens of rundown hotels and bars, transforming them into trendy nightspots that attracted Hollywood A-list celebrities, professional athletes, and starstruck tourists as well as local police and DEA and FBI agents.

But instead of avoiding contact with Roz Vargas, his law enforcement nemesis, Neil pursued her. He kept on paging her, and the two continued to have phone conversations through the waning days of May and beyond.

"Roz and Neil were in contact a lot," Barbara Gentile said. "He would page her. He would phone her." Gentile remembers Roz telling her about the many pages and the phone calls, many of which were after working hours. "From what she would tell me, nothing relevant [to our investigation] occurred during the conversations," the organized crime supervisor said. Roz also told Gentile that Neil was coming on to her.

"That's the impression we both had," Gentile revealed. "Even on the undercover meet, he wanted to play pool with her. He wanted to talk with her. He wanted to meet her alone."

Roz told her supervisor that Neil claimed to have a tape recording that would shed light on the December disappearances of Alvino Reyes and John Davidson, the two men arrested for receiving a shipment of illegal steroids for Neil. But it wasn't the MDPD's case. Miami Beach lawmen were handling the investigation as a missing-persons case.

Nevertheless, Roz wanted to listen to the tape. "We all did," Barbara Gentile said, so one week after Roz's second undercover meeting with him, Neil Napolitano appeared at the office of the Special Investigations Bureau on Northwest Twelfth Street. He was ushered into a tiny interview room, where Roz and Mark Liner questioned him, but Neil didn't bring the tape. Instead, he told the detectives about it. Joe Stracci, Neil said, confessed that he had murdered Reyes and Davidson.

Two days later Neil returned to the bureau. This time he was interviewed by Roz and Barbara Gentile, and this time he claimed that he had the tape with him. The detectives wanted to know about Junior Abbandando and Freddie Massaro and the others associated with the crew. Neil, however, was tight-lipped. He revealed nothing about his associates.

"We tried every which way to get information out of him, but nothing worked," Gentile remembered. "He talked in circles. Neil had a way of just talking and talking, and saying absolutely nothing."

Neil kept bringing the conversation around to the tape.

It was in his car, he said, and he would let only Roz Vargas listen to it, and only if she was alone with him in his car. Barbara Gentile wouldn't hear of it. She considered Neil Napolitano a very dangerous individual, someone who may have been responsible for two homicides, was involved with steroid trafficking and possibly burglaries and home-invasion robberies. Although she was anxious to listen to Joe Stracci's purported confession, she was not about to put one of her detectives in harm's way.

"For officer safety, we don't let anyone meet informants alone; we don't let anyone meet subjects alone," she explained.

Barbara Gentile's blood was boiling as Neil rambled on. To the sergeant it seemed that he had come to the SIB office under false pretenses; instead of giving them information, he appeared more intent on getting information. "He was on a fishing expedition," Gentile opined, trying to find out what the detectives had on *him*. After half an hour, Gentile ended the meeting.

"That's enough!" the exasperated sergeant shouted angrily. "This interview is over."

The meeting may have come to an end, but that didn't prevent Neil from contacting Roz. He continued to beep her at all hours of the day and night. When Gentile found out, she told her detectives that the MDPD was closing its investigation of Neil Napolitano.

"We're not getting anything from him," she told Roz. "This case has gone nowhere. We're going to cut our ties with the case. It's over with." The sergeant was adamant. Under no circumstances would Squad Two reopen its investigation of Neil Napolitano. If new leads developed, they would be passed to another squad or another bureau, or to another law enforcement agency. And Sergeant Gentile issued a direct order to Roz Vargas: "You will no longer have meetings with Neil Napolitano," she commanded.

"You will speak to him only during business hours by
phone. When you talk to him, you tell him that if he's got
any information to give the police, he can call you between
nine o'clock and five o'clock." Gentile's tone was stern and
resolute.

It was an order that Roz memorialized in a handwritten
report dated June 1.

> *7:14 P.M. Beeped to 861-5402/411. Called and spoke
> to Napolitano. Napolitano asked if Vargas had beeped
> him at 5:00 P.M. as he asked her to do. Vargas asked
> Napolitano if he got a beep. Napolitano said he didn't
> know because he had turned in his beeper at about
> 4:30 P.M. Vargas told Napolitano she did not beep
> him. Napolitano again asked Vargas about meeting
> with him and the C.I. at T.G.K.[4] Vargas again told
> the target it was not possible and didn't see the point
> anyway. Napolitano again told Vargas he wanted
> her to hear a tape recording of the C.I. talking about
> [Reyes and Davidson]. Napolitano continued to ask
> Vargas why he can't meet with Vargas alone. Napoli-
> tano appeared to be concerned about where and how
> Vargas met the C.I. and what the target has to do
> with anything. Vargas told Napolitano she could not
> tell him certain things because of an ongoing inves-
> tigation. Vargas told Napolitano she has nothing on
> him nor did she have anything against him. Vargas
> told Napolitano he could call during business hours
> (9 A.M.–5 P.M.), if he felt he had information to
> pass on or just say hello like friends and Napolitano
> said no, just acquaintances and Vargas replied yes
> acquaintances. Napolitano told Vargas he would call
> on 06-02-95 sometime in the afternoon.*

---

4   The Turner Guilford Knight Correctional Center.

But Neil Napolitano did not listen. He didn't have to obey Gentile's order, so he continued to page and phone Roz at all hours whenever he wanted to. He may have been an outlaw, but he was a handsome one—physically fit with a hard body and rippling muscles. Neil didn't smoke or drink, and he was meticulous about his appearance and personal hygiene. Despite a penchant for violence, the twenty-four-year-old Miami Beach bad boy could be sweet and charming. He was an alluring ladies' man, and he was coming on to forty-year-old Roz Vargas, a woman old enough to have given birth to him; someone who had been married for twenty years; a mother of three who, by her own words, had dedicated her life to her family, "cooking seven days a week," she said, "cleaning and ironing."

Roslyn Vargas wouldn't be the first woman whose passion was stirred by a handsome young rogue. It's natural, just as it's natural for men to be drawn to beauty. Perhaps Roz thought that she could rescue the bad boy from a life of crime, tame a tiger and turn him into a teddy bear. Despite Sergeant Gentile's direct order to restrict her contact with Neil to normal business hours, Roz and Neil continued talking at all hours of the day and night. Because he called from either borrowed cell phones or pay phones, the call-back number would be followed by "007," Neil's code. And they met secretly and alone on at least three occasions in August—outside Party Girls, Junior Abbandando's hang-out; in a parking lot on Biscayne Boulevard; and at Neil's apartment building.

MDPD rules and procedures regarding contacts with targets and informants were crystal clear. If Roz Vargas had any work-related contact with Neil Napolitano, whether before or after June 1, 1995, she was required to inform her supervisor and to file written reports. "She would have been required to document them," Barbara Gentile declared. "She would have written a report, and it would have been documented in her work sheets also." But

Roz did not document the phone calls or her rendezvous with Neil, nor did she inform Sergeant Gentile about them. She did, however, tell Barbara Gentile about an encounter she had with the Miami bad boy on June 26.

At the time, Roz was with another detective from her squad, Gary Porterfield. They were working another case when Roz spotted Neil pumping gas at a service station on Biscayne Boulevard. "I stopped," she remembered. "He saw me. He saw the vehicle. . . . We had a conversation at that time." According to Roz, Neil promised to give her information, but he said he could not be specific. Instead, it would lead her "in the right direction," but she "would have to figure out the rest" for herself.

Although Gentile knew about that encounter, she was in the dark about the others. She would learn of them soon enough, and the discovery would rock the squad and the department. It would tie up South Florida law enforcement resources for years to come, and it would lead to murder.

7

THE RUNAWAY DETECTIVE

The summer of 1995 had been exceptionally hot, insufferably humid, and especially wet in South Florida, so residents were looking forward to Labor Day. It signals the coming of fall and the promise of relief from blistering heat and oppressive humidity. The change is subtle at first, hardly noticeable to visitors, but it's apparent to "year-rounders," many of whom planned to take to the roadways and waterways over the long holiday.

Roz and Julio Vargas had the Labor Day weekend off. The couple and two of their three children had plans to travel to Orlando, a three-hour drive from their home in Davie. Roz, along with her daughter and youngest son, drove there on Friday evening, September 1. Her husband was already there, having made the drive the day before. The family planned to stay with Roz's grandparents. The organized crime detective was not due back at work until Tuesday, September 5, but the night before she was scheduled to return to the squad, Roz phoned Barbara Gentile at home to ask for the day off. The two women had worked

together for nearly a year, and they had become close colleagues and friends. To Barbara Gentile, Roz didn't sound
like herself. Gentile asked if she was okay. Roz assured her
that she was, and Gentile granted the additional time off.
The conversation was brief, and Sergeant Gentile expected
to see Roz back at work on Wednesday, but on Tuesday
night Roz phoned her supervisor again. This time she
asked for the rest of the week off, and this time Gentile
sensed that Roz was depressed.

"Are you okay? Are you still at your grandparents'
house?" Sergeant Gentile asked.

"No, I'm alone." Roz answered. "Julio went home,"

Surmising that the couple had a spat, Gentile granted Roz's
request for additional time off, which meant that Roz would
not be returning to duty until Monday, September 11. But on
the night of September 10, Roz phoned her supervisor yet
again, and this time she asked for the entire next week off.

"Roz, are you still alone?" Gentile wanted to know.

"Yes."

"Is everything okay?"

"I might have to resign."

"Roz, don't say something like that," Gentile responded.
"We'll talk about it when you come home." But before the
sergeant could utter another word, Roz Vargas made a
startling confession: "I'm involved in a relationship with a
much younger man. He's not a cop. I might have to resign."

Barbara Gentile was stunned. As far as she knew, Roslyn
Vargas was a dedicated public servant, a veteran investigator who was committed to her family and her career. She
couldn't imagine why Roz would have to resign or why a
relationship with a younger man who was not a cop would
cause her to quit the MDPD.

"It doesn't matter," Gentile said, trying to be reassuring.
"We'll talk about it when you come home."

As soon as she finished speaking to Roz, Gentile put in
a call to Julio Vargas. He revealed that he had not heard

from his wife in days, and neither had Roz's frantic parents. But one of the couple's sons had, and Roz promised him that she would return home on Monday, September 11. Reluctant to intrude on their privacy, Gentile did not ask Julio if he and Roz were having marital problems, and she would hear nothing more about Roz until the morning of Wednesday, September 13. That's when Gentile had a phone conversation with Roz's mother, who told her that Roz had come home Monday evening. She spent the night, awoke on Tuesday morning to drive her oldest son to work, and took off again.

Gentile discussed the situation with her boss, Lieutenant Petow, briefing him for the first time about the squad's runaway detective. They decided to have Julio Vargas meet with them at the SIB office in the afternoon. At that meeting Julio disclosed that on the night of September 3, he and Roz were in an Orlando restaurant having a Saturday night dinner with their family when they quarreled. Roz stormed off. Julio said he had not seen his wife since, but his two sons had—they had met their mother the night before, at an Applebee's restaurant on Sunrise Boulevard.

The Vargas boys told their father that Roz did not come to the restaurant alone. She was with a much younger man, "a young, big male with a lot of money." They said he drove a black Lincoln Mark VIII with tinted windows, and his name was Neil.

Barbara Gentile wasted no time. She immediately sent two detectives to the Vargas home with a photo of Neil Napolitano. When the lawmen showed the Vargas boys the picture, they identified the Miami bad boy as the man who had been with their mother the night before. With confirmation that Roz was with Neil, Gentile paged the errant detective. Roz returned the page. Sergeant Gentile demanded a meeting. Roz, however, wouldn't hear of it.

"I told her it was important," Gentile recalled, but "she totally refused to meet me."

Later that night, Roz phoned her sergeant. She was very upset, clearly distraught. She said that she was at home and that Gentile could meet her there. At a little past ten, Barbara Gentile and another MDPD sergeant rang the doorbell at the Vargas residence. Gentile doesn't recall who let them in, but she does remember being directed to a bedroom toward the rear of the single-story stucco house.

According to Gentile, through tears Roz said, "I'm sorry I let you down," when the two MDPD sergeants entered the room. She threw her arms around Gentile and hugged her. Laid out neatly on the king-size bed were Roz's county-issued cell phone and pager, .38-caliber Smith and Wesson Police Special, badge, official MDPD identification, and the keys to her county-issued Toyota Camry. But Detective Roslyn Vargas was not resigning from the force. Instead, she was being relieved of duty for "an administrative violation," Sergeant Gentile said, for—allegedly—consorting with someone she was investigating, an individual lawmen believed was a criminal.

After filling out property receipts for the items on the bed, Gentile placed them in a case, and the two sergeants exited the Vargas home. They had been there for less than twenty minutes. Gentile did not ask Roz about what had happened between her and Neil, and Roz never claimed she had been kidnapped by Neil Napolitano. Nor did she say that she had been held against her will.

If she had, the MDPD would have launched a massive manhunt for Neil Napolitano. A SWAT team would have raided his apartment, and every policeman and policewoman in Florida would have been on the lookout for him. But Roz never indicated that she had not been with Neil voluntarily, so no one could fault Barbara Gentile for feeling betrayed. She had trusted Roz Vargas completely, regarded her as a valuable member of her team, an intrepid partner in the fight against organized crime, and a friend.

But Roz, it seemed, had crossed the line, and the MDPD was compelled to investigate. Detectives from the department's Internal Affairs (IA) unit would do that. It would be their job to determine if Roz had participated in any illegal activities with Neil Napolitano; if she revealed information about MDPD procedures and investigations; and, more ominously, if during the course of her relationship with the young mobster she had in any way jeopardized the lives of other police officers or informants. In the meantime, Roz Vargas, disarmed and stripped of her badge, would remain on the MDPD's payroll, assigned to fielding nonemergency calls at the MDPD's Alternate Response Unit pending the outcome of the IA investigation. It was about to get underway, and the deeper the lawmen delved, the more unsettling the story became.

Five days after Barbara Gentile relieved her of her badge and gun, the official complaint against Roz Vargas landed on the desk of Cynthia Truncale, a sergeant in the Internal Affairs unit. She would be joined in the investigation by veteran MDPD Detective Joe Gross, a Massachusetts native with a law degree and a member of the Florida Bar. IA's mission is to investigate allegations of officer misconduct and criminal activity. The complaint charged that Detective Roslyn Vargas had "knowingly associated with a person engaged in unlawful activity," a serious violation of departmental policies and rules.

Roz Vargas was no stranger to Cindy Truncale. Before becoming an Internal Affairs investigator, Truncale worked at the Intracoastal Station on Biscayne Boulevard, the same station where Roz Vargas worked before joining Barbara Gentile's squad. Although the two women were acquainted, they were assigned to different units and never worked together. Nevertheless, Truncale was very familiar with Roz's heretofore stellar reputation. "She was a good officer," the Internal Affairs detective recalled. "Someone you could depend on to back you up on calls."

In the days and weeks ahead, Truncale interviewed and took statements from Roz and her supervisor, Barbara Gentile. The sergeant brought the Internal Affairs investigator up to speed on Roz's aborted undercover assignment, her requests for additional time off, her confession that she was involved with a younger man who was not a cop, and her stunning statement that she might have to resign. Gentile also revealed that the Vargas boys' identified Neil Napolitano as the man who had accompanied their mother to dinner on September 12.

Sergeant Gentile recalled an incident that occurred the month before, on the morning of August 10, when she left her office to use the ladies room. It was situated off the lobby, across from a bank of elevators. Gentile was walking toward the restroom when she saw Neil Napolitano in the lobby, near the elevators, "just milling around."

She asked him why he was there. At first Neil didn't answer, but then he said he wanted to speak with Roz.

Gentile: "I went back to our office and I said, 'Roz, you're not going to believe who is here.' And she says, 'Oh, really?' She didn't know. I said, 'I'm going to get rid of him. He's not here to tell us anything. I don't know what he wants.' She says, 'Let me listen.' So she waited outside our lobby area when I went there and told him, 'Is there anything you want to say?' He says, 'No.' "

At the time, Gentile thought the incident was peculiar, but as the Internal Affairs investigation unfolded, the episode took on a more sinister significance. That's because Miami Beach detectives Tommy Moran and Mark Defusco had arranged to bring Joe Stracci from the county jail to Gentile's SIB office that morning. They wanted to take a sworn statement from Stracci regarding his knowledge of Neil Napolitano's criminal activities in Miami Beach.

Although the MDPD had shut down its investigation of Neil, Miami Beach lawmen had not closed theirs. Moran and Defusco wanted to know about Neil's alleged drug trafficking, his ties to Junior Abbandando and Fred Massaro, and his involvement in the December disappearance of Alvino Reyes and John Davidson. But the lawmen were barred from taking him from the jail because he was a documented source for Roz Vargas, which meant they needed her to sign Stracci out of the jail. According to Defusco, he had arranged for Roz to meet him and Moran at the jail at ten in the morning to sign, but Roz did not show up. After many phone calls, the Miami Beach lawmen were able to secure Stracci's release, but instead of taking him to the SIB bureau, they decided to drive him directly to the state attorney's office.

It seemed like a simple snafu at the time, but in hindsight investigators theorized that Neil had advance knowledge that Joe Stracci was to be brought to the SIB office and that he was lurking in the lobby to intimidate the aging mobster as he emerged from the elevator. They never learned who tipped Neil off, but their suspicions were aroused as more and more details of Roz's relationship with Neil became known.

After interviewing Barbara Gentile, Cindy Truncale spoke with Organized Crime detective Gary Porterfield. He told the Internal Affairs investigator that he had noticed a change in Roz's work habits in the weeks before the Labor Day weekend.

"He used to ride with her quite frequently," Truncale recalled Porterfield telling her. "They would go out, conduct interviews together, but she suddenly started disappearing from the office. She would tell him she's going out to conduct interviews on her own."

According to Truncale, Porterfield said that he offered to accompany her, but Roz declined. "I'll call you if I need you," she reportedly told her partner. Porterfield, Truncale said, "thought that was a little bit strange."

He did ride with her on July 7, when they interviewed Carmen Sanchez at a sandwich shop on Collins Avenue. The two organized crime detectives were there when she arrived. In a report, Porterfield wrote:

> When Carmen arrived, Detective Vargas and this investigator identified ourselves. Detective Vargas told Carmen that Neil Napolitan [sic] was involved in illegal activities and Carmen may be putting herself in the position where she could be arrested. Carmen stated that she had no knowledge of any activities of Neil Napolitan [sic], and that Neil was a very good guy. People had the wrong ideas about him. . . . Carmen did say she was planning on getting away from Neil as soon as she could get enough money together. Carmen also denied that Neil ever beat her. She said he may have slapped me [sic], but he never beat me [sic].

Later that month, on July 28, Carmen moved out of the apartment she shared with Neil. She never saw him again.

Less than two months later, under threat of disciplinary action, including the loss of her job, Roz Vargas was ordered to the Internal Affairs office on September 19 to give an administrative statement. She admitted to a "personal relationship" with Neil Napolitano, but she denied that she was involved with him prior to Labor Day, declaring that the liaison began "a week and a half before."

On September 25, the investigation into allegations of officer misconduct took an unexpected turn when Cindy Truncale received a phone call from Lieutenant Malec at the Intracoastal Station. He informed the Internal Affairs investigator that Rocco Napolitano, his sister Monica, and Neil's ex-girlfriend Carmen Sanchez had come to the station to file a complaint against Detective Roslyn Vargas.

"They were complaining that their brother was missing, that they believed that Roz Vargas may know his where-abouts," Truncale recalled. It was a Sunday night, and Truncale did not have the case file with her, so she told the lieutenant to tell them to meet with her at the Internal Affairs office in the morning.

Cindy Truncale was in her office early the next morning when the threesome appeared. Rocco was surly and guarded. He would not allow the women to say anything, barking at them to "shut up" whenever they tried to speak. Rocco told Truncale little more than that he had not seen his brother since September 13, when Neil had dropped him off at their mother's apartment in Hollywood. He said that at the time his brother "was in the presence of Detective Vargas," which was why he wanted to file a complaint against her, and he wanted to file a missing-persons report, too. Rocco became hostile and belligerent when Truncale told him he would have to file the missing-persons report with police in Hollywood.

He was on edge, frightened at the thought that his brother was dead. Before storming out of Truncale's office, Rocco accused the Internal Affairs sergeant of being more interested in protecting Roz Vargas than in helping him find his brother. He left without revealing anything more about the relationship between his brother and the MDPD detective. Three days later, the investigation took another unexpected turn when Cindy Truncale learned that Neil Napolitano was dead, his remains having washed up like driftwood on the sands of Miami Beach. She met with Miami Beach homicide detective Gary Schiaffo. The two investigators agreed to share information, but they would conduct separate investigations.

In the weeks and months that followed, investigators from both agencies painstakingly traced Roz's and Neil's activities and their phone calls. They interviewed dozens of people, from South Florida to Orlando. They learned that when Roz walked away from her family, she phoned Neil from a pay phone in Orlando. Three hours later he was by her side. In the wee hours of September 4, Neil and Roz checked into a room at the Holiday Inn Lake Buena Vista near Disney World. They stayed there through September 6, when they returned to the Miami area. Later that night, Roz and Neil had dinner at Villa Perrone, an Italian restaurant on Hallandale Beach Boulevard. The couple did not eat alone. Dining with them were Gambino crime family associate Freddie Massaro and Tony Pep Trentacosta, a Gambino capo. Two days later Roz and Neil drove back to Orlando. They checked into the same Holiday Inn, staying there for three nights.

While in Orlando the couple went to restaurants, nightclubs, and Disney World, where they were photographed enjoying themselves on Splash Mountain, one of the Magic Kingdom's most popular rides. They rode go-karts at another amusement park, and they went shopping.

In October, Miami Beach detective Lori Wander interviewed store clerk Glenn Corbitt at the Sergio Tacchini in Orlando. He easily identified photos of Neil and Roz. The store clerk told lawmen that Neil and Roz were holding hands when they entered the store, and they were very affectionate with each other the entire time they were there, "hugging and kissing" and "playing grab ass in the store." Corbitt remembered Neil telling him, "I'm with the Mob. This is my girlfriend. She's a cop in Miami."

While Wander was in Orlando talking to Corbitt, Gary Schiaffo interviewed workers at Junior Abbandando's hangout, Party Girls. Roz told Truncale that her personal relationship with Neil had begun in September, but Joann Walter, the fortysomething bar manager there, told the Miami Beach homicide detective a far different story, claiming that she had been aware of the liaison since July.

She said she had known Neil for more than a year. She spoke with him often, whenever he came to Party Girls. Neil, she said, confided in her about the torrid relationship. Walter recounted how Neil engineered a ruse that brought her face-to-face with the organized crime detective.

Said Walter: "Neil came into the bar, and he said, 'I would like you to do me a favor. I want you to come outside in about ten minutes and tell me that I have a phone call.' The ten minutes went by. I came outside. He was standing over by the sign talking to a woman, and I said, 'Excuse me for interrupting, but you have a phone call. Would you like me to take a message, or are you going to take the call?' He said, 'Take a message.'"

Roz, Walter said, ignored her. "She did not acknowledge me when I came up, which I thought was odd."

Once back inside, the sandy-haired bar manager resumed her place behind the Party Girls bar. Moments later Neil was standing in front of her.

"He asked me, 'What do you think?' and I said, 'What did I think about what?' I didn't understand the question. I didn't know the person. He asked me what I thought of her physically. Did I like her appearance physically, and I made a couple of comments. I said, 'Well, I didn't really look at her, Neil.' I remember she was a brunette and that she was tiny and plain. Within a week or two he would come in, and he now started making comments about her. That he was finding himself attracted to her and vice versa. And his pager would go off, and he would say, 'That's her,' and he would leave and make a phone call, or at least that is what he would tell me he was doing."

Walter said Neil explained why he was drawn to Roz: "He talked about being fascinated by her because she was a police officer, that she was married to a police officer, and she was investigating him, and she cared about him, and she was putting everything on the line for him. That was his attraction to her, that she would sacrifice all of this for him. He normally went out with pretty flashy, attractive women. So this was somewhat of a surprise, and he commented on that. He said, 'I know that she's not the most beautiful, but the fact that she would do all of this for me is what makes her so attractive to me. . . . I am ready to throw everything away for this woman.' "

Walter told Schiaffo that in early July, Neil phoned her and told her "that he did a terrible thing and was panicking." In his report, the lawman wrote: "Joann was afraid to ask what was wrong because she remembered the two missing people and Neil's possible involvement in it, and was afraid that he might tell her something bad. Neil finally told Joann that he went to bed with Roz and he had sex with her. He further said that since her husband was a cop, and he probably fools around, he may have contracted a disease and gave it to her, and now he, Neil, may get something. Joann calmed him down and advised him to get an AIDS test."

Joann never spoke to Roz, and she never saw her again at Party Girls. But she did see her again in September at Nick's at Night, an intimate after-hours bar on Collins Avenue that had a small dance floor. Walter remembers arriving there at eleven, taking a seat at the bar, and ordering a drink. Neil and Roz arrived around midnight.

Said Walter: "They both walked up to me when they arrived. He did all of the speaking. He had his arm around her, and he said, 'Hi. How are you?' and they were both very dressed up. He had a suit on. She had a short little minidress on and heels. They were both really nicely dressed, and I think they said they had just come from dinner."

Walter recalled Neil turning to Roz. "This is my sweetie," he said to the Party Girls bartender. Once again Roz paid no attention to Walter, who went back to nursing her drink, but from her vantage point at the bar she was able to keep an eye on Roz and Neil.

"They were affectionate. They were dancing, slow dancing. [It] looked like they were having a terrific time. They were kissing, and they never bothered talking to anybody else or coming back into the [main] room again. They had the place to themselves, and they were having a great time."

Walter remembered speaking to Neil at Party Girls the night of September 13. He told her that he and Roz were planning on going away again, "but they were unsure about where to go." He promised he would see Walter when he got back, but she never saw him again. She did speak with him on the telephone later that night when he called to talk to Abbandando, but the mobster wasn't there. Walter also told Detective Schiaffo about a brief discussion she had with Junior Abbandando after Neil went missing, when she casually mentioned to the Gambino soldier that he should ask Roz about Neil's whereabouts. Abbandando, Walter recalled, "looked at me and said, 'You know about her. How come no one ever told me he was dating her?'"

"I just assumed you knew," Walter recalled replying. She said she explained to the gangster that she assumed that Junior would have known because he and Neil were so close.

"He was an idiot," Junior declared. "What was he doing being involved with her?"

Despite what Junior Abbandando told Walter, he was well aware of what Neil had been doing with Roz. He had known about the relationship for weeks, having heard about it through the grapevine. He also knew that Neil had been lying to him, telling him that he was dating a doctor who worked odd hours at the hospital. It was an attempt to explain why she would page him at one, two, or three o'clock in the morning. Junior knew the truth, and he ordered Neil to end the relationship, but the headstrong bad boy, who disregarded school rules and disobeyed his Police Explorer commanders, defied his underworld mentor. "Nobody tells me what do," he reportedly told Junior Abbandando.

"I found out that Neil was ordered to stop seeing Roz because she's a cop and he was embarrassing the Gambino crime family," Gary Schiaffo said. "Instead of complying, Neil's attitude was, 'fuck you, you don't tell me what to do.'"

Meanwhile, Miami media was following the story, too.

DEATH INVESTIGATION TAKES NEW TURN
MAN WHOSE BONES WASHED UP ON BEACH
HAD RELATIONSHIP WITH OFFICER

That was the startling headline in the *Sun Sentinel* on October 12. Citing "police sources," the newspaper reported that at the time of his death, Neil Napolitano was "involved in a personal relationship with an undercover police officer." It identified Roslyn Vargas of the MDPD as the cop, and it reported that she had been reassigned.

Later that day, Gary Schiaffo interviewed Carmen Sanchez. She told the Miami Beach detective that she left Neil on July 28, "because she was tired of his abuse," that she knew Neil was seeing Roz, and that Roz had confronted her at a sub shop in July. At that time, Schiaffo recalled, Carmen said that Roz told her, "Neil is a murderer and a drug dealer." Said Schiaffo: "Every time Neil was mentioned, Carmen would begin to cry. I asked Carmen if she knew that Neil was introducing Roz as a doctor. Carmen said she did." When Schiaffo asked Carmen if Neil would have told his Gambino associates to "fuck off" if they ordered him to stop seeing Roz, she replied, "That would exactly have been his reaction."

In the days ahead, an anonymous caller to the TIPPS hotline claimed that Neil and another man had ripped off a major drug dealer for cash and several kilos of cocaine. Neil, the caller said, had been murdered in retaliation. Investigators followed up, but the tip proved unfounded. More and more, it looked to lawmen that it was Neil's relationship with Roslyn Vargas that was the reason for his demise, and that his fate had been sealed on Wednesday, September 6. On that day Neil Napolitano became a dead man walking.

8

THE LAST SUPPER

Food is important to wiseguys. Very important. They "love to eat," says Joe Pistone. So much so they don't eat just three meals a day, which may explain why so many mobsters buy their clothes in big men's stores.

"Maybe you start with coffee and a roll," former FBI undercover agent Pistone explains, "but then you maybe have another breakfast at home or at the club. You also eat a big lunch at the club, then go home for dinner with the family. Then you eat another dinner when you meet up with the wiseguys at night. And if there's a meeting with other wiseguys or bosses, that's another meal right there."

Their culinary delights include mountains of pasta swimming in freshly made tomato sauce. They prefer their meatballs big—"the sizes of pool balls," Pistone says. Other favorites are sausages, calamari, peppers, and cheeses, especially mozzarella, and they wash their meals down with fine Italian wine and a good cup of espresso.

South Florida wiseguys loved the food at Villa Perrone. The eatery offered generous portions of traditional gourmet Italian cuisine; a large private room (where they could discuss business); ornate, faux marble columns; flamboyant fountains; fake greenery; plaster statues; and busts of Roman emperors, gods, and goddesses. Its valet-parking concession was run by the son of a Lucchese family capo, and it had an historic connection to the South Florida underworld.

The restaurant was built on the site of what had been the Sea Inn, a restaurant that had once been owned by brothers Frank and Thomas Romano. They were convicted of racketeering in 1981, and the U.S. Justice Department seized the restaurant. It remained a vacant eyesore until 1987, when another pair of brothers, Frank and Dominic Perrone, bought the property. They tore the decaying Sea Inn down and replaced it with the gaudy Villa Perrone. Located in the heart of the South Florida Mob belt, it became a wiseguy favorite and a locale that the FBI's organized crime squad kept under surveillance. It was where Roz and Neil went the evening of September 6 for a late supper.

"Neil said, 'Come with me. We're going to grab a bite to eat,'" Roz remembered. Then he instructed her in how to behave: "Just sit there and be quiet. And don't say anything."

Neil had a brief phone conversation with Fred Massaro earlier. The Gambino associate invited him to the Villa Perrone, where Massaro was hosting a get-together for his longtime friend, Gambino soldier and acting capo Tony Pep Trentacosta. Although not a "made man," Fred Massaro was a big earner for the Gambino crime family, highly respected, and powerful enough to be able to arrange the introduction of a low-level wiseguy like Neil Napolitano to a capo.

"It's a way of letting him know he's being rewarded for his activities, that he's been recognized for contributing to the family [because] he's working hard and he has

a chance for advancement," said Detective Joseph Mc-
Mahon, the MDPD's then resident expert on Italian organized
crime. At the time, the twenty-year veteran was assigned to
the Criminal Intelligence Unit of the SIB. Its mission was
to coordinate and share information with its counterparts
in other law enforcement agencies. Information Criminal
Intelligence Unit detectives learned would then be passed
on to organized crime squads like Barbara Gentile's.

"It's very strict, very rigid," Detective McMahon said
of the protocol governing the introduction of a nonmember
associate to a capo. The meeting may be nothing more than
a brief handshake at a ball game or the racetrack, or over a
meal. Whatever the venue, the associate is not allowed to
speak to the capo, unless he's spoken to first.

Fred Massaro expected Neil to show up at Villa Perrone alone, so he was surprised when Neil arrived at nine
o'clock with Roz. The others—Tony Pep, Dr. Jeffrey Kamlet and his wife, Karen, and Massaro's girlfriend, Carol, a
waitress at Party Girls—were already seated in the restaurant's private room. "We were eating dinner, somewhere
between the salad and the main course, when they walked
in," Dr. Kamlet, a Miami Beach medical doctor, recalled.
Roz knew no one, so Neil introduced her to Massaro, telling
the Gambino gangster, "This is my new girlfriend, I'm in
love." Massaro in turn introduced the couple to the others.
No one asked Roz about her occupation or her last name,
and neither Neil nor Roz volunteered the information.

They were an eclectic group—a prominent physician
and his wife, two gangsters, a mobster's live-in girlfriend,
Neil Napolitano, and Organized Crime Squad detective
Roslyn Vargas. As Neil and Roz took seats opposite the
Kamlets, Neil realized that he and the medic had previ-
ously crossed paths.

"I met you before," he told the physician, who looked
at him quizzically. Clearly, Kamlet did not recall, so Neil

tried to jog his memory: "Junior brought me to the ER, and you took care of me as a patient." Neil reminded the doctor that he had sought medical attention after sustaining an injury while kickboxing, but the forty-year-old physician still didn't recall treating him. He did, however, recall taking care of Fred Massaro, telling investigators that "Freddie is my patient. He had diabetes and other problems, and I took care of that."

He also took care of Tony Pep Trentacosta some years before, when Massaro brought him to the ER for a sore throat. Spotting a polyp and suspecting cancer, Kamlet referred the Gambino capo to an ear, nose, and throat specialist, who diagnosed cancer of the esophagus. A grateful Trentacosta credited Kamlet with saving his life, and the Gambino capo continued to consult the physician for medical advice. The two men became friends, but Kamlet claimed he never heard Tony Pep, Junior Abbandando, or Fred Massaro discuss anything illegal, nor was he aware of any crimes they had committed.

Said Dr. Kamlet: "Right from the beginning, when I first met these guys, I always told them, 'Please don't ever mention anything around me. Don't ever say anything around me that I can't tell to anybody else at any other time because I have a family. I have kids and I would give you up in a heartbeat.' I told this to these guys. I said, 'If we ever have dinner, and if you ever have anything to discuss, don't talk about it in my presence,' and they never have."

Instead they made small talk. Roz hardly said a word, while the others chatted about cars—Lincolns and Lotuses— and about Villa Perrone's cuisine: the *pappardelle alle Perrone* (wide noodles with peas, ham, and mushrooms in a light tomato sauce) and the *spezzatino di pollo* (pieces of chicken in olive oil and white wine).

According to Dr. Kamlet, Neil and Roz were openly affectionate at Villa Perrone. "Kissie, kissie," he said, their loving behavior reminding him of "high school kids." Neil "seemed enamored of this woman . . . head over heels for her," which surprised the medic. "Though she isn't an unattractive woman," he explained, "she isn't a gorgeous woman, and with these kind of guys, you expect the blonds with the breast implants."

Gambino associate John Porcaro joined them for dessert. Afterward, Neil excused himself from the table. He returned minutes later, announcing to everyone's surprise that he had paid the four hundred dollar tab.

"Why did you do that?" Massaro, exclaimed. "That wasn't necessary." Then Neil presented Trentacosta with a box of Cuban cigars, expensive Montecristos.

"It impressed me," Dr. Kamlet said. "I had heard that Cuban cigars are $40 apiece, and this guy gave him a box of twenty, forty cigars, and that is a lot of money. When he offered them to Pep, I turned to Pep and said, 'Tony, who is this kid that he would pick up the bill and give you these cigars?' "

"You know, doc, I don't want them," the Gambino capo replied. "I don't even know this kid."

As he was about to leave, Neil showed the physician his tattoos. He asked Dr. Kamlet if knew anything about laser removal of the markings.

"Why do you want to do that?" the doctor asked.

"Because they are too identifiable to law enforcement," Neil answered.

Kamlet thought the reply bizarre—"Not the kind of thing a real Mob guy would say," the medic opined, but neither was bringing Roslyn Vargas, Organized Crime Detective Roslyn Vargas, to dinner with a Gambino capo.

After leaving Villa Perrone, Neil and Roz went clubbing until the wee hours of Thursday morning. They visited two South Florida nightspots: Bajas, in Coconut Grove, and Bermuda Triangle, on Las Olas Boulevard, Fort Lauderdale's Rodeo Drive.

On Friday the couple drove to the Dadeland Mall, in

Miami, where Roz bought clothes and makeup. In the evening they drove back to Orlando, checking into the same hotel they stayed in the week before. Neil registered under an alias, calling himself Cam Jackson. He paid for the room with cash. Over the next two days, Roz and Neil shopped, went clubbing, and visited Disney World. On Monday, September 11, they returned to South Florida. Roz went home for one night before returning to Neil's apartment the next day. She was in Neil's bed when Rocco Napolitano, newly arrived from New York where he had been living and dealing steroids, stopped by.

Just two days before, while Neil and Roz were on their second sojourn to Orlando, Rocco, at home in New York, took an ominous phone call from Frank Abbandando Jr. The gangster's words were chilling: "I don't know what I am going to do about your brother." Rocco needed no explanation. He knew the Mob's rules, and he knew exactly what Junior meant. His brother's life was in the gangster's hands, and it was because of his relationship with the MDPD detective.

Rocco knew that Neil had been seeing Roz long before Junior phoned him. Joe Stracci had told him. And Neil told him weeks before, when Rocco was last in South Florida. He was riding with Neil when his brother's pager went off. "I just got a beep. I have to go see Roz," he remembers his brother saying. In those days, Rocco told investigators, Neil would not bring the organized crime detective to his apartment. Instead, they would rendezvous at a hotel or a motel.

———————————

With Junior Abbandando's words ringing in his ears, Rocco hurriedly packed a bag for the long drive to South Florida. He drove straight through, stopping only to buy gasoline and to relieve himself. It was a grueling ride. He arrived in the early hours of Monday, September 11. Exhausted, he rested at his mother's apartment. Later that day, Rocco drove to his brother's apartment, where Roz was lounging under the covers in his brother's bed.

They had spoken previously on the phone, when his brother called him. At the time, Roz and Neil were on their way to Disney World. Rocco spoke first to Neil, and he didn't like what he heard.

"That's it. I'm finished. I'm done. I'm out. I'm changing my life," Rocco said his brother told him. To Rocco, Neil sounded depressed and confused. Rocco was alarmed, because Neil was talking about turning his back on Junior Abbandando and Fred Massaro, and Rocco knew that no one walks away from men like Junior Abbandando and Fred Massaro. But before he could say anything, Neil handed the phone to Roz, who wasted no time declaring her strong feelings for Neil.

"I really care about your brother," Rocco remembered her saying. "I'm in love with him. I never felt this way about anyone before."

Rocco wasn't the first member of Neil's family to hear Roz gush about her feelings for the young wiseguy. On Wednesday, August 30, Roz was with Neil when he used her cell phone to call his oldest sister, Monica, who was living in San Diego, California.

Neil hardly ever called her, so Monica was shocked when she heard her brother's voice. "I thought someone had died," she recalled.

"Neil, why are you calling me?" Monica asked.

"I want you to talk to somebody. Her name is Roslyn," Neil said.

"Why?" Monica remembers asking, but it was too late. Neil had already handed the phone to Roz.

Monica said that Roz was crying hysterically as she professed her love for Neil, and declared "that she was going to leave her husband, that she was going to leave her children, and she was going to leave her job."

The conversation left Monica shaken. Roz, she said, sounded "like a mental case." They would speak a second time, while Roz and Neil were in Orlando. Roz, Monica said, told her that she and Neil had not left their hotel room "in a couple of days." When she heard that, Monica cut the conversation short. "I was really uncomfortable . . . I didn't think that was an appropriate thing to say to his sister; that it would make my mind wander to a place I did not want it to go."

Neil's relationship with the married, forty-year-old organized crime detective who had been assigned to investigate him for murder was a continuing source of friction between the Napolitano brothers. They argued about Roz whenever they spoke, but Neil would not listen to his younger sibling. Rocco believed that no good could come from the relationship. His brother, he feared, would eventually wind up in prison—or dead.

———————

For the most part, unless they are involved in a serious relationship, young men like Neil Napolitano do not bring women home to meet their mothers, but this is just what Neil did. Fifty-six-year-old Velma Byrne told investigators that she was fast asleep one night when she was awakened by a ringing doorbell.

"I looked through the peephole," she recalled. "I only saw Neil, so I let him in. Right behind him comes Roslyn Vargas."

Roz and Neil were dressed to the nines, Velma remembered. Roz carried a purse, "a nice one with a shoulder strap; could have been a Gucci," she said.

"Neil, what do you want?" Velma asked. "It's two in the morning."

"Ma, I want you to get the picture albums." Then he introduced Roz.

"This is Roslyn. I want you to get out all the albums and show Roslyn pictures of when you were young, how beautiful you were."

While Neil played with Booboo, his mother's dog, Velma went to retrieve the album. At first Velma thought that Neil had brought a stripper to her apartment. Or a hooker.

"Does Roslyn work at a club?" she wanted to know, as she returned with the album.

"Mom, you will never believe what she does," Neil answered.

"I have no idea," Velma replied.

Neil hinted: "She's been in court many, many, many times." When his mother shrugged her shoulders, indicating that she still had no idea, Neil turned toward Roz.

"Show her who you are," he commanded. Roz complied. She opened her purse, removed her badge, and showed it to Velma.

"She's a lady cop. Organized crime. And she's investigating me," Neil said boastfully.

The revelation was a jaw-dropper. It left Velma speechless. Roz removed her gun from her purse and handed it to Velma, assuring her that the gun was not loaded.

"She's a police officer, and she's investigating me," Neil boasted again, as his mother carefully examined the Smith and Wesson.

While Neil and Roz looked through the album, Roz was "hugging him like a little baby girl, like she was in love," Velma observed. Roz "was just dizzy about him . . . like a dizzy little girl for being a fifty-year-old woman, or however old she was."

According to Velma, Roz and Neil stayed for an hour, the visit ending when Neil said, "Ma, we've got to go." On his way out, Neil placed a roll of cash in his mother's hand.

"Nice meeting you," Velma called out to Roz as the couple left her apartment.

"Nice meeting you, too," Roz responded.

The two women would meet again, sooner than either expected, and the circumstances would not be as pleasant.

9

SEPTEMBER 13, THE LAST DAY

It had been a very hectic week for Roz Vargas and Neil Napolitano. On Wednesday they had supper with Fred Massaro and Tony Trentacosta, after which they went clubbing in South Florida. They drove to Orlando on Friday. They spent Saturday at Disney World. On Sunday they went shopping, with Neil purchasing a pair of jeans and two jogging suits at the Sergio Tacchini store. Later that night Roz phoned Barbara Gentile, telling her sergeant that she might have to resign. On Monday Roz and Neil checked out of their hotel and returned to Neil's apartment. Later, Roz phoned home and arranged to meet her son at a sandwich shop in Hollywood. She spent that night at home, then returned to Neil's apartment the next day. In the evening Neil and Roz had dinner with her sons, but instead of going home again, she left with Neil.

On Wednesday, September 13, Roz and Neil awoke to a bright blue sky. The weatherman promised the mercury would not top ninety degrees and predicted scattered showers later in the day. Floridians were paying attention to the eastern Caribbean, where Tropical Storm Marilyn, the thirteenth named storm of the season, was churning its way toward the Florida Peninsula, while across the country in Los Angeles, Americans were still paying attention to the O. J. Simpson double-murder trial, which was in its eighth month.

Despite the sunny weather, Neil was on edge and irritable from the moment he opened his eyes, but his mood had nothing to do with storms in the Caribbean or the long-running trial in California. The fact of the matter was that Neil had been jittery for some time. His close friend Joe Defuria took notice. The twenty-eight-year-old bouncer at Bermuda Triangle was interviewed by MDPD Internal Affairs Detective Joe Gross.

> *Defuria considered [Neil Napolitano] to be his best friend. Defuria stated that Neil would often come visit him at his job at the nightclub and spend hours with Defuria just hanging out. Defuria stated that he knew generally that Neil was involved with organized crime but that he never asked any questions about it and Neil never volunteered any information.*
>
> *Defuria stated that during the summer of 1995, Neil told him that he had fallen in love with a police-woman. Neil told him that he had just seen her in a car and struck up a conversation with her. Defuria encouraged Neil to bring her to the club, and finally Neil did so. Defuria met her only for a moment and described her as being a brunette and older than Neil. They spent some time in the club, and Defuria recalled that they sat together at a table, and Neil had a non-alcohol beverage while the officer (Roz Vargas) had at least one drink containing alcohol. Defuria placed this visit to the club to be about two months prior to Neil's disappearance and death. After the visit, Neil continued to stop by and*

Roslyn Vargas at Disney World.
Miami-Dade state attorney's office

Roslyn Vargas
Miami-Dade Police Department

Neil Napolitano's booking photo.
Miami-Dade Department of Corrections

Napolitano's bones washed up on Miami Beach on September 27, 1995.

Miami Beach Police Department

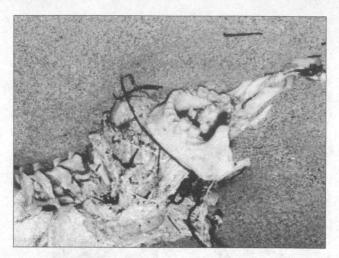

Napolitano's jawbone on the beach.
Miami Beach Police Department

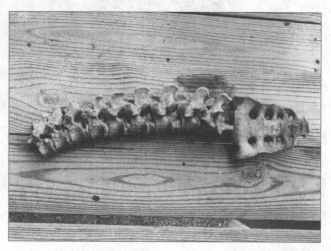

A section of Napolitano's vertebrae.
Miami Beach Police Department

LEFT: Anthony "Tony Pep" Trentacosta booking photo from
September 26, 2000.
Federal Bureau of Investigation

RIGHT: Ariel Hernandez
Miami-Dade Department of Corrections

LEFT: Joe Stracci
Miami-Dade Department of Corrections

RIGHT: Fred Massaro booking photo from September 26, 2000.
Federal Bureau of Investigation

Assistant U.S. Attorneys Jeffrey Sloman (left) and Lawrence LaVecchio
Author

FBI Special Agent Terry Feisthammel
Federal Bureau of Investigation

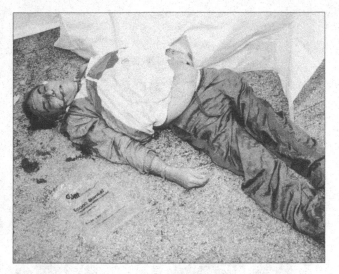

Frank Abbandando Jr., minutes after he was gunned down in a Miami parking lot.
Miami-Dade state attorney's office

Rocco Napolitano
Miami-Dade Department of Corrections

The stereo box that held the body of Jeanette Smith floats in a murky Everglades canal.

Broward Sheriff's Office (BSO)

see Defuria. He talked about being in love with the policewoman. Defuria advised Neil to stop seeing the police officer because it could lead to trouble for Neil considering Neil's line of work, but Neil ignored this advice.

Defuria stated that for the bulk of the time that he associated with Neil, Neil was perfectly groomed and impeccably dressed. Shortly before his disappearance and death, however, Neil had begun to neglect both his grooming and dress. This was to such an extent that Defuria pulled Neil in front of a mirror at the club and remonstrated with him for letting a woman bring him to such depths.

Others who saw Neil in the days before he went missing confirmed Defuria's observations. Some even thought that Neil had taken to drinking or had been taking pills.

Reynaldo Gispert, the Napolitano boys' foster brother, told investigators that Neil was wary of Roz, even though she vowed that she would leave her family to be with him.

"Neil didn't trust anybody," said Reynaldo, an auto mechanic and church youth director. Neil visited with him at his auto repair shop about two weeks before he disappeared. Gispert recalled Neil telling him that "he didn't know if Roz really loved him or if she was just having sex with him to crack a case." Cops, he added, "will give blow jobs just to crack a case."

And Neil thought he had been marked for murder.

Reynaldo: "I asked him, 'Why are your days numbered?' And he said, 'It's just all going to be over. I need to get out of all this.' I looked at his car, and his car was just a mess. It was all dusty. I knew something was wrong because he is very meticulous about his things, cleans everything up. He said, 'I don't care about any of this anymore. I just want to get out of all this." And before he left, Neil said he wanted to go to church.

Reynaldo never saw Neil again, but the foster brothers spoke on the telephone on September 6, about an hour before Neil and Roz went to the Villa Perrone. Neil phoned Reynaldo.

"Hey, listen," Neil said. "Roz doesn't believe that I want to go to church. Can you talk to her? I'll put her on."

The next thing Gispert heard was a woman's voice.

"Hi, I am Roz."

"You are the one dating my brother?" he asked.

"Yeah, he talks about you all the time."

"How are you doing? Are you guys killing each other?" Reynaldo asked jokingly, referring to Neil's revelation the week before that he feared for his life.

"No, we're not," Roz answered, laughing, too.

"If you kill him, make sure that we can have an open casket for him," Gispert recalled saying.

Then the conversation turned to church.

"He really wants to go?" Roz asked.

"Yes, he does," was the response, after which Neil came back on the line. He made plans to go to church with Gispert the following Sunday, but he never showed up. He went with Roz to Orlando instead, and the two men never spoke again.

Although Defuria and Gispert attributed Neil's edginess and slide into slovenliness to being torn between his feelings for Roz and the lure of the underworld, the one who knew him best, his brother, Rocco, told FBI Special Agent Howe Grover that he had noticed subtle changes in Neil's demeanor as far back as December 1994, not long after Reyes and Davidson went missing. According to the G-man, Rocco said that Neil never admitted to him that he was involved in the suspected murder of the two men, nor did he tell him that he wasn't.

On Neil's agenda this morning, one week after his final phone conversation with Gispert, was a meeting with Junior

Abbandando, his Mob mentor. Junior had been avoiding Neil for weeks, refusing to take his phone calls or see him. Neil had made a life-changing decision, and he was going to tell the Gambino gangster what it was and explain to him that he had nothing to worry about. Afterward, he planned to meet his brother at an auto body shop in Hialeah, where Rocco was having work done on the Lincoln Mark VIII that Neil had been driving months before, when he was under surveillance by Barbara Gentile's organized crime squad. Neil had gotten a new Lincoln in the summer. He gave the old one to Rocco, who had it in New York until he drove it back to South Florida in response to Junior's phone call.

Neil picked Rocco up at about one o'clock in the afternoon. Roz was with him, sitting in the front passenger seat. Rocco climbed into the back. From the body shop they drove to lawyer Angelo Ali's office in downtown Miami. At first, the talk inside the car during the twenty-minute drive was all about Neil's morning meeting with Junior.

Said Rocco: "The last day, September 13, Roslyn went with my brother to Party Girls and sat in the car when my brother went in and told Abbandando, 'This is the cop, this is the lady that I have been seeing all the time.' But Junior knew about Roslyn Vargas from the beginning."

According to Rocco, Neil tried to reassure the gangster, telling Abbandando, "I know you guys are upset, but I'm changing my life. I'm finished. I don't know what you're paranoid for. She knows all about the drug deals. She knows everything. She's with me now. There is nothing to worry about."

But Junior didn't wish Neil luck. He didn't congratulate him, and he didn't hug and kiss him on the cheeks like wiseguys do. Instead, he looked up at Neil and said, "I have no idea what you are talking about." Then Junior turned his back on his protégé and walked away.

Rocco took Junior's reaction as a dire omen, "a sign that they felt that my brother couldn't be trusted. It was a very dangerous situation."

And he was disturbed by Roz's reaction. "She should have known better. As an organized crime detective, she should have protected him." Instead, Rocco said, "She was laughing, as if [there was] nothing to worry about. Roslyn, while I was in the car, was discussing it as well. She participated in the conversation, as I said, and she felt there was nothing out of the ordinary with Abbandando's reaction to what had taken place, and I was very bothered by that."

Rocco said he was also bothered by Neil's attitude, describing it as "blasé."

"It was as if it was a joke, and Roslyn turned to the side in the front seat so she could see me as well as talk to my brother, and she was joking about it as well, and she had made a comment as to, 'Yes, I mean, who is he kidding? I mean, they're all drug dealers.'"

The discussion about Neil's meeting with Junior Abbandando continued until they arrived at Angelo Ali's office. The seventy-four-year-old criminal defense attorney knew the Napolitano boys well, and he knew their mother, too. On their way in, Neil handed Roz a Rolex that belonged to Rocco.

"Here," he said. "Hold on to this, so I can change the face on it." She put it into her purse.

Once inside the attorney's office, Rocco sat on a chair in front of the attorney's desk, while Neil and Roz sat on a sofa directly behind Rocco.

"They were lying on the couch, kissing," Rocco recalled, describing their interaction as "bubbly, giggly, very affectionate," and "mutual." They were acting "as if they were newlyweds on a honeymoon."

After ten minutes, Roz and Neil left the office, holding hands and hugging, while Rocco remained with the lawyer. He caught up with Roz and his brother later in the Seybold

Building, a ten-story structure on NE 1st Street that serves
as the hub of Miami's jewelry industry. Roz, Rocco recalled,
was trying on an expensive pair of diamond earrings that
Neil offered to buy for her, but they left the store without
making a purchase. From there they drove to Velma Byrne's
apartment in Hollywood, arriving at four thirty. When Neil
pulled the Lincoln into the parking lot at Velma's building, the brothers stepped out of the car while Roz remained
inside. Neil and Rocco hugged and kissed.

"I'll see you later," Neil said, confirming the brothers'
plans to meet up later that evening. Then Neil got back into
the Lincoln and drove off. Rocco never saw him again.

At six o'clock Neil and Roz were at a restaurant in Broward County. Roz arranged to have her mother meet her
there to drive her home, and it would be the last time she
saw Neil, too. In his case file notes, Miami Beach detective
Gary Schiaffo summarized what he learned from Mildred
Rivera:

> *Roz told her mother she was at a restaurant and did
> not have a ride. Mrs. Rivera told Roz she would come
> and get her. Mrs. Rivera drove to the Macaroni Grill
> on University and Broward Boulevard to pick up
> Roz. When she arrived she saw Roz standing in front
> with a W/M [white male] wearing a black and white
> "Fila" jumpsuit. As Mrs. Rivera walked toward Roz,
> she could see that Roz was upset and looked as if
> she had been crying. Roz introduced the W/M to her
> mother as Neil and the mother just said hello. Mrs.
> Rivera began to argue with her daughter about her
> behavior lately and Neil came over to them and said,
> "Why don't we go inside, calm down, and have some
> soup?" Mrs. Rivera snapped back, "If I want soup
> I'll go home and make some," and told her daugh-
> ter to get into the car. Mrs. Rivera noticed Neil walk
> over to a black Lincoln and get in.*

*As Roz and her mother were driving, Mrs. Rivera
demanded to know what was going on, and began to
tell Roz about her behavior and her lack of responsibility with her children. Roz yelled back, "I don't
want to talk about it" and kept quiet all the way
home.*

It is not known where Neil went after dropping Roz off,
but he was seen later that night at Party Girls. He went
there looking for Junior Abbandando. Witnesses say the
gangster wasn't at the nude bar, and Neil left alone. Meanwhile, Rocco, who was expecting to hear from his brother,
became alarmed when dinnertime passed without a phone
call from Neil. He paged his brother several times, then
drove to Party Girls and Nick's at Night looking for him.

And he phoned Roz Vargas.

Rocco: "Now when I spoke to Roslyn, she's an entirely
different person. Now she doesn't want to speak to me. I
even went as far as to tell her that, 'If you don't speak to me
I'm going to the law. I don't care if you're a cop. I don't care
if my brother goes to jail.' I told her, stressed to her over
and over again, 'I'm going to the law,' but she didn't care."

Rocco phoned her again. This time, he recalled, she said,
"Speak to my attorney."

Believing that Roz was involved in Neil's disappearance, Rocco tried another tack. Using a different phone, he
dialed Roz again, but this time he entered his brother's 007
code. Roz called back immediately. Now Rocco began to
think that Roz Vargas really did not know what had happened to Neil. Over the next several days Velma and Rocco
continued to page Neil, to no avail. Phone records revealed
that Roz paged him, too. Then on the morning of Sunday,
September 17, Roz drove from her home in Davie to Velma
Byrne's apartment in Hollywood, arriving there between
six and seven. When she knocked on the door, Velma let
her in.

"Something is wrong. They got Neil," Velma remembers Roz saying.

"Who got Neil?" Velma demanded, but Roz did not answer.

Roz, Velma said, was "crying hysterically." And she was shaking. She asked Velma for the key to Neil's apartment. When Velma told her that she did not have one, Roz turned to leave.

Said Velma: "I got her little hands, her wrists. I said, 'You are not going anywhere.' She was shaking, weeping, frantic. I took her back to my bed, a double bed that Rocco bought me, the only thing in the apartment because I just moved. I said, 'You better tell me what is going on. Wait until I get dressed. I'll go with you. We will go look for Neil.' She said, 'No, no, you can't come with me.'"

As she headed for the door, Roz reached into her pocket. She handed Velma the gold Rolex wristwatch Neil had given her as they walked into Angelo Ali's office four days before.

"If you find Neil, are you going to come back and tell me?" Velma pleaded.

"Yes, I'll come back," Roz promised.

The next day, Velma phoned Roz. "Neil is missing on account of you."

"You're right. You're right," Velma remembered her saying. She sounded contrite, remorseful.

"If anything happens to Neil, you're going to have to answer to me," Velma warned.

"Are you threatening me?" Roz asked icily, contrition and remorse gone from her voice.

Before Velma could utter another word, the phone went dead. It left Velma angry and worried, and with good reason. Her oldest son had not been seen or heard from for five days, while her youngest, Rocco, believed that his life was in danger, too. Velma and Rocco's worst fears about Neil were confirmed on September 29, when Dr. Richard

Souviron, the forensic dentist, matched Neil's dental records to the teeth and jawbone that washed up on the beach on September 27. But despite his fears for his own life, Rocco didn't run and hide. Instead, he did what his fiery-tempered brother would have done if it had been Rocco's bones that washed up on the beach instead—he sought out the person he believed responsible for Neil's death.

10

JUNIOR'S DEMISE

By November 1, Miami Beach homicide detective Gary Schiaffo was stymied. His investigation into the death of Neil Napolitano had hit a brick wall. The one person who could shed light on Neil's last hours, Roz Vargas, declined to speak to him, even though she had been eliminated as a suspect. He did, however, interview her husband, her children, and her mother.

"That was how I found out about the Disney trip," the homicide detective recalled.

And he learned about Roz's undercover assignment from Barbara Gentile. Schiaffo: "Roz was initially working Neil for the disappearance of Reyes and Davidson, and for the import and export of the drugs he was dealing. Then we find out information from Carmen, from Rocco, from Monica, from the mother, that Roz was the girlfriend of Neil, and we have Roz in Orlando, and the fight with Julio on the fourth [of September]. We have Roz at the meeting when they met with Tony Pep and Freddie. We have Roz . . . having dinner with Neil and the kids. Then we have Roz being picked up by her mother on the thirteenth [of September]. Then we have Roz showing up at Neil's mother's house crying, and saying, 'They got him,' and she has this [Rolex] watch that belonged, she said, to Rocco. So we have Roz from back in June or July with him. We have Roz's belongings at his apartment."

Schiaffo hoped Roz would "give me a light into things that might have been discussed with her by Neil, since they were together at Disney World."

He explained why: "They spent the night together, the night before he disappeared. They were together the whole day. The night he disappeared, the mother told me that when she went to Macaroni Grill, Roz was crying, and Neil was there. So I don't know if maybe Neil said something to her . . . because she did tell Sergeant Gentile, a day or two before, that she was in love with another man, she may have to resign . . . I thought maybe she could shed some light. I felt being a police officer, she should have cooperated in a homicide investigation."

But Roz apparently felt otherwise, and without her help all the lawman had were body parts. No indication of the cause of death. No murder weapon. No eyewitnesses. And no proof that Neil Napolitano had been murdered, let alone whodunit. The criminalists from the Broward Sheriff's Office who went through Neil's Lincoln turned up nothing helpful even though they took the vehicle apart. They did, however, identify the green liquid as Gatorade, but the vehicle had been wiped clean of fingerprints.

Nevertheless, Schiaffo assumed that Neil had been the victim of foul play. And he had a theory. He believed Neil was murdered as he sat inside his car. It would have taken at least two people, one in the front seat and the other in the back. The detective speculated that Neil was drinking from an open container of Gatorade when the backseat passenger wrapped the driver's side seatbelt around his neck. When the belt was suddenly yanked back, Neil's arms jerked up reflexively, causing the sports drink to spill and splash the interior of the car. After he was strangled, Schiaffo theorized, Neil's body was carried to a boat, weighed down, and dumped at sea, most likely off Haulover Beach Park.

From an anonymous caller Gary Schiaffo learned that Junior Abbandando owned a small power boat, but when Miami Beach lawmen went to examine it, they discovered that it had sunk two weeks before. It was fifty yards out in Biscayne Bay, just a half a football field from where it had been docked behind Junior Abbandando's waterfront residence on Bay Harbor Island. Was it a coincidence? Lawmen don't believe in coincidences. Investigators, however, decided to let the sunken craft remain at the bottom of the bay because the salt water and the current would have washed away any useful evidence.

Nevertheless, Schiaffo concluded that Neil Napolitano had been murdered, whacked by his Mob cronies because of his relationship with organized crime detective Roslyn Vargas.

Neil and Roz, Schiaffo said, were "taunting" the Gambino wiseguys, "throwing it in their faces." Neil even had the audacity to bring her to Villa Perrone on September 6, where she met Tony Pep Trentacosta. Neil had been warned by Junior, but he chose her over them, and despite his assurance—"She's with me now. There is nothing to worry about"—the mobsters felt threatened, concerned that he was spilling secrets about their illicit businesses.

"The Mob," Detective Schiaffo said, "takes no chances. They don't trust anyone. To them, Neil was a rat, and they feared that he would roll over on them."

So it was decided that Neil Napolitano would disappear, but it wouldn't be the first time a South Florida wiseguy vanished, his car found abandoned at one of the area's airports. In 1976, Johnny Roselli's car was found in a parking garage at Miami International Airport. His dismembered body turned up floating in a barrel in Biscayne Bay.

Nor would it be the last. On June 13, 1998, more than four years after Neil's remains washed up on Miami Beach, thirty-nine-year-old John Porcaro disappeared.

Bronx-born Porcaro was a fearsome-looking five-foot-seven, two-hundred-pound Gambino associate who sported a glass right eye and a horseshoe-shaped scar on his face. He made a fortune in the moving business operating a string of companies including Father and Son Moving and Storage of Florida Inc. and A Nice Jewish Boy Transfer and Storage Inc. Porcaro's companies racked up loads of complaints for lowballing estimates then holding furniture and other items hostage until customers paid hundreds of dollars in extra fees. Tony Pep operated Father and Son Moving and Storage in Georgia, while Fred Massaro was a principal in Father and Son Moving and Storage of Jacksonville Inc.

Porcaro also ran a South Florida boiler-room scam that lawmen say bilked investors out of millions of dollars. Operating as Trump Financial Group, the bogus Miami currency-trading operation had no connection to Donald Trump or any of his companies.

Lawmen said that Porcaro, who lived with his wife and daughter in a sprawling four thousand square foot waterfront home, paid tribute to Tony Pep Trentacosta and worked with Freddie Massaro. He also owned five cars, including a Rolls-Royce convertible, and three boats—one of which was a cigarette boat. And he enjoyed the company of South Beach models. "John Porcaro lives a lifestyle well beyond his means," narcotics detective Edward Goldbach wrote in a 1990 report.

Although lawmen suspected that Porcaro was dealing drugs—a suspicion the moving-and-storage magnate vehemently denied—what may have gotten him whacked was something else: he had persuaded several made men and associates to invest in an offshore-gambling operation that turned out to be bogus. When the gangsters realized that they had been conned, Porcaro was ordered to reimburse them for their investments. He refused.

On the morning he vanished, Porcaro, an avid fisherman, left a note for his wife, Filemena: "Fil, went fishing, got call, swordfish are biting. Love, J. I'll call later." Next to the note, he left his wedding ring and Rolex watch. His Mercedes convertible was found at the Fort Lauderdale International Airport by Massaro. A few days later, Massaro walked into the boiler room's offices in Aventura and announced that he had taken over. He also took over Porcaro's Miami-based moving-and-storage company.

Lawmen suspect that the Mob sent Porcaro to a watery grave, but unlike Neil, he stayed there. Neil was supposed to sleep with the fishes, too. If he had remained among the missing, there would have been little law enforcement could or would have done. But even in death, the rebellious Miami bad boy refused to do what he was supposed to do. His remains rose from the sea, and his postmortem act of defiance would haunt the mobsters. It brought a lot of heat from lawmen. Investigators from three agencies—the FBI, the MDPD, and the Miami Beach Police Department—zeroed in on Junior Abbandando and Fred Massaro and the rest of the South Florida crew.

They showed up at their homes, at Party Girls, and at other Mob haunts in South Florida, asking questions and serving subpoenas. Nearly four years would pass before the entire crew would be brought down, undone by yet another shocking episode of gangland violence—the gruesome murder of Jeanette Smith. But before that happened, South Florida lawmen would be rocked by more gangland violence.

On October 22, one month after Neil Napolitano's body parts washed up out of the Atlantic Ocean, two bullet-riddled bodies were discovered in a Fort Lauderdale apartment, while a third was found in a Boca Raton condo. The victims knew each other, and the bullets that killed them came from the same gun. All were shot while they slept. Cops believed the same gunman committed the three murders.

The Fort Lauderdale victims were twenty-seven-year-old Vincent D'Angola, a muscular six-foot-five, two-hundred-pound strip club bouncer and bodyguard, and his twenty-four-year-old girlfriend Jami Schneider. The third victim was D'Angola's close friend, twenty-six-year-old Mark Rizzuto.

The men were Mob wannabes with connections to a violent underworld crew known as the Ozone Park Boys, who reported to Ronald "One Arm" Trucchio, a Gambino capo. Lawmen suspected that D'Angola took part in a Fort Lauderdale jewelry store heist that netted two hundred and fifty thousand dollars in gold, diamonds, and other precious jewels. It was led by members of the Ozone Park Boys. D'Angola, investigators said, drove the getaway car.

At the time of the slaying, Schneider was wearing a necklace that had been taken in the jewelry store robbery. Investigators cleared Schneider, who was visiting from New Jersey and had no part in the heist. She died because she happened to be in D'Angola's apartment when the killing went down. Investigators theorized that D'Angola and Rizzuto were murdered to keep them from talking to investigators about the heist or, possibly, something else—the murder of Neil Napolitano. His body parts had washed up on the beach less than one month before. Was it a coincidence? Lawmen don't believe in coincidences, and they say that it's not unusual for a hit to be outsourced to another crew. Although detectives were unable to establish a link, they never discounted the possibility that the deaths were connected.

One month later, on Friday, December 22, while lawmen were still scrambling to solve the murders of D'Angola, Schneider, and Rizzuto, Frank Abbandando Jr. decided to walk to a drugstore one block from Party Girls. It was 11:25 A.M. when he emerged from the nude bar where he made his headquarters. As the Gambino gangster approached the driveway of Giordy's Country Kitchen, the driver of a red Nissan pickup truck gunned the engine and ran him down, striking him from behind as horrified bystanders looked on. The driver had been watching the club for several days, on the lookout for Abbandando, and he was armed with a shotgun, two semiautomatic handguns, and a revolver. Moreover, he was dressed in stealth mode—all in black, ninja-style. Instead of fleeing after running Abbandando down, the driver stopped, exited the truck, and walked back to the crumpled mobster. He fired seven rounds into Abbandando's body before returning to his vehicle and driving away.

North Miami detective Jerome "Jerry" Brown was on the road when his police radio crackled with a report of a shooting on Biscayne Boulevard. Siren screaming, he was on the scene in minutes. Paramedics were already there when Brown pulled up at 11:40. "I arrived on the scene and found the parking lot taped off with the victim covered by a yellow blanket," the lawman remembered.

As the first detective to arrive, Brown immediately took command. Twenty minutes later, his police radio crackled again, this time with news that the Nissan pickup had been found abandoned in a motel parking lot only a block away. Minutes later Detective Brown learned that a uniformed cop on routine patrol had a suspect in custody just five blocks away.

"I think you're looking for me," Rocco Napolitano said when he surrendered to the cop.

Witnesses brought to the location from the crime scene
had no trouble identifying Rocco as the shooter. One eyewitness, Elias Sussman, was at the restaurant with his wife
when he watched in horror as the Nissan struck Abbandando, knocking him to the pavement. In his report, Brown
summarized what Sussman told him:

> The driver of the vehicle climbed out with a gun
> in his right hand. [Sussman] noted the offender
> appeared calm as he spread his legs to be steady on
> his feet, pointed the handgun at the victim with his
> right hand, and took what appeared to be careful
> aim as he fired three to four shots at the victim. The
> suspect then drove away south on Biscayne Boule-
> vard. Mr. Sussman was driven to the location of the
> stop and immediately identified the offender. He was
> then driven a short distance to the subject's vehicle,
> which was parked. He identified the vehicle as the
> one used.

Linda Benway, a waitress at the eatery, wrote down the
Nissan's license tag on the back of her guest check pad. She
was driven to where the Nissan was parked and identified
it as the one that struck Abbandando.

In the days after his brother's bones washed up on Miami
Beach, Rocco Napolitano appeared on television station
WSVN, Channel Seven. He talked about the events that
led up to his brother's disappearance and his relationship
with MDPD detective Roz Vargas. Rocco also provided the
station with a photo of Neil and Detective Roslyn Vargas
enjoying themselves on the Splash Mountain ride at Disney
World, and he complained bitterly about the investigation.

"My brother was murdered," Rocco declared on camera. He angrily accused authorities of a cover-up to protect
one of their own.

Unhappy with Schiaffo's handling of the case, Rocco launched his own investigation, asking questions and trying to meet with Abbandando. But the old-time mobster kept blowing him off, which led Rocco to conclude that Junior was behind his brother's death. And he came up with a new theory of Neil's demise, one that differed from Gary Schiaffo's.

Rocco believed that two men were waiting for Neil inside his apartment the evening of September 13 and into the wee hours of September 14. Once inside, Neil was attacked, subdued and killed, then wrapped in a blanket and carried out through the service entrance. From there he was taken to a boat and tossed overboard.

Rocco based his theory on what he observed when he entered the apartment on September 27, along with Neil's ex-girlfriend Carmen Sanchez: muddy footprints on the carpet and inside the bathroom; a set of car keys for a Lincoln—but not his brother's Lincoln—next to the bathroom sink; a blanket missing from the bed. His meticulous brother, he says, would never have left the apartment that way. Moreover, Rocco learned that the service entrance lock had been mysteriously broken on September 13, and the security cameras that monitored the building's service entrance and lobby were inexplicably out of order, too, which meant that there was no surveillance tape for that night.

When he left Neil's apartment that day, Rocco took with him video equipment and tape recordings, including the one that Neil had wanted to play for Roz Vargas back in August, in which he claimed that Joe Stracci confessed to murdering Alvino Reyes and John Davidson. Rocco turned the tape over to the FBI. If Rocco hoped the tape recording would lift the veil of suspicion from his brother, he was mistaken. The FBI passed it on to Gary Schiaffo, who dismissed it.

"We didn't think it was true," Detective Schiaffo explained. "We thought it was set up by Neil." Stracci "sounded drunk or stoned." Schiaffo dismissed Rocco's theory, too, but he remembers telling Rocco, "You and I both know what happened here. Your brother defied these people, but there's nothing I can do. I need proof."

Under Mafia rules, it fell to Junior to do something about Neil. That's because it was Junior Abbandando who brought Neil into the Gambino crew. He vouched for Neil, schooled him in the ways of the Mob, and was grooming him for a life of crime. And because it was Junior who brought him in, it was Junior's responsibility to eliminate him, either by arranging for others to kill him or by doing it himself. Unhappy with the investigation into his brother's death and fearful that he, too, was in danger after narrowly escaping two attempts on his life, Rocco concluded that Junior wanted him dead, too, so he went gunning for the mobster.

Junior Abbandando's bullet-riddled body remained on the sidewalk for hours while investigators processed the crime scene. Finally, staffers from the medical examiner's office arrived and moved it to the morgue, where they would conduct an autopsy.

———

Autopsies, or postmortems, are smelly and gruesome. They are performed by forensic pathologists—doctors whose medical specialty is pathology and whose subspecialty is medicine as it relates to the law, most often criminal law. There is a standard protocol for autopsies. After arriving at the morgue, a body is removed from the body bag and placed on a stainless steel autopsy table. The body bag isn't discarded. Instead it's sent to the crime lab, where criminalists will examine it for trace evidence—fibers, dirt, hair, or paint chips, for example, that may have been transferred to it from the body.

The first phase in the actual postmortem procedure is

the external examination. The pathologist will examine the corpse while it is still clothed so that damaged clothing can be matched to corresponding wounds to the body. After carefully removing the clothing, the pathologist sends the garments to the laboratory for processing, after which the corpse's height and weight are recorded.

Next, the pathologist will perform a very careful external examination. X-rays may be taken in order to find broken bones or unseen evidence, like bullet fragments. The pathologist will also search for additional trace evidence that may have become embedded in the body. If found, it, too, will be collected and sent to the lab for processing.

If there are indications that there had been a struggle, a homicide victim's fingernails will be clipped and processed because the assailant's hair, blood, or tissue may have gotten under them. If a sexual assault is suspected, the pathologist will comb the corpse's pubic hair, looking for hairs from the attacker that may have become entangled with the victim's. In addition, the pathologist will check for semen by obtaining anal and vaginal swabs.

Next, the pathologist will painstakingly examine each wound and injury, measuring them one by one for length and depth. Their locations will be precisely marked on an anatomical diagram. In addition, each will be photographed. If weapons have been found that investigators believe are connected to the corpse, they will be compared to the wounds and injuries on the body.

The second phase of the postmortem is not for the weak-kneed or the faint of heart. It involves dissecting the corpse. The pathologist makes a Y-shaped incision on the front of the body from the shoulders in a downward direction toward the breastbone, then a straight incision down toward the pubis. Using a saw, the pathologist will cut the ribs and collarbone to remove the breastplate, exposing the heart and lungs. They will be removed and weighed and sent to the toxicology lab for testing.

Next, the pathologist will examine the abdomen, weighing each organ and taking tissue samples for microscopic examination. The contents of the stomach will be examined along with other body fluids including urine, bile, and liver samples, all of which may be sent for toxicological testing.

The pathologist will look for brain injuries, too, by opening the skull with an incision from behind one ear, crossing over the top of the head to a point behind the other ear. Using a saw, the pathologist then removes a section of skull to expose the brain, which will be removed, weighed, and from which tissue samples will be taken. Finally, each removed organ is returned to the body, and the incisions are sutured. When all the results are in from the toxicology lab, the medical examiner will write and file an official report.

There was nothing unusual about the postmortem examination of Frank Abbandando Jr. Associate Medical Examiner Sam Gulino began it promptly at nine the next morning. In addition to Dr. Gulino and his assistant, Detective Jerry Brown, the lead detective in the case, was on hand along with a photographer from his department's crime scene unit. They were there to witness the postmortem and to assist the pathologist by filling him in on details of the crime scene as he performed the procedure and to immediately take custody of any evidence found on or in the body.

Dr. Guilino followed the standard protocol for postmortems. He began by measuring and weighing the body. In his report he wrote: "The body is that of a well-developed, well-nourished white male who measures five feet four inches in length, weighs 152 pounds, and appears consistent with the stated age of sixty years."

The pathologist noted a 15-centimeter scar over the left buttock and hip and a 1.4 centimeter scar on the right anterior chest, just below and to the right of the sterna notch. He described the abdomen as "protuberant." Further examination revealed a tattoo of an eagle and the number "1954" on the left arm, and "the left middle finger is amputated at the proximal interphalangeal joint."

The pathologist also noted dozens of lacerations and abrasions from head to toe, the result of having been run over. Moreover, Abbandando's left leg had been broken in two places. Seven bullet wounds were pumped into the gangster, who was lying face down on the sidewalk when he was shot. Two slugs went into his head, while four went into his back and penetrated through to his chest. One slug lodged in his neck.

Although the gunshots killed him, the autopsy also revealed that Abbandando was not a well man. Dr. Gulino summarized his findings in a ten-page report:

- Multiple gunshot wounds of the head, neck, back, and chest.
- Multiple blunt force injuries, predominantly of head and extremities.
- Severe calcific coronary atherosclerosis [hardening of the arteries].[5]
- Old subendocardial myocardial infarct of anteroseptal and apical left ventricle [evidence of a previous heart attack].
- Moderate concentric left ventricle hypertrophy [enlarged muscle tissue that makes up the wall of the left ventricle, the heart's main pumping chamber].
- Arteriolar nephrosclerosis [kidney impairment caused by hypertension].
- Severe calcific aortic atherosclerosis with ulceration [weak spot in the wall of the aorta].
- Cholelithiasis [gallstones].

---

5   Remarks in brackets have been added by the author.

- Mild benign prostatic hyperplasia [enlargement of the prostate].

- Cavernous hemangioma [tumor] of the liver.

- Lungs: atelectasis [collapse of lung tissue]; tobacco pneumonitis [blackened lungs caused by smoking].

- Coronary artery: 90 percent obstructed by an atherosclerotic plaque.

The pathologist concluded that Abbandando died from "multiple gunshot wounds associated with blunt trauma."

At 5:50 P.M. on the day he mowed Abbandando down, Rocco spoke with Jerry Brown in an interview room at North Miami police headquarters. In his report, the detective wrote:

I was advised by Lt. Clint Shannon that the offender had indicated that he wanted to speak to me. Lt. Shannon introduced me to the offender. I asked him if this was in fact his decision to cooperate by giving a statement. He stated that he had turned himself in to a uniform officer and from the beginning had indicated his desire to speak with the investigator handling the case. I then escorted him to the detective bureau's interview room where I asked if he had been advised of his rights earlier. He stated that he had and indicated that he never actually invoked that right. I explained that I had been told that he had told a uniform officer that he thought he should speak to an attorney. I further explained that I felt that this could be construed to be an invocation of this right to remain silent until he spoke with an attorney. He stated that wasn't his desire at that time and at this time was interested and speaking to me. I then went over a written Miranda Form which I read to him and which he read back stating that he understood this right. He stated that he wished to show that he had cooperated with the police. He signed the form expressing his desire to speak with me and Det. Glenn Kinsey, who witnessed this waiver.

Subject Napolitano then explained how he had learned that the victim was responsible for the recent death of his brother, who was murdered. He wouldn't provide facts to show how he knew for sure that the victim had his brother killed, stating that at the right time he would provide further information. He admitted that he had stalked the victim with the intention of causing a confrontation which he had hoped would lead to his ability to kill the victim. He had armed himself with a recently purchased shotgun, two semiauto handguns, and one revolver. Subject Napolitano stated that he was driving in the area of the Club owned by the victim, Party Girl's at 11340 Biscayne Blvd., in search of the victim. He added that he was northbound just past the club when he observed the victim walking south on the sidewalk just east of Biscayne Blvd. He made the decision to kill the victim. Subject Napolitano explained that he swerved his vehicle into the victim. The right front of the Subject's Vehicle collided with the victim, knocking him over the hood, against the windshield, then back to the pavement where he laid [sic] motionless.

Subject Napolitano stated that he walked up to the victim with his 9 MM semiautomatic handgun in his right hand. He took close careful aim and fired at least three times at the victim's upper torso. He explained that he wasn't a great marksman and aimed all the shots at the largest part of the victim's body to insure that he had been hit. Subject Napolitano added that he drove out of the area, parked his *vehicle, then started to walk back to the shooting scene when he realized police were in the area.*

He stated that his intentions were to turn himself in and wanted the safety of the police to protect him from the criminal friends of the victim. He then explained how he made eye contact with an officer and raised his hands to "show that he was unarmed and not a threat to him." He then turned himself in to this uniform officer. Subject Napolitano agreed to give a recorded statement. I went over the facts surrounding the subject's surrender and his decision to speak with the lead investigators. I then went over his Miranda rights again and he verbally waived them and repeated the confession.

Later that day, a shackled Rocco Napolitano made his first appearance in court. He would remain jailed without bond on a charge of first-degree murder and possession of a firearm in the commission of a felony. The stakes were high for the twenty-three-year-old. Conviction could put him on Florida's death row. The brutal murder in broad daylight on a bustling South Florida boulevard sparked a media sensation in South Florida.

BAR OWNER'S KILLING
TIED TO BODY PARTS CASE

the *Miami Herald* reported on the front page of its local section. The newspaper linked Abbandando to organized crime and recounted his criminal past.

BROTHER QUESTIONED IN SLAYING
MAN WAS SHOT DOWN OUTSIDE RESTAURANT

trumpeted the *Sun Sentinel.* Both papers reminded readers that the bones of Neil Napolitano, Rocco's brother, had washed up on Miami Beach in September, and that MDPD detective Roslyn Vargas was under investigation for her involvement with Neil. Two weeks later, a front page article in the *Herald* profiled the slain gangster.

LIKE FATHER LIKE SON:
MOBSTER'S LIFE STEEPED IN VIOLENCE.

"Following in his father's footsteps, Frank 'Junior' Abbandando was mean, ugly, and a hit man for the Mob," the paper declared. "Murder was his birthright. It's also how he died."

"It couldn't happen to a better person," Mob turncoat Joe "Dogs" Iannuzzi told the *Herald* reporter. "He was a son of a bitch, a "butcher," Iannuzzi said, someone who would "chop your body up" if ordered to. "That's the kind of moron he was."

Meanwhile Rocco, unwilling to reveal how he knew that Abbandando murdered his brother, was cooling his heels in the county jail, which is where he was on Friday, January 5, when his brother's remains were laid to rest at Our Lady Queen of Heaven Cemetery in Broward County. Velma, her daughters, and Carmen Sanchez attended the brief cryptside service.

Roz Vargas did not attend. No one had been closer to Neil Napolitano or spent more time with him during the last two weeks of his life than the organized crime detective, which is why investigators wanted to question her about her relationship with him. Even though she had been eliminated as a suspect in Neil's death, Roz's attrorney Douglas Hartman insisted on immunity for her. After weeks of legal wrangling, Hartman and Assistant State Attorney Mary Cagle reached an agreement—anything Roz said could not be used against her except to prosecute her for perjury, trafficking in narcotics, murder, attempted murder, or any other crimes of violence. Her sworn statement was set for Thursday, February 22, 1996.

11

TO TELL THE TRUTH

It had been five months since Barbara Gentile relieved her of duty, but Roz Vargas was still on the MDPD's payroll when she appeared at the office of the Miami-Dade state attorney to answer questions. She arrived that Thursday morning, February 22, 1996, at 9:30, accompanied by her lawyer, Douglas Hartman

Two veteran prosecutors, Mary Cagle and Flora Seff, were waiting to question her. Both had cut their teeth as prosecutors under six-foot two inch Janet Reno, the first female state attorney in Florida.

There is no glass ceiling in the Miami-Dade state attorney's office, which, from 1978 until 1993, was headed by Reno. The gangly Miami native cast a giant shadow over law enforcement in South Florida until President Bill Clinton chose her to be the first female attorney general of the United States. Governor Lawton Chiles named Katherine Fernandez Rundle, Reno's top deputy and protégé, to succeed her. She has held the office ever since. By the mid-1990s, the Miami-Dade state attorney's office employed more than 1,100 paralegals, investigators, support staff, and assistant state attorneys, more than half of whom were women.

Mary Cagle headed for South Florida after graduating from law school in her native Michigan. She joined the state attorney's office in 1981. A tall redhead with sparkling blue eyes and a friendly smile, in 1984 she became senior prosecutor in the state attorney's organized crime and public corruption unit.

Assistant State Attorney Flora Seff had been assigned to prosecute Rocco Napolitano for the murder of Junior Abbandando. A graduate of Florida International University and the University of Miami School of Law, she joined the state attorney's office as a student intern in 1977 and became a prosecutor in 1980. It wasn't long before Seff established herself as a tough litigator. By 1989 she was prosecuting death penalty cases for the Major Crimes Unit. In 1985, the U.S. Marshall Service named Seff Law Enforcement Officer of the Year "for her work on an investigation that spanned six years." Also on hand in the fifth-floor interview room were MDPD homicide detective Victor Pidermann, Miami Beach detective Tommy Moran, and court reporter Margie Johnson.

At 10 A.M. Roz Vargas raised her right hand and swore to tell the truth. To the lawmen in the room that day, many of her answers were evasive and disingenuous, while others seemed superfluous and self-serving.

"They were bullshit," Detective Tommy Moran said bluntly. Assistant State Attorney Flora Seff put it differently. Roz Vargas's answers, she said, "contradicted all the evidence we had and all the other people we had spoken to." Her story, Seff added, "made absolutely no sense."

Mary Cagle began the questioning with Roz's first days as an organized crime detective.

"When did you first get involved in an investigation into Neil Napolitano?"

"Mid-November."

"Can you tell us briefly why he was being targeted by your squad."

"You would have to ask them. This was an investigation that apparently was started prior to my getting there."

"The investigation was ongoing?"

"Apparently so."

"Did your squad have some meetings about Neil Napolitano? Were you made aware of his criminal background?"

"Not completely, no."

Roz admitted that she was aware that Neil was close to Frank Abbandando Jr., but she claimed she did not know who Frank Abbandando was when she first joined Barbara Gentile's squad and that she only learned more about the Gambino gangster much later, after he was gunned down.

"At some point during the time period that you worked there, did you find out that Frank Abbandando was involved in organized crime, and who he was and all of that?" Cagle asked.

"Not to the extent of what I know now from the newspapers," Detective Vargas answered.

Her response prompted a question from Flora Seff: "I just want to ask something, because I'm not familiar with how your unit works. When you were working a case, whether the investigation had started prior to your being there, or once you got there . . . wasn't there a meeting with every member of your squad where everyone shared information?"

"Unfortunately not," Roz replied.

When asked if she had learned that Neil Napolitano was involved with crack dealers, that he had possibly taken part in at least one home-invasion robbery, and that he had been involved in Rolex strong-arm robberies, Roz replied that she had, but it came from Joe Stracci, her confidential informant, whose information she characterized as "maybe credible," adding gratuitously that he "was playing two sides."

PETER DAVIDSON

146

"How about from Miami Beach [detectives]?" she was asked.

"No," she answered. "I was never actually told."

"So you never knew about the crack dealers that Neil Napolitano was involved with on Miami Beach?"

"No. And the only story was from Stracci, and Stracci's stories are a lot different than [how] everybody else would put it."

Listening, Tommy Moran knew better. He remembered bringing Roz up to speed on Neil's underworld activities in the days before she went undercover.

Next, Mary Cagle wanted to know what Roz knew about Neil's suspected role in the disappearances of Ryes and Davidson. "At some point during the time that you were involved with your squad, working him as a target, you became aware of the fact that he was the prime suspect in what everyone believed was the murder of those two people, is that accurate?"

"I wouldn't say that's how it was put," Roz responded. "It was put that there were two people that were missing and they felt that he *may* have had something to do with it."

Roz knew more about Neil's suspected ties to Reyes and Davidson than she was letting on, and the prosecutor wanted it on the record so she bored in, reminding the organized crime detective that she and her partner, Detective Mark Liner, were at Miami Beach police headquarters the night Reyes and Davidson were arrested. The reminder must have jogged her memory. Said Roz: "When we got there Davidson was in one room; Reyes was in another."

She recalled being in the interview room with Davidson. "He was talking to a blond female officer from the Beach. . . . At that point in time, Mark Liner started talking to him. You have to understand this is like a month after I'm there, with not much information, and I don't know all the people they are discussing. So therefore, Mark Liner started taking notes from whatever Davidson told him."

"What did Reyes and Davidson say that night about Neil Napolitano's involvement that you were aware of?" Cagle asked.

"The only thing I knew was they were paid to receive the packages."

"Who paid them?"

"Neil did."

"So, through interviews with Davidson and Reyes, you became aware of the fact that Neil Napolitano was the one who paid them, and that they worked for Neil Napolitano, and [you became aware of] Neil's involvement in this steroid organization, correct?"

"Correct."

Flora Seff had a question: "They handed Neil Napolitano up that night, those two guys?"

"Right," Roz answered.

"And within two weeks of Davidson and Reyes handing up Neil Napolitano, Davidson and Reyes disappeared?"

"Right."

"And you were aware of all of that, right?"

"We became aware of it."

The prosecutors didn't let up. They wanted it on the record that Roz knew that Neil was much more than a surveillance target; he was a suspect in the disappearance and suspected murders of two men.

"When you put together the fact that Reyes and Davidson hand up Neil Napolitano, two days later Reyes and Davidson disappear, Neil Napolitano was the guy you were working, were you immediately concerned about whether or not Neil Napolitano was involved in that?"

"Sure."

"Did you have discussions personally with other people in the squad about that? "

"Yes."

"And that became another focus of the investigation?"

"Yes, to a certain extent, because, actually, it was the Beach's case."

"But it certainly made Neil Napolitano an even worthier target in terms of your squad, now that he was implicated in this missing-persons case?"

"Right."

"And these two people were probably dead?"

"Correct."

Next, Mary Cagle probed Roz's feelings for the young wiseguy. Cagle had read investigators' reports of interviews with Rocco and Joann Walter, and she knew that Barbara Gentile told Internal Affairs detectives that Roz told her that she was in a relationship with a younger man and might have to leave the MDPD. Cagle also knew that Roz had shared personal information about her background with Neil, which explained how his sister Monica knew that Roz was twenty years old when she married Julio, who, like her, was a police officer.

"Did there come a point in time where your relationship with Neil Napolitano changed from where you were working him as a target to a personal relationship?" Mary Cagle asked.

"Define *personal*," Roz shot back.

"Friends. Somebody you had an affair with. Somebody you talked to, liked, cared about. Any of the above."

Roz pondered before answering. "No. Not quite any of the above, the way you put it. What happened was he was becoming a source of information."

She admitted to having contact with the young wiseguy in June and through the summer, but she insisted that all the contacts were "work-related."

"Did there come a point in time when your relationship with Neil Napolitano changed?" Mary Cagle asked again.

Said Roz: "It was in the beginning of August, maybe the

first two weeks in August. He claimed that he had had it. And he spoke of not living a long time," and he told her he was tired of living. She added, "A lot of conversations went back and forth where he felt female officers were not really ladies, or they were more into, you know, being bisexual, or being gay, and blah, blah. And these are the conversations that went back and forth in between bits and pieces [of] work-related stuff."

But as far as the relationship changing, Roz declared that it had, but "it was on his end," not hers.

"Did you ever look at pictures of him when he was a kid? Did you get together with him then and talk about personal stuff with him?" Cagle asked.

"His personal stuff. Not my personal stuff," Roz said. She was adamant, and she said it happened during the first two weeks of August, when they met on Biscayne Boulevard. Said Roz: "He called to say, 'I have information.' Everybody in that district knows me. It wasn't like I was hiding somewhere. It was like out in the open. Yeah, I saw the pictures. Nice. Give me what you are going to give me, and that was the end of it. . . . It was personal but it was personal on his part. I mean he gave me this whole story. I didn't sit here for hours and tell you all the things he told me when he was a kid and how his life got all messed up. Okay. So what?"

Roz admitted that she met with Neil alone on the day she left for Orlando, and on the day before, in the lobby of his apartment building and in the parking lot. Both meetings were work-related, she insisted, and Neil used her personal cell phone to call his sister in California and his brother in New York.

"Were these meetings documented?" Cagle asked.

"No."

Cagle pressed her for an explanation.

"It wasn't a thing where it was part of surveillance," Roz said, adding that "you have to understand I had a county phone; I have a county beeper. And I know if we want to get phone records, if I needed anything, it would be easy for anybody to look at the records. You could go back and see where the phone calls are made and I could tell you exactly what the phone conversations were at that point. So, no, I didn't, you know, sit down and write a whole life story."

"So you didn't document the meetings in August that you had with Neil Napolitano?

"No."

"And those meetings in your mind were personal meetings or work-related meetings, or a combination?"

"Work-related. I was still on county time."

"You didn't write reports of the meetings and document them?"

"Other than what I had in my head and documentation that I knew that I could go back and get."

"So in August you continued to meet with him although Barbara Gentile and the squad didn't know really that that's going on?"

"Right."

"But your testimony is you were doing it for work-related purposes?"

"Yes."

"Did your squad, and did Barbara Gentile specifically, know that you continued to have meetings with Neil Napolitano, and that you were talking to him, and that you were on the phone with him?"

"No."

"Was there any specific reasons why you didn't tell her about the meetings?"

"Everybody was really afraid of Neil."

If Mary Cagle wondered what that had to do with Roz's failure to either document or tell Sergeant Gentile about the meetings, she didn't ask. Instead the prosecutor wanted Roz to explain why Neil was so feared.

"Because apparently he had a roundhouse kick that could hurt somebody," Roz said.

"And everybody knew that he was at least the main suspect in the Reyes and Davidson thing, right?"

"Right."

"You knew Frank Abbandando could be dangerous, too?"

"I never knew anything about any of Abbandando's past and what he had done to people. Maybe I should be a little more fearful of people [but] I didn't feel threatened."

"In August you continue to have meetings and conversations with Neil. Where were those meetings?"

"Right. One was in front of Party Girls. One was on 163rd between Dixie and Biscayne Boulevard. . . . In the open."

"Did you ever meet with him in his apartment?"

"I met with him at the apartment building. . . . There were people around all the time. And maybe that's why I didn't feel threatened."

———————

Cagle and Doug Hartman had agreed to a three-hour time limit, and the clock was running out, but the prosecutor had not yet delved into what happened in Orlando over Labor Day weekend. "Tell me what happens toward the end of August. Does the relationship at that point in your mind change?" Cagle asked.

"What happened was my family and I were going up to Orlando to see someone that was ill, that wasn't given much time to live, and we were trying to make it up there prior to their death," Roz recalled. "But that didn't happen. In fact, the weekend before we were supposed to go up was when the person died. And so arrangements had to be made to go up there. . . . On my way to Orlando I had gotten beeped, so I called the number not recognizing it. And it was Neil. He said he had some information. And I said,

'Well, I'm on my way to Orlando. I'm out of town. When I get back I'll get ahold of you.' He said, 'You got to call me back later.' I said, 'All right, if I can I'll get back with you and I'll call."

She did, the very next day, and that's when Neil told her that he had a falling out with Junior Abbandando, that he'd "had it with the Mafia," and "he was going to give me all kinds of stuff."

"So Neil Napolitano himself told you at that point in time that he had had it with the Mafia? Did he give you details about that?"

"No."

The next night, Sunday, Roz was in Orlando when she and her husband had a spat. Cagle asked what the argument was about. It was about their daughter, Roz said. "She wanted to go with Julio's nephew to a party because he lived on campus. And everybody said no. I said, 'It's her cousin.'"

"Did you actually on the way to dinner get out of the car that night?"

"Yes."

"What happened when you got out of the car?"

"I was pissed. And then my husband tried chasing me down. And I was a stubborn person. I wasn't getting in the car. And I have been married for twenty years. My life has been dedicated for my family, cooking seven days a week, cleaning and ironing, and I kind of got bent out of shape when he said, 'Get the fuck out of the car.' And that just threw me for a loop. And so that's what I did. And I refused to get back in."

"But at some point you get back in the car. You go to dinner?"

"We battled back and forth. And he chased me. And my daughter got upset. I have a son who is diabetic. He's got to eat. I told him, 'I'll get back in the car. I will go to dinner with your sister. After dinner I am leaving. I'm not staying.'"

"And that's what you did?" Mary Cagle asked.

"Yes."

It was nearly midnight when Roz walked away from her family. All she carried with her was her purse. Inside was her gun, her badge, a nearly dead cell phone, and five hundred dollars that her grandmother had given her to help defray the four-thousand-dollar cost of an insulin pump for her son.

Roz said she was angry and upset, and she reached out to Neil Napolitano, calling him from a pay phone inside a Denny's restaurant in Orlando. Said Roz: "I beeped him and he called me back. And he said, 'What's wrong?' And that's where my biggest mistake was, because I just started venting about personal stuff. . . . And went on and on and on. And in the conversation, [he asked] 'Where are you?' I said I'm in Orlando. I'm near the airport. I'm going home. And it was just one of those conversations. I just let it out. And it was like that was somebody that was listening. And I just kept going. And this was the hard part, I know everybody has a hard time believing, because I had a hard time believing in the conversation. . . . I said I'm at Denny's at the airport. . . . And I had a three-hour conversation. And the next thing I know he's in Orlando."

It was three o'clock in the morning.

Roz said she and Neil left Denny's and had breakfast at a nearby Waffle House. When they were finished eating, Roz told the young wiseguy to "take me to the nearest hotel," and he did. Roz waited in the car while Neil checked into the Holiday Inn Sun Spree Resort in Lake Buena Vista, registering as Cam Jackson of North Bay Village, Florida. He paid $144.31 cash for a two-night stay.

"Did he go into the room with you?"

"Yes, he did."

"How long did you stay there with him?"

"Monday, Tuesday. I left Wednesday."

"And did he stay there with you the entire time?

"Yes, he did."

"Did you guys have a relationship that night and those nights?"

"No."

"But you stayed together in the same room?"

"Yes."

"But you didn't sleep together?"

"No."

"Your testimony is it was separate beds?"

"At that point, yes."

Roz said she did a lot of sleeping and a lot of crying in room 311 over the next two days.

"Were all the conversations you had with him at this point in time personal conversations on both sides?" the prosecutor asked. Roz said they were, adding without being asked that "absolutely nothing was spoken about work, nor did he ask." But at one point Neil told her that if his Mob pals ever learned that he was in Orlando with a cop, "he would probably be killed."

On Labor Day night, Roz said she phoned Barbara Gentile at home to ask for Tuesday off, telling the listening investigators that the sergeant asked if she was okay "because it was kind of obvious that I didn't sound okay." Tuesday evening she phoned Gentile again, this time asking for the rest of the week off.

Said Roz: "She asked me if I was in Orlando. I said yes. She asked, 'Are you with your family?' I said no. She said, 'Are you okay? You don't sound okay.' And I said, 'Look, I just got to go.' "

On Wednesday, September 6, Roz and Neil were back in South Florida. Later that night they went to Villa Perrone.

"Tell me about the meeting [at the Italian restaurant]," Mary Cagle commanded.

Said Roz: "On Wednesday he said . . . come with me. We're going to grab a bite to eat. . . . You want to know stuff, this is your time. Just sit there and be quiet, and don't say nothing.' " At the restaurant they were greeted by Freddie Massaro. Neil introduced Roz to the Gambino associate and to Dr. Kamlet and his wife, Karen; to Massaro's girlfriend, Carol; and to another man whose name Roz didn't recall exactly—"Pep I think was what they called him," she said.

Roz remembered that she had heard of Fred Massaro through Mark Liner, but, as with Junior Abbandando, she said she knew nothing specific about his ties to organized crime, and she never bothered to ask Neil about his relationship with the portly gangster.

"Why not?" Cagle asked.

"Because it almost became the entire time that I was there, don't ask me questions, I'm not asking you anything." She added, "I'm not going to sit there and pump."

Cagle pressed her. "You didn't ask him why he was having dinner with Freddie Massaro? What's your relationship with Freddie Massaro?"

"No."

"Afterward, did he discuss with you his relationship with Tony Pep?"

"No. I don't even know who Tony Pep is," Roz answered.

Cagle was incredulous. So was every lawman in the room. They couldn't believe that organized crime detective Roz Vargas did not jump at the chance to learn more about the Gambino mobsters she was face-to-face with at Villa Perrone. Nor did they believe that she knew so little about the crew and its illicit activities.

"Knowing everything you knew about Neil Napolitano from the investigation, stuff from the Beach, stuff about Reyes and Davidson, all of that, and knowing at least the name Freddie Massaro and having had a meeting with him, with these people, and knowing that he had a relationship with Frank Abbandando and all of that, wasn't the cop in you curious?" Mary Cagle asked.

"By nature I am a very curious person," Roz answered.

"Didn't you have conversations with him about all of that during this period of time that you were spending with him?

"No. You have to understand there was a part of me that knew, you know, I couldn't believe half the things that were going on. Was there fear there? Was I afraid of him? Yes. At one point in time he got my driver's license and was actually writing my name. So I questioned that. And it was just basically don't ask me anything because you are not getting anything. Was there fear there? Yes."

Over the next two days Roz and Neil were virtually inseparable. They visited Velma at her apartment, went to a bookstore in Boca Raton, and took in a movie, *A Walk in the Clouds*. It starred Keanu Reeves and Aitana Sánchez-Gijón as star-crossed lovers from very different backgrounds—he's Anglo; she's Latina. They are forced to confront overwhelming odds to be together. Afterward, Roz and Neil dined at restaurants and shopped at the Dadeland Mall, in Miami. And they slept at Neil's place but, Roz said, not together.

"I got the mattress, he took the floor," she declared. On Friday, September 8, they drove back to Orlando.

"Does there come a point in time when you sleep with him?" Mary Cagle asked.

"Yes," Roz replied. It was on Saturday, at the Holiday Inn, but it was not because she wanted to.

"Is it your testimony that he rapes you or that you do it consensually?" Cagle asked.

"Define *rape*," Roz replied.

"Did you have sex with him out of choice?"

"No."

After exploring other aspects of their relationship, Cagle brought her questions back to their sexual relationship. "I've got to stop you a second. There is something that's not clear to me from your testimony about the ninth, which is the Saturday you say you slept with him. Your testimony is that you didn't really consent, is that right?"

"That's correct."

"Did you ever tell him you didn't want to have sex with him?" she asked.

"Yes, I did," Roz insisted.

"Did he force himself on you?"

"Was there force? No, because out of fear I just let it happen."

"But from your testimony I think you are trying to tell us that he basically raped you that night?"

"It was not something that I really wanted to do. And from fear, yes, I let him."

And fear was why she stayed with him.

"Was there ever a time that you wanted to leave or tried to leave and you didn't feel like you could leave?" Cagle asked.

"Yes."

"When was that?"

"That was Monday, Tuesday, I said, 'Look, I've got to go get clothes. I can't be here with you. It's not right.'"

"But did you try to leave at any point?

"Yes, I did."

"When did you try and leave?"

"It was an incident in Orlando,"

"What day?"

"I believe it was Tuesday."

"What happens on Tuesday when you try and leave?"

"That was after the mall. I had gotten a change of clothes. Went back to the hotel. Said, 'I can't stay here.' And he said, 'Well, there are two beds.' And there were. The first room had a bed and a couch because he was on the couch. He said, 'You are not doing anything wrong.' I said, 'It isn't right. My family life isn't right.' When I went to get my purse he grabbed my purse from me. He knew I had a firearm and he claims that he believed that I was going to take it out and use it. I would never kill myself for anybody."

"Did he take the gun away from you?"

"Yes, he did."

"Did he give it back to you?"

"Yes, he did. . . . It was a little bit of a struggle [but] I got it back."

"Right then?"

"Yes."

"Did he actually try to overpower you and keep the gun but you overpowered him?"

"Yes. Even to the point that I don't know what marks are still around, but his left shoulder should have had a mark from my ring that cut him. He thought it was funny because he thought I was just kind of feisty. He's a big guy."

"But did you overpower him to get the gun back, or did he give you the gun back?"

"He gave it back to me with no ammo."

"You didn't try to leave?"

"No more at that point."

"During the following day did you want to leave and you only stayed there because he was . . .

"From fear." Roz interrupted.

"So when you were in the shopping malls and all of that, and at Disney and all of that you didn't feel you could walk away?"

"No."

"Why not?"

"He's not a small guy. He never left my side."

Next, the prosecutor questioned Roz about her September 10 phone call to Barbara Gentile, when she told her sergeant she might have to resign.

"Did Neil force you to do that, or did you do that out of choice?"

"Anybody that knows me knows how I feel about my job, and just wouldn't believe that that was something I would do."

The prosecutor followed up. "I'm not clear on that. When you called Barbara were you trying to give her a message in telling her that?"

Cagle was looking for a simple yes or no answer. Instead, Roz seemed to blame Barbara Gentile: "Anybody that knows me, knows how I feel about my work, would know that there is something wrong."

Neil and Roz left Orlando in the wee hours of Monday, September 11. They drove back to South Florida. Later that day Rocco, recently arrived from New York, stopped at Neil's apartment. In the afternoon, Roz called her son, who picked her up at a sub shop and drove her home.

"Is there any reason you couldn't have done that the prior week?" Cagle asked.

"He just wouldn't let me."

"Did he ever tell you that?"

"It was just the fear, like I told you before. In his mind it was a totally different relationship than what it actually was." But the next morning her pager went off. Roz returned the call. "I have your stuff. . . . Come get your stuff," Neil said.

And despite her fear, Roz said she drove to Neil's to pick up what she'd left there—a black-and-white dress, a black pants outfit, a tunic top, and makeup.

"And you were not afraid to go there alone for fear that he wouldn't let you leave?" Mary Cagle asked, her voice betraying disbelief.

"No," Roz replied. "Because if he let me leave the first time, he would let me leave again."

Her answer made no sense to Cagle or any of the other investigators. What also made no sense was what Roz said next, that instead of gathering her things and leaving, Roz spent most of the day with Neil in his apartment, arguing about their relationship.

"Neil's whole idea," she said, "was this was a totally different relationship than it was."

"So in your mind he had fallen in love and wanted to go away with you?"

"That's what he said to other people."

"Did he ever say anything like that to you?"

"No."

"Did you ever get to the point where that happened, your view of the relationship?"

"Absolutely not."

"You never had any intention of leaving with him?"

"No."

Roz said she finally left Neil's apartment at about 3:30 in the afternoon, driving to the video store where her son worked.

"I went to my son's job, and [Neil] shows up behind me," Roz said.

"He followed you to your son's job?" Cagle asked. Roz nodded yes.

She called her youngest son, who met them there, and the four of them—Neil, Roz, and her two sons, Julio Jr. and Nick—went to dinner at Applebee's, driving there in Neil's Lincoln. They made small talk in the car and at dinner, chatting mostly about music and movies. After dinner they drove back to the video store. Roz said it was her intention to go home that night with her sons, but Neil ordered her into his car, and she returned with him to his apartment instead.

"Was there a reason you didn't get into the car with one of the kids?

"Yes."

"What was the reason?"

"Neil."

"Did he say anything? Did he tell you to get into the car with him?"

"Yes.

"When did he tell you that?"

"After we got back to Blockbuster and we got in the parking lot and we were getting out of the car."

"Did he have a weapon?"

"Not that I remember."

"Are you trying to tell us that he kidnapped you in front of your kids?"

"Did he hold something to me? Did he physically force me into the car? No, he didn't. But it was the fear again. And I said leave them alone, and let them do whatever it is they have to do. Just leave my kids alone."

"So you didn't go into the car with Neil by choice?"

Roz answered by shaking her head, indicating no. She returned with Neil to his apartment and spent the night there.

"Did you have sex with him?" Mary Cagle asked.

"I really don't remember," Roz Vargas replied.

———

Seven people had been closeted in the stuffy fifth floor interview room for nearly three hours. Everyone was hungry and tired, but there were still a few more avenues the investigators wanted to explore. The first was August 10, 1995, when Barbara Gentile, on her way to the ladies room, found Neil lurking in the hallway outside the SIB office on the very day that Miami Beach detectives were to bring Joe Stracci there for a sworn statement.

"Did you know that [Neil] was coming to the office?" Cagle asked.

"No, I did not."

"Did you talk to him when he got there?"

"Absolutely not."

"Did you talk to him that day?" Flora Seff wanted to know.

"It's possible, but did I discuss anything about Joe Stracci? No."

But the prosecutors had phone records. And they knew that Roz had spoken with Neil both before and after he appeared at the SIB office.

"Do you have any recollection of what you talked to him about?" Seff asked.

"No," Roz answered. "Like I told you, a lot of times he beeped me. Supposedly, he was going to give me information. He did a lot of fishing, and he got absolutely nothing from me."

And they wanted to know about the afternoon of September 13, the last time Roz saw Neil Napolitano.

Said Roz: "My mother had beeped me during the day . . . and asked me to meet her for lunch. And naturally he was like listening on the phone. And I said, 'I can't meet you for lunch. I'll call you back later.' . . . And then again, my mother beeped me and I told her, 'These people are worried. I got to do something. It's not like they don't know.' I even told him, Barbara beeped me that same day, and I spoke to Barbara, and it was again like trying to let her know. I even said to him, 'Look, it's obvious, my kids saw you. My children aren't stupid. I need to leave.' He agreed to let me go meet my mother."

"When is the last time you saw Neil?" Cagle asked.

"At Macaroni Grill, in the parking lot."

"Did you have any contact with him at all after the thirteenth?

"No."

"Did you have any contact with him at all after the fourteenth?"

"No. In fact, on Wednesday, when he left me there, as crazy as it sounds, I even said thank you. It was thank you for just letting me go. I said, 'I'll talk to you another time.' And Thursday, I think Friday, I tried contacting him. You know, I tried beeping him."

"Why?"

"Just to say I'm not going to say anything. I had to worry about myself and I had to worry about my kids."

It was a startling response from a veteran detective. The lawmen in the room winced when they heard it. According to Tommy Moran, all cops worth their salt would have gone after Neil themselves if they believed he posed a threat to their family. It prompted Cagle to ask, "Did you have some feelings for him also?"

"No."

Finally, the prosecutor asked Roz if she knew who killed Neil. She offered two possible suspects: His brother, Rocco, or Junior Abbandando.

"Why would you say his brother?" Cagle wondered.

"I have never seen two people so angry at each other," Roz declared. She described Rocco as "really bent out of shape" when Neil told him he was done with the Mob.[6]

Mary Cagle was nearly finished. The prosecutor had just one more question for the detective.

"In August, when you were talking to Neil, and not documenting it at all in terms of work, your phone records show that you are beeping him in the middle of the night. Do you have any explanation for that?"

Roz seemed to beat around the bush, talking first about her son's diabetes, and voice mail from her office phone forwarding to her pager, and how Joe Stracci had once beeped her at 2 A.M. Cagle pressed her again for an explanation, and this time Roz said: "All the calls with the beeper and the county phone number, it's all county stuff. [If] I really wanted to do something bad, I would never use a county phone or beeper."

---

6 In a subsequent deposition, Roz would be asked a similar question. "I don't know who did it," she said. "I have no reason to believe who could have done it, who would have done it, [or] why they would have done it."

Her testimony ended minutes later. After Roz and her lawyer were gone, the investigators discussed what they'd heard and observed.

Mary Cagle was struck by Roz's coldness and by her defiant attitude. They all agreed that her answers to many of their questions had been evasive and disingenuous, clearly at odds with photographs that showed Roz looking relaxed and happy while in Orlando with Neil, and with reports from investigators that were based on interviews with witnesses who told a far different story, one very much like the plot in the romantic drama *A Walk in the Clouds*. But in the real-life romance, the rules and traditions of the Mafia would prove too difficult an obstacle for Neil and Roz to overcome. As the FBI's Joe Pistone, aka Donnie Brasco, noted, "Anything more than 'Nice day, officer,' is grounds for execution."

Flora Seff took notes while Roz testified. In the upper right-hand corner of one of the pages, the prosecutor wrote, "This is BS or she's stupid." Later, Seff, her tone indicating skepticism and disbelief, summed up what she heard that day: "She was in organized crime . . . and she really had no idea why she was being sent to do a surveillance of [Neil Napolitano], nobody clued her in on any of the information. And nobody told her about the different crimes that Neil was suspected of, or [what] some of these other people [were suspected of], and she was totally in the dark. She was riding around, following this guy, who she didn't know. When it got to be maybe more, she was doing it because that was part of her job, to get him involved with her, and not in a sexual way, and get to know her. She was getting to know him, and this was going to help the investigation somehow, which she, of course, knew nothing about."

Roz's explanations, Seff said, were "contradicted by all the evidence we had, and [by] all the other people we had spoken to. All of the evidence we had, none of it supported her story. Her story made absolutely no sense."

Based on her testimony that day, prosecutors would file charges against Roslyn Vargas, but more than three years would pass before she would have her day in court. In the meantime, investigators from three agencies—the MDPD, the Miami Beach Police Department, and the FBI—were closing in on the South Florida Gambinos.

12

THE HEAT IS ON

For the Gambino wiseguys in South Florida, Neil Napolitano's death meant increased scrutiny from law enforcement. Federal and local investigators visited Party Girls
and other Mob hangouts, asking questions, watching, and
listening. It didn't take long for lawmen to realize just how
dangerous the crew was.

"They were very violent, into everything," FBI Special
Agent Howe Grover recalled; among their crimes were
bank and credit card fraud, gambling, arson, loan-sharking,
extortion, pornography, forgery, stolen merchandise, drug
dealing, and murder.

Lawmen wanted to talk to Abbandando, but the aging
gangster managed to elude them until the day he died.
Not so Fred Massaro. He liked to play cat and mouse with
investigators, but by surveilling him, lawmen learned
about Tony Pep, the Atlanta-based Gambino soldier who
flew into Miami twice a month to check on the crew and
collect his share of their illicit earnings. And by talking to

Massaro, they were able to confirm what they suspected: Neil Napolitano had been murdered by the Mob.

MDPD Internal Affairs detectives Cindy Truncale and Joe Gross interviewed Fred Massaro at his residence in Hollywood. Gross remembers asking Massaro who had ordered the hit on Neil. The gangster leaned back in his chair, raised his hands palms upward, and shrugged his shoulders. "Tony Pep didn't even know the kid," he declared. It was a bizarre response, an answer that incriminated no one, but the detective interpreted it as a clear signal that Anthony "Tony Pep" Trentacosta had ordered the killing.

Massaro told investigators that he had known Neil for three years. They had been introduced by Junior Abbandando. Massaro said he would see Neil "two or three times a month, at least." Neil, the Gambino gangster explained, "liked my company."

And Fred Massaro liked his company, too.

"I didn't think he was a bad kid," Massaro said in a sworn statement. But during all the time that they spent together, they never talked about business.

"Did you ever discuss with him what he did for a living?" an investigator wanted to know.

"None of my business."

"Did Neil ever bring it up to you?"

"Never."

"You never asked him?"

"No."

"Were you aware of any interests of Neil, such as hobbies or anything like that?"

"Not really."

"Did you have an occasion to meet a woman named Roslyn Vargas?"

"Yes."

"On how many occasions did you meet Miss Vargas?"

"One."

"Where did you meet her?"

"Met her in a restaurant . . . Villa Perrone on Hallandale Beach Boulevard."

"Who introduced you?"

"Neil."

"What was the purpose of dinner at Villa Perrone?"

"There was no purpose. We were having dinner. A couple of guys getting together with the wives, girlfriend."

Massaro named the others who were with him at Villa Perrone, including Trentacosta, describing Tony Pep as "a friend of mine from New York" who was living in Atlanta.

"Was he down on a trip, on vacation?"

"On vacation."

"How often would you see Mr. Trentacosta?"

"Probably once, twice a month."

"Here or there? Here being in Miami, there being Atlanta."

"Mostly here."

"At some point in time, Neil joined you. Correct?"

"Yes."

"Who invited him?"

"I got a beep. And when he beeped me he said, 'What are you doing?' I said, 'We are having a little bite to eat at the Villa Perrone.' He said, 'Do you mind if I stop by?' I said, 'No.' "

When Neil arrived with Roz, Massaro invited them to join him and the others at their table.

"Did you know she was a police officer at that point in time?"

"Wasn't even thinking about it."

"At some point in time you learned that she was a police officer?"

"Yes, I did."

"If you had known [then] that she was a police officer, would you have been uncomfortable with her presence?"

"No. . . . What we were doing was eating."

"Did you ever have a conversation with Anthony

Trentacosta about the fact that Neil had brought the cop he was dating to that dinner at Villa Perrone?"

"There was a conversation of that effect, that the woman who was at the dinner with him was a police officer."

"What was his reaction?"

"So what?"

"Did you ever discuss the fact that Neil brought a police officer to a social gathering with Mr. Abbandando?"

"I didn't make a big deal about it."

"Did anybody make a big deal about it?"

"Not that I know of, no."

━━━━━━

Fred Massaro would be hard-pressed to find even one organized crime investigator or Mafia expert to believe his contention that no one made "a big deal about it." It's far more likely that the fiery-tempered Trentacosta was furious and worried, concerned that Neil was working with the police. Under Mob rules, Trentacosta had no choice but to give the order to whack Neil Napolitano. The young wiseguy was out of control. He knew too much. He was dating an organized crime detective. He couldn't be trusted. Moreover, when he brought Roz to Villa Perrone, Neil committed an act of disrespect, "a betrayal of everything they believe in," said Detective Joseph McMahon, the MDPD's Italian organized crime expert. They had to make him an example to others. They couldn't take the chance that he would rat them out.

Massaro never saw Neil again after the dinner at the Villa Perrone. He claimed he learned that Neil had been murdered by reading the newspapers, but he had no idea who would have done it. "I was very surprised. Very surprised . . . and I just couldn't see anything like that happening. It's not a normal thing to happen. I felt bad. I liked the kid." Massaro recalled discussing Neil's death with Junior. He was, Massaro said, very, very upset about it.

"Where did you encounter Junior when he was upset? Was it at Party Girls or Nick's at Night?" an investigator asked.

"Could have been in both," the gangster replied. "Could have been also in a restaurant here and there because we ate together once in awhile. We talk. He was very upset about it, from what I can recall."

"Did he have any theories about what led to Neil's death?"

"No, he did not. He was very concerned about that. He said he would like to know, but he had no theory about what had happened to him."

"How about Mr. Trentacosta, did he offer any theories?"

"No."

═══════════

It didn't take long for lawmen to realize that while Fred Massaro was outranked by Tony Pep Trentacosta, Trentacosta was outranked by Nicholas "The Little Guy" Corozzo. Investigators following Fred Massaro watched as Massaro picked up his Mob bosses whenever they visited South Florida. He chauffeured them around, picked up the tab when they went out to dinner, even ran errands for them. The FBI also had wiretaps and a Mob insider, a bagman and enforcer named Louis Maione. He had known Corozzo, his brother JoJo, and Tony Pep Trentacosta for forty years, and he had known Massaro since 1983. Maione had been informing on his Mob pals since 1988, regularly reporting on what he knew about Gambino crime family criminal activities in New York, Florida, and Georgia. The information he provided would lead to the indictment and conviction of Gambino capos and associates.

In February 1996, Maione reported to his FBI handlers in Miami, agents Howe Grover and Terry Feisthammel, that Nick Corozzo had been chosen to take the reins of the Gambino crime family from John Gotti. During March

and April, Corozzo himself told Maione that he would be
the boss. Maione also reported that on March 13, he met
Corozzo at the Sonesta Beach Resort. The G-men summarized what Maione told them:

> *Corozzo provided Maione with the following infor-
> mation: Frederick Massaro had picked up Corozzo
> and Ralph Davino at the airport and transported
> them to the hotel. Corozzo had questioned Massaro
> concerning the activities in which Massaro was cur-
> rently involved in the South Florida area. Massaro
> implied that he was not earning any money. Corozzo
> stated that he was lying, and that Corozzo had heard
> that Massaro owned half of South Florida.*
>
> *Massaro told Corozzo that he was selling Party
> Girls for approximately $250 thousand. Corozzo
> asked Massaro how much money Massaro was
> sending to Corozzo's brother Joseph Corozzo, a
> Gambino capo. Massaro told Nicholas Corozzo
> that he was sending $500 per week. Nicholas
> Corozzo instructed Massaro to immediately travel
> to New York and to contact Joseph Corozzo regard-
> ing the amount which Massaro should be paying per
> week.*
>
> *According to Maione, on March 13, 1996, at the
> same meeting described above, Nicholas Corozzo
> advised Maione of the following additional infor-
> mation: Corozzo did not like Anthony Trentacosta,
> and stated that if Corozzo was the boss years ago, he
> never would have allowed Trentacosta to leave New
> York. Corozzo complained that Trentacosta was all
> over the place, indicating Trentacosta's influence
> and control in New York, in Atlanta, Georgia, and
> in South Florida. Corozzo advised that Trentacosta
> made a "ton" of money in the oil business with . . .*

an incarcerated Gambino capo. Trentacosta was supposed to pay $100,000 toward [the capo's] legal fees, and Corozzo had to sit down with Trentacosta just to get $25,000 out of him.

On March 15, 1996, Nicholas Corozzo advised Maione that Corozzo was taking Massaro away from Anthony Ruggiano's crew and placing Massaro in the crew of Trentacosta. Maione told Corozzo that Fat Andy Ruggiano would not be happy about this change, to which Corozzo replied that he was the boss, and that they would deal with Ruggiano when he got out of prison.

On March 18, 1996, Maione met Nicholas Corozzo, Anthony Trentacosta, and several other Gambino members and associates at the Fontainebleau Hilton Hotel, Miami Beach, Florida. This meeting was directly observed by agents of the FBI. According to Maione, he obtained the following information during this meeting: Trentacosta was told by Corozzo that Trentacosta had to either spend more time in Florida working for the Family or stay retired in Georgia. Corozzo told Maione that Trentacosta indicated his intent to have a more active role in South Florida. Corozzo told Maione that Trentacosta had to be respected because he "did his work" (a reference to Trentacosta having previously been involved in the commission of a murder for the LCN).

On March 20, 1996, Maione met Frederick Massaro at the Fontainebleau Hilton Hotel, Miami Beach, Florida. According to Maione, Massaro was at the hotel to assist in transporting Nicholas Corozzo, Leonard DiMaria (a Gambino capo), and their wives to the airport for their return flight to New York.

A seemingly modest man, Corozzo listed his occupation as contractor and landscaper and lived quietly in the Canarsie section of Brooklyn, New York. He was a staunch Gotti loyalist. In 1986, Corozzo stood trial with The Dapper Don on federal racketeering charges. Both men were acquitted. When Gotti was convicted in 1992 and sentenced to life in prison, he made Corozzo a member of a governing triumvirate whose other members were his twenty-eight-year-old son, John, and brother Peter. Together they would oversee the crime family's day-to-day operations, while Gotti called the shots from his prison cell. By 1996 the four heads of the other New York families that made up the Mafia Commission became convinced that disarray at the top of the Gambino crime family was hurting their own rackets. They ordered Gotti to name a successor. In October The Dapper Don passed the baton to Corozzo.

By then the FBI in Miami had had Corozzo in their crosshairs for nearly two years. They were well aware that he was making frequent trips to South Florida to expand the Gambino crime family's underworld ventures in the Sunshine State, a clear violation of the RICO Act, which made it a federal crime to cross state lines to participate in an ongoing criminal enterprise. By December they were ready to charge the newly named godfather.

At 1:00 P.M. on December 18, 1996, a Wednesday, only two months after he was declared godfather and just two days after his arrival in Miami, FBI agents Howe Grover and Michael Leverock arrested Corozzo and Ralph Davino Jr., his right-hand man in South Florida, as they emerged from the surf at the Sonesta Beach Hotel, a swanky resort on Miami's Key Biscayne.

"It was obvious they weren't expecting us," recalled Leverock, a Brad Pitt look-alike. The agents allowed the surprised gangsters to don T-shirts and cover their handcuffs with beach towels; then they led the mobsters through the hotel's lobby to waiting cars for the short ride to the FBI's field office, where they were booked on charges stemming from a sealed federal indictment. Corozzo, Davino, and seven other Gambino soldiers and associates (Fred Massaro and Tony Pep Trentacosta were not among them) were charged with RICO Act violations—participating in an ongoing criminal enterprise whose racketeering activities included an interstate loan-sharking operation and fencing stolen merchandise. Corozzo was also charged with masterminding the attempted kidnapping and murder of Louis Maione, whom he believed had skimmed twenty thousand dollars from the loan-sharking operation.

Lawmen had amassed a mountain of evidence: wiretaps on which Corozzo could be heard proclaiming that he was the new boss of the Gambino crime family and boasting of his plans to expand their illicit activities in Florida; tape recordings of extortionate threats made by crew members to pressure their loan-sharking debtors to pay up; documents that revealed that Corozzo took as much as forty thousand dollars monthly as his cut from the proceeds of the operation; and sworn statements from Mob informant Louis Maione, who was prepared to testify against Corozzo and the other gangsters, as were several loan-shark victims. At a bond hearing, U.S. Magistrate Judge Barry S. Seltzer decreed that prosecutors presented "credible evidence that the defendant committed the offenses with which he has been charged." Said the court:

The defendant is the self-described boss of the Gambino crime family and successor to John Gotti. Corozzo told an informant ("CI") that he had been put up to the position by "family Capos." According to Corozzo, he had agreed to accept the position if Peter Gotti supported him. He stated that [t]here would be "a lot of changes in the next year or so."

All major decisions involving this operation, including the hiring of the CI as a strong-arm

collector, were cleared through the defendant.
The operation charged borrowers 2 percent to 5
percent per week and up to 260 percent. Borrowers
who were late with their payment were threatened
with physical violence. Upon suspecting that the
CI was cooperating with the government, codefen-
dants likened him (in their words) to "Sammy the
fucking bull" (Gravano), whom they regarded as a
traitor. The defendant approved his abduction and
murder.

Judge Seltzer ordered the fifty-six-year-old godfather
held without bail. Facing twenty years behind bars, on
October 31, 1997, the Gambino boss pleaded guilty to one
count of conspiracy to engage in racketeering. Appear-
ing before U.S. District Court Judge Norman C. Roettger
Jr., Corozzo was sentenced to seventy months in federal
prison, to be followed by three years' probation. Five of his
codefendants, including Ralph Davino, pleaded guilty, too,
and received similar sentences.

Five weeks later, on December 8, Roz Vargas was
arrested by internal affairs detectives Joe Gross and Cindy
Truncale on three counts of perjury stemming from her
statement of February 22, 1996. Her husband, Julio, was
with her when she was taken into custody at the MDPD's
internal affairs office. Roz was handcuffed and led to a
police car for the drive to the county jail, a trip she had
made many times during her eleven-year career. This time,
however, she was the prisoner in the back of an MDPD
cruiser. In less than one hour Roslyn Vargas was booked,
released, and on her way home after posting a $15,000
bond. A bail bondsman was at the jail when she arrived,
his presence there having been arranged for by her new
lawyer, Joel Kaplan. The defense attorney was at her side
when she was arraigned on December 29. Roz Vargas
pleaded not guilty.

Joel Kaplan began practicing law in Miami in 1976. Over the years, he built a reputation as the go-to guy for cops charged with perjury after successfully defending City of Miami police officer Dawn Campbell in 1991. His blistering cross-examination of eyewitnesses led to the acquittal of the twenty-six-year-old cop, who was accused of lying under oath to protect her partner, William Lozano. He was charged with manslaughter after shooting a speeding motorcyclist he said was bearing down on him as he stood in a roadway in Miami's Overtown section. Campbell corroborated Lozano's claim that he shot in self-defense.

The incident—for which Lozano was convicted, then retried and acquitted—took place shortly after 6 P.M., on January 16, 1989, Martin Luther King Day. It began when twenty-three-year-old Clement Anthony Lloyd allegedly ran a stop sign and then revved his Kawasaki Ninja 600R motorcycle past a police car driven by Police Officer John Mervolion. A passenger on the bike, Allan Blanchard, purportedly showed the officer his middle finger. The cop turned on his lights and siren and give chase. Lloyd steered the bike north on Northwest Third Avenue, a route that led him directly to Lozano and Campbell, who were standing near their parked cruiser, which was facing south on the avenue near Sixteenth Street.

Hearing the siren and the roar of the Kawasaki, Lozano stepped into the street. He removed his Glock 9mm automatic pistol from its holster, aimed, and fired one round. The bullet struck Lloyd in the head and killed him. Blanchard died later from injuries he sustained when the speeding motorcycle crashed. Both men were black, and their deaths touched off three days of violence in the predominantly black inner-city neighborhood.

Like Roz Vargas, Dawn Campbell faced three counts of perjury and a long prison sentence. She was suspended but resumed her career as a Miami cop when an Orlando jury (because of intense media coverage, the trial was moved out of Miami) found her not guilty. Roz Vargas was hoping for a similar result when she retained the six-foot-five-inch Kaplan, a Cincinnati native who played varsity basketball at Brandeis University before moving to South Florida to study law at the University of Miami. More than one year would pass before her case would come to trial, but its outcome would reverberate through the MDPD for years to come.

13

A BODY IN A BOX

FBI Special Agent Terrence "Terry" Feisthammel began investigating the Gambinos in 1995. Born in Cincinnati, Ohio, the youngest of five children, he grew up in South Florida. He graduated from North Miami Senior High in 1974 and served a four-year hitch in the U.S. Air Force, after which he enrolled at Miami-Dade Community College and the University of Florida, where he majored in chemistry. Graduating with honors in 1982, he was commissioned a second lieutenant in the U.S. Army, where he was assigned to an elite airborne unit and taught military tactics. His hitch up in 1986, Feisthammel decided to pursue a career in law enforcement, following in the footsteps of older brothers Rick and Gerry, who were police officers in South Florida. In 1987, Terry joined the FBI. After assignments in Dallas, Texas, and San Juan, Puerto Rico, the bureau sent him to Miami, where he was assigned to Organized Crime Unit 1, partnering with agents Howe Grover and Mike Leverock and others. His sister Roxanne and sister-in-law Alicia worked there, too.

The agents of Organized Crime Unit 1 brought down Nicholas Corozzo's South Florida loan-sharking ring, but another had taken root, and the Gambino mobster behind that criminal enterprise was Fred Massaro. Among his crew was an ex-marine named Ariel Hernandez.

Crew headquarters was the back room of Beachside Mario's, the Collins Avenue pizzeria owned by Massaro. From there the Gambino gangster ran a lucrative loan-sharking operation that made short-term loans at exorbitant interest rates to cash-strapped gamblers and businessmen. When they fell behind in their payments, Massaro sent enforcers to collect. Hernandez, aka Richard Martinez, was one of them, as was Neil Napolitano before he died. But strong-arming borrowers wasn't Hernandez's only talent. The ex-marine was also a skilled forger. Also involved was Jeanette Smith, a twenty-two-year-old exotic dancer who performed at Thee Dollhouse, a strip club in Sunny Isles Beach. Lawmen hoped to build a RICO case against Trentacosta, Massaro, and the rest of the crew, but their efforts to put the gangsters behind bars would not come in time to save Smith's life.

It was after 8 P.M. on Friday, March 19, 1999, when Jeanette Smith left the Pembroke Pines apartment she shared with her sister Krissy. Driving her black 1997 Mazda 626 to Thee Dollhouse, the smoky strip club where she performed as Jade, Jeanette had every reason to believe that she was in for yet another lucrative night. The hotels along Collins Avenue were brimming with visitors out for a good time. By midnight, Thee Dollhouse was packed with big spenders willing to part with their cash.

By all accounts, Smith was very good at what she did, confidently strutting and gyrating across the stage to rock music. She was one of the top earners at the club, and all she needed was a silver pole, a G-string, and an overhead disco ball spraying her with rapidly flickering rays of light. Ariel Hernandez, a club regular who in 1996 was charged with stalking a Thee Dollhouse stripper, was in the club that night, too, downing shots of Scotch and beer chasers and plying Smith with hundred dollar bills. When she was on stage, Hernandez was heard boasting that he would be taking her home. When she wasn't performing, Smith sat with Hernandez at a table. The ex-marine seemed attentive and generous with his money at a time when Jeanette was especially vulnerable, having broken up just days before with her longtime boyfriend, Jason Rodriguez.

No one knows what pretext Hernandez used to persuade Smith to leave Thee Dollhouse with him. What is known is that Smith kept mostly to herself. She didn't socialize with the other dancers; was not known to drink, smoke, or use drugs; and she never dated or left the club with a customer. Instead, when her shift ended, Smith went home.

"She was a sweetheart, a really nice girl," said Eric Bock, the strip club's floor manager. "She never got into arguments with anybody. She never bothered anybody. She was always smiling, and she always made good money when she worked."

If she had a weakness, Bock suggested, it was being "attracted to bad-boy kind of guys. And someone who talks like Ariel and presents himself in that way, I could see being attractive to Jeanette."

When she left the club at 5:30 on Saturday morning, Ariel Hernandez was waiting for her in the parking lot. Bock walked her to her car. Before Smith slid behind the wheel of her Mazda, Bock asked if everything was okay. "Yeah," she replied. "He's a friend. We're going to breakfast."

They drove to a nearby Denny's, then went to the Olympia Motel, a run-down, single-story motel within walking distance of Beachside Mario's and Thee Dollhouse. Hernandez had been living there in a sixty-dollar-a-night room for three weeks, filling it with cartons from merchandise that had been purchased with phony checks.

Later that afternoon, lawmen from the joint federal and local task force investigating the Gambino crime family in South Florida were on duty at the FBI's Miami field office. They were inside the "wire room," the electronic listening post where lawmen intercepted wiretapped telephone calls. Just two days earlier, U.S. District Court Judge William Dimitrouleas had authorized a tap of Fred Massaro's phones.

The bureau had been investigating the mobster since October 1995, just days after Neil Napolitano's bones washed up on Miami Beach. The investigation was dubbed Operation Gemstone, and lead case agent Terry Feisthammel drew up the request for the wiretap. In it he declared that there was probable cause to suspect that Fred Massaro and others associated with him were involved in bank fraud, mail and wire fraud, extortion, and drug trafficking. Feisthammel linked Massaro to the Gambinos. He wrote: "Frederick J. Massaro . . . is an associate of Gambino soldier Anthony Trentacosta and in the crew of Anthony Ruggiano. . . . Numerous surveillances have documented Massaro meeting with Trentacosta. Confidential source information indicates that Massaro has had hidden ownership interests in adult entertainment clubs. In addition to numerous arrests, Massaro was convicted in the 13th Judicial Circuit of Florida, on June 25, 1985, of passing forged instruments (five counts)."

Feisthammel also named Massaro associate Ariel Hernandez: "Confidential source information indicates that Massaro and Hernandez are conspiring to obtain victim bank account information in order to produce forged personal checks and identification documents in order to cash forged checks."

Lawmen were listening at 3:43 P.M. on March 20, when Fred Massaro placed a call to the Olympia Motel. He was responding to a page from Ariel Hernandez's pager. Massaro asked to be connected to room 121. A man later identified as Ariel Hernandez answered. An FBI tape recorder captured the call.

> *HERNANDEZ: Listen, uh, things got a little messy yesterday. Remember that, a detective from the thing?*
> *MASSARO: From what thing?*
> *HERNANDEZ: The homicide.*
> *MASSARO: Yeah.*
> *HERNANDEZ: Well, the thing is this. I tied up the loose end and I got a package I gotta get rid of. Oh man, I haven't been able to sleep. My stomach is all fuckin' turned around.*
> *MASSARO: Uh huh.*
> *HERNANDEZ: What should I do?*
> *MASSARO: I don't know. I'll talk to you in person. Let me shower and shave and I'll be out there. All right?*
> *HERNANDEZ: All right.*

Detective Howard Roble of the Broward Sheriff's Office (BSO) heard the call. The lawman, a member of a joint FBI-BSO task force, was convinced that they were talking about a dead body, but he didn't know whose it was. The next day, listening lawmen intercepted a noontime phone call to Massaro from Sonny Silverman, a man investigators identified as a Massaro enforcer. They heard Silverman tell Massaro that the experience of moving the body was a "shockeroo," and he vowed that he would never reveal what he saw.

———

It was warm and clear just before 8 A.M. on Sunday, March 21, 1999, when Orlando Maytin cast his line into the murky canal beside Mile Marker 31 on Alligator Alley, the straight-as-an-arrow, flat-as-a-pancake, eighty-four-mile stretch of I-75 that crosses the Florida Everglades, connecting Miami and Fort Lauderdale with the Gulf Coast city of Naples and points north. As Maytin waited for a fish to bite, he couldn't help but notice a large, half-submerged carton floating nearby. Curious, he reeled in the cardboard box.

The fisherman tried to lift the carton out of the water, but it was too waterlogged and too heavy. It immediately broke apart, releasing a corpse and several white towels. Horrified, Maytin watched as the bound and bent body of what appeared to be a woman splashed into the murky water and floated away. He called 911.

The first lawman to arrive was Florida Highway Patrol trooper Phillipe Coralles. He immediately broke out the yellow police tape, marked off the scene, and alerted the Broward Sheriff's Office, the BSO. Among the responders were homicide detective Frank Ilarraza and dive-team deputy George Furguson. A team from the medical examiner's office arrived, too. As Deputy Furguson prepared to go into the water to retrieve the body, Ilarraza examined the box. It measured 35 by 22 by 18 inches. The barcode was clearly visible, and the printing on the outside of the box indicated that it had once contained a Sony Mini Hi-Fi system with Surround Sound. As crime scene investigators photographed the scene from the ground, a BSO helicopter hovered overhead so that a police photographer onboard could take aerial photos, too. While other deputies kept an eye out for alligators, Deputy Furguson removed the body from the water and placed it on a plastic liner.

It was the battered corpse of a thin young woman, about five-foot-three, a brunette with bright red fingernails. Her skin was wrinkled from being in the water. Her face, neck, and chin were bruised and battered. Her arms were tied behind her back, while both ankles were tightly bound together by a single shoelace. The only item of clothing she had on was a gray sweatshirt, which was twisted and inside out. A gold ankle chain bore the name "Jeanette."

As Ilarraza stood on dry land watching the recovery of the body, a call came in over the police radio. Boaters at Mile Marker 41 had found a black backpack. Ilarraza dispatched BSO deputy Tom Sheridan to retrieve it. Inside were business cards from Thee Dollhouse. By noon the still unidentified body was on its way to the Broward County Medical Examiner's office in Fort Lauderdale, where Dr. Lisa Flannagan prepared to perform the postmortem examination. It began at 1:45. While a BSO detective took photographs of the body, the pathologist began with the external examination. She noted hemorrhaging in various areas of the neck, blunt head trauma with contusions of the left frontal scalp and right temporoparietal scalp, multiple injuries under the chin and along the jaw, and bruising and contusions of the lips. She also noted severe bruising of the anus—"anal trauma with acute hemorrhage and force lacerations."

The internal examination revealed that Smith's larynx had been crushed. A large amount of semen was found in her mouth. Her tongue was nearly sliced in two. No water was found in her lungs. Toxicology tests found no presence of drugs. Dr. Flannagan concluded that death was caused by strangulation, and it occurred before the body went into the water.

Later that evening, Detective Ilarraza was at Thee Dollhouse. The mustachioed lawman brought a photo—a Polaroid headshot of the corpse—which he showed to the strip club's manager.

"That's Jeanette Smith," the shaken manager said. Club employees told the detective about Smith's last appearance there, how at the end of the night she happily counted out $1,400 in cash. The lawman learned that the exotic dancer known as Jade was "straitlaced." She didn't drink or do drugs, and when her shift ended, she went home—except for the morning she left the club at 5:30 A.M. with Hernandez, telling Eric Bock that they were on their way to

Denny's for breakfast. Ilarraza went to the eatery, where a waitress recalled serving them.

With a name and an address for the body in the box, Ilarraza drove to Pembroke Pines, to the apartment Jeanette Smith shared with her older sister Krissy. He showed her the Polaroid. Distraught and grief-stricken, Krissy phoned her parents. The next day a parking enforcement agent in the city of Surfside found Smith's abandoned Mazda.

On Friday, March 26, Detective Ilarraza listened to the phone call Detective Roble intercepted the afternoon of March 20. Roble told Ilarraza that the call came from Ariel Hernandez's room at the Olympia Motel. Ilarraza recognized the caller's voice. He had heard it the day after Jeanette Smith's body was found, when an anonymous caller claimed that "the girl in the box" had been tortured by two Columbians who forced women to perform oral sex by shoving wine bottles up their rectums.

Ilarraza and a team of lawmen headed for the Sunny Isles motel, but Hernandez was long gone, having checked out two days before. Inside the room investigators found towels similar to the ones recovered from the canal. They also found blood in the room and a receipt for a Sony Mini Hi-Fi system with Surround Sound bearing the same bar code as the one on the box that held Jeanette Smith's body. It was from a Sharper Image store located in the Sawgrass Mills shopping center in Sunrise, and Ariel Hernandez's name was on it. Clerks there remembered the ex-marine.

Two days later, Hernandez was in police custody. He had not gone far. Lawmen tracked him to an apartment house at 172nd Street and Collins Avenue, less than a mile from the Olympia Motel, nine blocks from Thee Dollhouse, and around the corner from Beachside Mario's. At 9 A.M. a team of eight lawmen from the BSO and the Sunny Isles Beach Police took up positions around the apartment. They had been alerted to the ex-marine's whereabouts by the FBI's tap of Fred Massaro's phones. When police came knocking, Hernandez was fast asleep inside the apartment of his twenty-six-year-old lady friend, Tami Bubel, a legal secretary. Among the lawmen who took Hernandez in that Sunday morning were BSO Detective Ilarraza and Sunny Isles police lieutenant Rick Feisthammel, Terry's brother. Hernandez offered no resistance. A search of the apartment yielded a single shoelace. It matched the shoelace used to bind Jeanette Smith's ankles.

Taken to BSO headquarters in Fort Lauderdale, Hernandez was placed in an interview room and read his Miranda rights. He admitted leaving Thee Dollhouse with Smith but claimed that she had dropped him off on Collins Avenue and drove off. As he exited her car, he said, he noticed a suspicious vehicle following her.

When Frank Ilarraza made it clear that he didn't buy his story, Hernandez changed it, this time claiming that he brought Smith to his room at the Olympia Motel but waited outside while two men, Columbians named Enrique and Francisco, tortured her with a wine bottle, then strangled her with a belt.

Ilarraza didn't buy that story either, and he told the ex-marine that he knew he was lying. Finally, Hernandez told detectives that he wanted to level with them. After breakfast at Denny's, Smith said she wanted to spend the day with him. He gave her five hundred dollars and took her to his hotel room, where they engaged in rough sex. Smith, he said, died accidentally, choking to death when Hernandez's muscular arm accidentally pressed against her neck as he mounted her. He heard a crack, after which Smith began struggling to breathe.

Hernandez told lawmen that Smith sustained bruises on her body when he put her in the bathtub. Afterward, he hog-tied her so she would fit inside the stereo box, taped the carton, and drove to Mile Marker 31 on Alligator Alley. He told the detective that he thought hungry alligators would devour the evidence, but March and June are mating months for the reptiles, and the amorous gators didn't bite.

Ilarraza didn't buy the ex-marine's third story either, but because Hernandez implicated himself in Jeanette Smith's homicide, the lawman could charge him. At 2:28 P.M. Ariel Hernandez was booked into the Broward County Jail. The charge: murder. The next day, Detective Ilarraza and his boss, Broward Sheriff Ken Jenne, held a news conference.

"We have a confession," the sheriff announced. "We think this is a good case."

The sheriff revealed details of what Ariel Hernandez told his detectives, that he paid Smith five hundred dollars for sex. "By Mr. Hernandez's account, the sex got rough and resulted in Miss Smith's strangulation," he said.

Ilarraza reminded reporters that police had only the ex-marine's version of what happened inside the cramped hotel room. Before the press conference ended, Sheriff Jenne hinted that others may have been involved. "There is a potential for more arrests," he declared.

The owner of Thee Dollhouse wasted no time defending the dead dancer. "I have a hard time believing that this was about rough sex for money," Steven Lesnick said. "This has nothing to do with prostitution. She was a clean-cut, nice kid." Ariel Hernandez, he declared "is trying to make her look like a bad girl."

The strip club owner was right, but it would be a while before lawmen would reveal the truth behind Jeanette Smith's murder.

14

"WE WHO LABOR HERE SEEK ONLY TRUTH"

SIGN ABOVE CIRCUIT COURT JUDGE
RONALD DRESNICK'S BENCH

South Florida was in the grip of an emergency on Wednesday, May 26, 1999. Dozens of lightning strikes the week before and a large brush fire the previous day had sparked grass fires in Florida's River of Grass, the Everglades. Although most of the fires had burned out, thousands of acres of bone-dry marshland were still smoldering, sending thick smoke skyward for the wind to push into Miami and Fort Lauderdale. The smoky conditions prompted officials to urge those with respiratory ailments and the elderly to remain indoors.

The acrid smoke drifted to Miami. It hung over the nine-story Richard E. Gerstein Justice Building, where the perjury trial of Roslyn Vargas was about to begin. Believing that she had been blowing smoke when she gave her sworn statement to investigators on February 22, 1996, prosecutors charged the MDPD detective with three counts of violating Florida Statute 837.02. It says, "Whoever makes a false statement, which he or she does not believe to be true, under oath in an official proceeding in regard to any material matter, commits a felony of the third degree."

Prosecutors alleged that Roz Vargas made false statements under oath when she said that her meetings with Neil Napolitano in August 1995 were for work-related purposes (count 1); that she was not with Napolitano voluntarily from September 5 through 11, 1995 (count 2); and that she did not go with Neil Napolitano voluntarily on September 12, 1995 (count 3). The stakes were high. If convicted, Roz Vargas faced five years in prison for each count.

Six jurors had been empanelled to hear the case in Circuit Court Judge Ronald Dresnick's third-floor courtroom. Representing the State of Florida were veteran prosecutors Mary Cagle and Michael Von Zamft. Seated with them was MDPD Detective Joe Gross, the lead investigator on the Vargas perjury case. Roz Vargas sat at the defense table flanked by her lawyers, lead attorney Joel Kaplan and co-counsel Stuart Kaufman. Julio Vargas, Roz's husband, positioned himself directly behind Roz, in the first row of wooden bench seats reserved for the public. He would be there throughout the four-day trial, joined at times by their children and Roz's parents.

In the weeks and months leading up to the trial, Kaplan sought to have the case thrown out, arguing, among other things, that his client's alleged false statements on February 22, 1996, were immaterial to the reason she was called on to give a statement under oath—the investigation into the death of Neil Napolitano. Throughout the pretrial wrangling, prosecutors argued that Vargas's alleged perjury about her relationship with Neil Napolitano adversely impacted the investigation into his death. After a morning of motions and discussions of procedural matters, and a recess for lunch, Judge Dresnick took the bench at 1:30 P.M. *State of Florida v. Roslyn Vargas* was underway.

"All right, Mr. Von Zamft," the jurist commanded, and the fifty-two-year-old assistant state attorney, a graduate

of the University of Miami and the University of Miami
Law School, rose from his seat at the prosecution table. He
crossed the room to the jury box and began his opening
statement.

"On September 27, 1995, the body parts of Neil Napolitano washed up on the shores of Miami Beach. He was
identified on September 29 through those body parts. Neil
Napolitano was last seen September 13 of 1995, and one of
the last people to have seen Neil was the defendant Roslyn
Vargas."

Next, Von Zamft explained why the MDPD detective
was on trial: "It's that death and the surrounding circumstances that brings us to this, brings us here. It's the odys-
sey of their relationship that you're going to hear about that
culminated on February 22, 1996, in Roslyn Vargas being
given an opportunity to testify truthfully and choosing
not to."

The burly prosecutor offered specifics. Roz Vargas, he
said, "was not truthful when she was asked certain questions. She was not truthful when she said that she met with
Neil Napolitano during the month of August only for the
purpose of work. She was not truthful when she said that
she was not with Neil Napolitano voluntarily from September 5 of 1995 to September 11, 1995 . . . [and she] was
not truthful when she said that she did not go with Neil
Napolitano voluntarily on September 12, 1995, when she
left Applebee's restaurant after having dinner with Neil
Napolitano and her children."

Von Zamft told jurors that Detective Vargas became an
organized crime detective on October 31, 1994, and he told
them about Neil Napolitano's suspected drug trafficking,
about Alvino Reyes and John Davidson, and the nagging
suspicion among lawmen that Neil Napolitano was responsible for their disappearance. He also told them about Joe
Stracci and about Roz Vargas's undercover assignment.
Its purpose, he said, was "to get more information about

[Neil Napolitano's] drug deals and the deaths of Reyes and Davidson."

And he told them about the relationship between Neil and Vargas that seemed to blossom after the undercover operation was shut down.

Von Zamft: "By June 1, it was clear to her sergeant that the undercover role was gone . . . so on June 1, she writes her last report . . . and one of the things that takes place approximately June 1 is she's informed by her sergeant, 'You will no longer have meetings with Neil Napolitano. You will speak to him only during business hours by phone, approximately eight to five.' She was not supposed to have any further contact."

But in July 1995, Von Zamft said, Roz Vargas was having "occasional" contact with Neil by telephone. By the following month she was having "extensive" phone contact, with "calls to his beeper, calls to his home."

Von Zamft: "You'll find out about dates she had with Neil Napolitano. You're going to find out about the fact she went to people's homes as his date for dinner, that she went to bars with him as his date during August 1995. Yet in her statement of February 22, 1996, which you are going to have introduced to you, you will see where, when she's asked about it, she says, 'I only met with Neil for work-related purposes.' "

The prosecutor told them about Roz's Orlando trip. She went there on September 1, 1995, "ostensibly to go to a family gathering." While there, she and her husband argued. "She starts contacting the only person she could think of who was going to be sympathetic—her former target, her subject, Neil Napolitano," Von Zamft declared, his tone brimming with disbelief. "While she's talking to him from the pay phone in Denny's, according to her statements, suddenly he appears. He's there. He's so sympathetic."

They checked into a hotel, the Holiday Inn. They stayed together in the same room, went to a mall, and phoned

Neil's sister Monica in San Diego. Two days later, they
drove back to South Florida. They visited Neil's mother
Velma.

Von Zamft: "Now, keep in mind, that on February 22,
when asked about this, she's saying: 'I am not with him
voluntarily.' So she's telling us and you, when you read the
statement, 'I'm not with him voluntarily in the hotel room.
I am not with him voluntarily when I go to the mall. I am
not with him voluntarily when I drive back to Broward
County.'" Then, the prosecutor said, "comes what was probably the beginning of the demise of Neil Napolitano's life."

With those words the six jurors, three men and three
women, who until then were paying rapt attention, sat
straight up in their chairs.

Von Zamft: "Neil Napolitano takes Roslyn Vargas,
police officer, to dinner at a place called Villa Perrone, an
Italian restaurant . . . a place where a lot of people like to
eat, especially some people who are known by the authorities to be members of organized crime. And at that dinner . . . there's a man by the name of Freddie Massaro,
and another man whose nickname is Tony Pep, and you're
going to hear testimony from people who do surveillance
and work on organized crime, and have for years, that
Freddie Massaro and Tony Pep are known members of the
Gambino crime family, and Neil Napolitano chose to bring
Roz Vargas, a police officer, to that dinner."

Von Zamft told the jurors what happened the next day,
September 7. Neil and Roz went to a bookstore, a movie,
and spent the night together at his apartment. With a tinge
of sarcasm, the veteran prosecutor urged the jurors to
"keep in mind the focus of this, which is her statement to
the State Attorney's Office, all of these events are transpir-
ing while she is not with him voluntarily."

On September 8, they return to Orlando. "They check
into a hotel, the same hotel that they checked into the first
time they were in Orlando. . . . They go to Paradise Island,

to a place called Mannequin's. They go to the Waffle House, spend the night at the Holiday Inn. The next day they go to Disney World. They're having a good time in Disney World. . . . We know this because we have photographs of Roslyn Vargas sitting on a bench at Disney World, looking very happy, and certainly not looking like someone who was forced to be there, and Neil Napolitano, again, with his photograph, looking very happy."

Then, pointing to a poster-sized photo that Mary Cagle placed on an easel, Von Zamft said, "We have another photograph. Anybody that's ever been to Disney recognizes this. That's Splash Mountain. There she is, with Neil Napolitano, against her will, riding Splash Mountain," Von Zamft said derisively. "The next day they go shopping, and this is very interesting. Now again, keep in mind that she said this whole time, 'I'm not with him voluntarily.' You would think she would be looking for a way to get loose, get away, [but] she says she never could get away. . . . They check out of the Holiday Inn and drive back to Broward. They go to his apartment."

On September 11, Von Zamft noted, "She is free . . . and where does she go? She goes home. And what does she do? Well, the next morning, she talks to Neil. Then she drives to Neil's apartment. You will hear testimony that at no time did she tell her husband what had happened, did she call her sergeant and tell her what happened, did she report the fact that she had been held against her will, did she ever report any of the things that a police officer, who had been forced against their will or was not with someone voluntarily, would have and should have done. Then, on that day, at Neil's apartment, she goes to get some clothes, but she spends the day there . . . meets her children at Block-buster with Neil Napolitano, the man who had been forcing her . . . the one she had been with involuntarily. She calls her children. She has them meet her, and they go to dinner together, Roz, Neil, and her two sons. They finish dinner.

They go back from Applebee's to where the cars are, and she leaves with Neil and spends the night at his apartment. Her children go home."

On September 13, Barbara Gentile relieved Roz Vargas of duty. "Does she take this opportunity and say he forced me to go with him?" Von Zamft asked rhetorically. "[Do] you know what she says? 'Gee, I'm sorry. I'm sorry.' "

September 19: "She's called in and she gives a statement to Internal Affairs, and nowhere in that statement does she say she'd been held against her will, or say that to any of the Internal Affairs people that are there."

November 3: "Everybody, the police, are still trying to figure out what to do. They have a body that's come up. They have Roz Vargas, who had participated in this undercover operation and is now associating with this known criminal. The defendant, Roz Vargas goes in for another statement at Internal Affairs. . . . But did Roz Vargas tell the Internal Affairs detectives that she was with Neil involuntarily? Never," Von Zamft thundered, "did she say 'I was not with him voluntarily.' "

Von Zamft told the jurors that they would hear from Neil's brother, Rocco. He had been charged with the murder of mobster Junior Abbandando, and he would tell them what happened when Neil informed the Gambino gangster that he was done with the Mob and that Roz "knows all about the drug deals" but "isn't going to do anything about it."

Pointing at the defendant, Von Zamft said, "Her relationship with Neil Napolitano may well have been the catalyst for his death. Her relationship with Neil Napolitano may have potentially injured other investigations. [Investigators] needed to know. So on February 22, 1996, Roz Vargas, with her lawyer, comes to the State Attorney's Office with a grant of immunity. . . . It was at that statement on February the 22nd, 1996, that Roz Vargas committed perjury. She lied. She lied in a couple of areas. She's charged with specifically lying in those three areas I've told you about. You're going to hear from people who have seen them together, watched them together, saw them dancing together at nightclubs, holding hands, cuddling, kissing. You're going to hear from people that were at the dinner at Villa Perrone. You're going to hear from Rocco Napolitano, his brother. When we're done, you're going to realize that Roz Vargas, who had the opportunity to be truthful, chose not to."

Finally, the prosecutor pointed to the sign above Judge Dresnick's bench. He read out loud what it said: "We who labor here seek only truth." Then, turning toward Roz Vargas, he said, "She chose the opposite."

Von Zamft's opening was powerful, but opening statements are not evidence. They give jurors a preview of the case. Lawyers liken them to the pictures on the outside of jigsaw-puzzle boxes. They help puzzle solvers fit the pieces together. Likewise, opening statements help jurors put the evidence together. When his turn came, defense attorney Joel Kaplan painted a very different picture. His tone was matter-of-fact. Unlike prosecutor Von Zamft, he avoided polemics.

"Good afternoon, ladies and gentlemen," he began. "Roslyn Vargas did not, I repeat, did not lie and commit perjury about her activities with Neil Napolitano when she gave this statement under oath on February 22, 1996. Plain and simple, she came forward as requested, without compulsion, and told the investigators who were examining his death everything they wanted to know and, as the evidence will show, she was the one and the only one who provided that window into his activities which led up to his demise. She raised her right hand, swore to tell the truth, and she did."

Neil, Kaplan said, "Was a mafia wannabe, and you will hear him so described by the people he associated with, including his brother."

He was also a target of the MDPD. "They surveilled

him. They observed him. They dissected him. They scrutinized him, and they found nothing, nothing to charge him with. Part of the investigation was into his associations. Part of it was into his activities, lots of suspicion, and even so much so that notwithstanding the fact, as you will hear, that he was considered by law enforcement to be a dangerous, violent individual, they sent [Roslyn Vargas] in undercover to make contact with him, to see if she could offer him the opportunity to commit a crime for which he could be arrested. Nothing happened."

About Roz's statement of February 22, 1996, Kaplan said, "Roz went on that date to the State Attorney's Office under no compulsion. . . . She was so honest and thorough, things no one else could have talked about because there was just two of them, and one of them was around to provide this information. Why would she do this? Because she was telling the truth. She was helping the authorities. She was cooperating."

As an attorney with extensive experience defending cops accused of perjury, Joel Kaplan knew that under Florida law, a false statement was not perjury unless it was material to the purpose of the proceeding at which it was made. The defense attorney argued that even if Roz had made false statements on February 22, 1996, the statements were immaterial to the purpose of the proceeding—the investigation into the death of Neil Napolitano. Therefore, under Florida law they did not constitute perjury. The reason his client was called to give a sworn statement, Kaplan said, "was not about Roz. [Neil] died a particularly gruesome death. And then, several months later, one of his associates [also] died a particularly gruesome death, a man by the name of Junior Abbandando, and [investigators] wanted to see if there was a connection, because Rocco Napolitano believed Junior Abbandando killed his brother, and Rocco had been arrested and awaits trial for Junior Abbandando's death."

Said Kaplan: "Now, there had to be a why. There had to be a theory pursued into why Neil was killed. That started this chain reaction, and that theory, as you will hear, is a pretty simple one: when Neil brought Roz to the dinner you're about to hear about, he committed a great act of disrespect. If you believe these people were truly, in fact, Gambino family members, organized crime types, Mafia types, what have you, the bringing of a police officer into their midst knowingly, somebody who is undercover, is an incredible act of disrespect, and it's obvious why. Neil's association with a police officer scared these people and led them to believe that he posed a threat to them, to their freedom, to their operations. Roz's testimony on February 22, 1996, locked in that theory, because they didn't know about Neil's activities, this dinner and all these things until she gave them one hundred and twenty-eight pages of answers to their questions."

The defense attorney implored the jurors to consider the charges against Roslyn Vargas "in the context of the case" because "the focus of this investigation at the time this statement was taken was on why Neil was killed and not the fact that Roz and Neil had been together voluntarily or not."

He reviewed the charges, and he read from the statement transcript.

"Count 1 states that Roz committed perjury when she stated she met Neil Napolitano in August of 1995 . . . for work-related purposes. She has never said . . . it was for work-related purposes. Only, in fact, that she was *authorized* to meet with Napolitano for work-related purposes during work hours.

"Count 2 tells us that Roz committed perjury when she said that she was not with Neil Napolitano voluntarily from September 5, 1995, to September 11, 1995. Roz was neither asked a question, nor did Roz give an answer on all one hundred twenty-eight pages, as I read the statement, in which she used the word *voluntary*. . . . What she said was that on Tuesday, September 5, the second day in Orlando, she said to Neil, 'You know, this is not right. I shouldn't be here. I've got to go.' She reached for her purse, and in her purse was her gun. He grabbed the purse, removed the gun. There was a little bit of a tussle. He gave her back the gun. He gave her back the gun without ammunition, and from thereafter, he never left her side . . . [and] the evidence will show she was never asked the question."

Referring to the third count, Kaplan declared: "Roz is charged with perjury by virtue of the fact she stated that she did not go with Neil Napolitano voluntarily on September 12, 1995, after she, her sons, and Neil Napolitano had dinner at Applebee's restaurant. The evidence will show that when that question was asked, when that topic was discussed, she was asked if Neil said anything, and she said, 'Yes, he told me to get in the car.' 'Did he have a weapon?' She said, 'No.' And then the questioner said, 'Are you trying to tell us that he kidnapped you that day in front of your kids?' Answer: 'No. Did he hold something on me? Did he physically force me in the car? No, he didn't. It was the fear.' The very fear the police had instilled in her that this guy may be capable of violence if he doesn't get what he wants. Question: 'So you didn't go in the car with Neil by choice?' And the response was negative. As the evidence will show, Roz shook her head, indicating no.

"Ladies and gentlemen, you will hear from an array of witnesses, most of them or lots of them who Roz helped identify. You will see and hear a lot of evidence she helped identify, but you know, none of them will tell you that she said these things. What she said is in the record, all right, and, you know, she was truthful in her perceptions, her subjective feelings, as the evidence will show, about some of these events, because she was truthful about everything, as the evidence will show, truthful about the most intimate things only she could tell the authorities, and if she was that thorough in her truthfulness, ladies and gentlemen, I submit, the evidence will show to you she did not commit perjury in this case. Thank you."

"Call your first witness," Judge Dresnick commanded. The prosecutors called Dr. Jeffrey Kamlet.

The Miami Beach physician testified that he recalled dining at the Villa Perrone in September 1995 with his patients Freddy Massaro and Anthony Trentacosta. Kamlet said he knew they were mobsters. Napolitano arrived halfway through the dinner, and he was not alone. He was with a woman. Dr. Kamlet said he had not seen her since that night, but he identified Roslyn Vargas as the woman he met that night at Villa Perrone. Asked to describe how Neil Napolitano acted toward Roz and how Roz acted toward Neil, the doctor said, "Mr. Napolitano was very upbeat, very happy, in a jovial sort of mood, had his arm around Mrs. Vargas, seemed to be very proud that this was his girlfriend, very happy that this was his girlfriend. He said to me, 'This is my girlfriend.' "

Dr. Kamlet was followed to the stand by his wife, Karen, who corroborated her husband's testimony about the dinner. It was late afternoon when Mrs. Kamlet stepped down from the witness stand. Judge Dresnick adjourned court for the day.

15

STATE OF FLORIDA
V. ROSLYN VARGAS

DAY TWO

The muck in the Everglades was still burning the next morning, shrouding the region in a smoky haze and sending hundreds of South Floridians to hospital emergency rooms for relief from respiratory problems. The *Miami Herald* reported that smoky conditions were expected to last throughout the day. Although the fires in the Everglades made the front pages, the *Herald*'s local section recapped the first day of *State of Florida v. Roslyn Vargas*.

PROSECUTOR: POLICEWOMAN LIED
ABOUT RELATIONSHIP WITH SUSPECT

Miami-Dade Police Detective Roslyn Vargas was given the opportunity to testify truthfully about her personal relationship with a suspected criminal whose body parts washed ashore on Miami Beach, but she chose to lie under oath, a prosecutor told jurors Wednesday in opening statements of Vargas' perjury trial. But Vargas' lawyer, Joel Kaplan, said no lying occurred.

The newspaper reported that the proceeding began with "a dramatic flourish" when prosecutor Michael Von Zamft displayed two poster-sized photographs of Roslyn Vargas "looking very happy at Disney World" with Neil Napolitano, "whom Vargas had been assigned to investigate." The paper also noted that Roz Vargas "occasionally shook her head in disagreement as Von Zamft spoke."

Despite the acrid air outside, court convened at 10:30 A.M. MDPD detective Joseph McMahon was to be the state's first witness, but before he could take the stand, a juror had a question.

"Can we take notes?" the juror wanted to know.

"That's an interesting question," Judge Dresnick replied. "Would you like to?"

"There's a lot of information here, and I would like to."

The judge turned to the lawyers. "Any objection?"

"Whatever the court decides," Joel Kaplan said.

"It's okay with me," Mary Cagle announced.

"I am going to let them," the judge declared.

Addressing the jurors, Judge Dresnick said jurors could take notes if they wished. "We will pass out notepads and pens. Every time we take a recess, you will need to leave your notepad in the courtroom. We'll collect them. Don't write anything on the front of your notepad except your name."

And he issued an instruction: "Your notes are only a tool to aid your own individual memory and should not be compared with any other juror's notes in determining the contents of any testimony or in evaluating the importance of any evidence."

The judge urged the jurors to rely on their memories "above all" when it came time to deliberate. Take notes "if you want," the jurist said, "but your memory is what you need to rely upon and not your notes."

While a bailiff distributed pads and pens, Detective McMahon waited to be sworn in. As soon as the bailiff was done, the lawman took the witness stand. His testimony would give jurors a crash course on the history, structure, and rules of the Mafia, and he would link Neil Napolitano to the Gambino crime family.

Responding to the prosecutor's questions, the lawman testified that he was assigned to the MDPD's Criminal Intelligence Bureau. "My field is Italian organized crime. Cosa Nostra. The Mafia. We monitor activities of identified individuals that are visiting, operating, working, or living in South Florida."

McMahon said he began studying the activities of Italian organized crime families in South Florida in 1992. He learned about their "very structured, very rigid" hierarchy and the rules under which they operated. He told about the five families and the Commission and about bosses, underbosses, capos, soldiers, and member associates. Using a chart, McMahon explained the pyramid-like hierarchy of the families, comparing their command structures to the military. All the Mob families, he said, "are involved in illegal activity, from gambling to extortion to murder to credit card fraud."

"Law enforcement authorities have identified twenty-four La Cosa Nostra crime families throughout the United States," McMahon said. "There are probably fourteen hundred made members within those crime families."

And he explained how member associates become made men: "Either by following orders to eliminate an individual—kill someone who has betrayed their trust—serv[ing] jail time, keeping your mouth shut . . . or having made a financial success."

McMahon identified Anthony "Tony Pep" Trentacosta as a soldier and an acting capo in the Gambino crime family, Frank "Junior" Abbandando as a "soldier/member" of the Gambino family, and Freddie Massaro as a "member associate" under Trentacosta.

"Have you ever heard of Neil Napolitano?" Von Zamft asked. The lawman said he had. He explained: "I was

contacted by an agent in the FBI. We had information that
Mr. Napolitano was involved in illegal activities in the area
of Collins Avenue and Sixty-second Street, at a Denny's
restaurant there. We proceeded to do surveillances to verify
the information, talked to our confidential sources. I was
able to determine that Mr. Napolitano . . . was involved in
the sale of narcotics, prescription drugs, and some rip-offs
of checks from some of the hotels."

Q. *How would you have classified Neil Napolitano?*
A. *[We] classified him as a wannabe. We carried him as
below Mr. Massaro.*
Q. *Assume, for example that a wannabe brings an
undercover, or introduces an undercover police
officer to a member of the Gambino crime family,
a soldier or a capo, and then they learn that that
person is an undercover officer. What is, generally,
the outcome of that kind of a situation?*
A. *Based on my years of experience, everything I know,
it's a sentence of death.*
Q. *Excuse me?*
A. *Based on everything I know, it's a sentence of death.*
Q. *For whom?*
A. *The person who brought the undercover. . . . They
consider him a rat, a fink, a turncoat, a traitor. He's
betrayed the whole family. There is no other way they
would look at it.*
Q. *Assuming that Neil Napolitano spoke to Junior
Abbandando on September 13, 1995, and explained
to Junior Abbandando, "I want out of the business.
Roz is a police officer. Roz knows all about the drug
dealing, but she's cool. She's not going to do anything.
We're getting out together. She's not going to say anything, and neither am I." What would you anticipate
the result would be from Junior Abbandando, or any
other member of a known crime family?"*

A. *If any individual involved in La Cosa Nostra tried to get out, it's impossible. . . . It's impossible for a person that is brought into this crime family to walk away.*

Q. *What would you expect would happen to somebody like Neil Napolitano who tried to do that?*

A. *He would be killed, assassinated.*

When his turn came to cross-examine the lawman, defense attorney Joel Kaplan pounded away at the likely motive behind Neil's death.

Q. *Would it be fair to say that Neil Napolitano's action in bringing a police officer to a Mafia dinner was an act of disrespect?"*

A. *Yes, sir.*

Q. *An incredible act of disrespect, right?*

A. *In their eyes, yes, sir.*

Q. *That would violate every tenet by which organized crime, the Mafia, La Cosa Nostra, conducts its business, correct?*

A. *Yes, sir.*

Having established a plausible "why" for Neil's death, the defense lawyer turned his attention to who might have done it.

Q. *And who would be most disrespected by that act?*

A. *Mr. Massaro, because he was the one that brought Neil Napolitano over to meet Mr. Trentacosta.*

Q. *Who would be responsible for remedying or rectifying this act of disrespect?*

A. *The people that are involved in that faction. Neil worked with Junior Abbandando for a while before he worked with Mr. Massaro [and] a variety of things could occur there [with] Abbandando, Massaro, anyone who is on a lower level and wants to impress*

Mr. Trentacosta and try and elevate his status in the
family and takes it on his own and commits murder.

Q. *So in all likelihood, Mr. Massaro or Mr. Abbandando*
was responsible for Napolitano's death, correct?

A. *It could be one of the theories, yes, sir . . . and at this*
point that's what it is, a theory.

Q. *An IA [Internal Affairs] theory?*

A. *Correct.*

Q. *Now, in addition to being disrespectful, this act of*
bringing a police officer to a get-together threatened
the well-being of these people in the sense that it
might expose them to some criminal prosecution,
correct?

A. *Yes, sir.*

Q. *At least in their minds, correct?*

A. *Yes, sir.*

Q. *And that was intolerable, correct?*

A. *Yes, sir.*

Q. *That kind of threatening behavior which could com-*
promise the activities of these people, that's punish-
able by death, is it not?

A. *Yes, sir. . . . It violates the code of silence.*

Q. *How important is this code of silence to the organized*
crime types you were talking about?

A. *If it's not adhered to it could result in the La Cosa*
Nostra individuals being incarcerated. The testimony
can be used against them for previous murders, illegal
acts. It's very threatening to them.

Having established a possible "why" and "who" regarding Neil Napolitano's death, Kaplan moved on. He pressed the lawman on whether Mob business would have been discussed at the table at the Villa Perrone in front of Roz Vargas.

"At dinner, no," McMahon said.

And Kaplan asked Detective McMahon about his work

in criminal intelligence. "As I understand it, in 1995 you were in your current position, correct?"

"Yes, sir."

"And in that capacity you acquire and exchange information about organized crime figures with federal authorities and the FDLE,[7] correct?"

"Yes, sir."

"And then you forward the information to particular squads that might be working a case involving the subject of the intelligence?"

"If the intelligence is germane to their specific case and I get it, I generally would contact detectives I know."

"Well, in June of 1995, do you recollect forwarding any intelligence information to Sergeant Gentile's squad, and anyone on it, including Detective Vargas?"

"It could have been during that time. . . . It could have been prior to and including June or July and subsequent to."

"And it was regarding what or whom?"

"Just some activities that sources knew of Mr. Napolitano's whereabouts and what activity he may have been involved in."

That line of questioning opened the door for Michael Von Zamft, on redirect, to ask the lawman about his source. "Mr. Kaplan just asked you about information that you were giving to the Strategic Information Bureau and from your sources. Was one of those sources that gave you information about Neil Napolitano the same source that told you about the dinner at Villa Perrone where Roslyn Vargas, Neil Napolitano, Tony Pep, and Freddie Massaro were?"

"Yes, sir," McMahon replied.

"Was it a reliable source, in your opinion?"

"Yes, sir, it was."

---

7   Florida Department of Law Enforcement, the state's statewide investigative agency.

"Let me get to the point here. You mentioned that having an undercover officer at a dinner like that would be useful, even if [there was no discussion of] actual criminal activity in front of that person?

"Yes, sir."

"Is that so they could detail who was there and their relationships?"

"Yes, sir. . . . Also, sometimes when you're preparing affidavits, whether they're for court authorized state intercepts or Title IIIs[8] under the federal system, it could help with conspiracies."

"And the normal way that such an undercover person would give that information would be what, a report?"

"Yes, either a report or they'd be equipped with a mini recorder, a tape, a bug that would be monitored by someone on the outside."

"So if Roslyn Vargas goes to dinner at Villa Perrone with Neil Napolitano on her own, not working undercover and not writing a report, that wouldn't be job-related, would it, based upon your experience?

"Not under those circumstances, no, sir."

The lawman's response was a jaw-dropper, a stunning answer. Jurors who had opted for pads and pens made notes.

"No further questions," the prosecutor announced. When Kaplan said that he, too, had no further questions, Detective McMahon stepped down from the witness stand. The State called Rocco Napolitano.

———————

It was high courtroom drama when Rocco Napolitano, shackled and wearing an orange prison jumpsuit, took the witness stand at 2:30. He had been behind bars since

———————

8   Title III of the Omnibus Crime Control and Safe Streets Act of 1968 requires federal lawmen to obtain court permission to install wiretaps.

surrendering to police on December 22, 1995. No one
knew Neil better than Rocco, and no one had better insight
into his brother's relationship with the organized crime
detective than he had. In January 1998, Rocco confided to
a cell mate that Neil had originally planned to blackmail
Roz. The cell mate reported what Rocco told him to police.
According to a police affidavit,

> *Rocco Napolitano told the informant that his brother,
> Neil Napolitano, had entered into a relationship
> with the female detective that was investigating Neil.
> Neil Napolitano had concealed a video camera in
> the ceiling of his apartment and had surreptitiously
> filmed himself and the female detective engaged in
> sexual activity. Neil Napolitano's plan was to black-
> mail the detective into providing Neil with confiden-
> tial police information upon the threat of revealing
> the relationship to the detective's superior officers.
> Rocco Napolitano told the informant that it had not
> been necessary to actually use this plan because the
> detective fell in love with Neil Napolitano.*

If true, it would explain the wires and the mini tape
recorder that the FBI found in the ceiling of Neil's apartment when it was searched on October 3, 1995. But Rocco
wasn't in court to testify about electronic surveillance
equipment. Instead he was there to bear witness to his
brother's relationship with Roz Vargas.

"Keeping your voice up loud and clear so that everybody
can hear you, tell the jury your name, please," Michael Von
Zamft commanded.

A. *Rocco Napolitano.*
Q. *And where are you presently living?*
A. *Presently I am being housed at the Federal Detention
   Center.*

Q. Are you presently facing any criminal charges?

A. Yes, I am. A first-degree murder charge.

Q. Have we made any agreement with you to have you testify here today?

A. No.

Q. Are you hoping to get some benefit by this?

A. Yes. I expect after my testimony is given it will help clear any doubt as to what happened in the fall of 1995.

Q. Do you expect either Ms. Cagle or I or Detective Gross to do anything on your behalf in your first-degree murder prosecution?

A. Yes, I do. I expect the charges to be reduced.

Q. And has Ms. Cagle or Detective Gross or I promised you that would happen?

A. No.

Q. Is that a hope and an expectation, or is that something someone has promised you?

A. No one has promised me anything.

Q. Has any deal been reached for you to testify to this jury?

A. No.

With that out of the way, Rocco testified that he was Neil's younger brother and his partner in crime. Neil, he said, sold drugs, stole, committed credit card fraud, and engaged in loan-sharking and racketeering. Von Zamft continued his questioning.

Q. Have you ever met someone by the name of Roz Vargas?

A. Yes, I have.

Q. Do you see her here in court?

A. Yes, I do.

Q. Where is she?

A. *She's sitting at that table wearing a blue blazer and a blue shirt.*

Q. *And when was the first time you ever saw Roz Vargas?*

A. *The first time I saw Roz was inside my brother's apartment.*

Q. *And where was she inside your brother's apartment?*

A. *She was lying in my brother's bed, underneath the covers.*

It was in September 1995, "the eleventh or twelfth," Rocco said, but he wasn't certain about the exact date. He saw her again the next day, in the lobby of his brother's apartment building. "She came up to me, exchanged a few words."

Q. *The person you spoke to in your brother's lobby, did you recognize her as being the same person you saw in your brother's bed?*

A. *Yes.*

Q. *The person you spoke to in your brother's lobby, had you ever spoken to that person before?*

A. *Yes, I had.*

Q. *When?*

A. *Sometime in September.*

Q. *In person or by phone?*

A. *By telephone.*

Q. *Tell us about that conversation.*

A. *Either I received a call or I called my brother while I was in New York. I spoke to my brother, and my brother was on his way to Orlando, to Disney World, and after speaking to my brother he handed the phone to Roz Vargas.*

Q. *Now, you say he handed the phone to Roz Vargas. . . . You didn't see him do that?*

After conceding that he had not, Rocco said that a woman's voice came through the phone. He recalled what she said, that "she cared for my brother and that she was madly in love with him" and "they were on their way to Disney World."

Rocco testified that what he heard made him uncomfortable. It prompted him to say, "Roz, would you please put my brother back on the phone."

"When you said that, did the person on the phone say my name is not Roz?" Von Zamft asked.

"No."

Rocco testified that he saw Roz Vargas again, on September 13, 1995, when Neil and Roz drove with him to attorney Angelo Ali's office.

Von Zamft: "Let's talk about the conversation when your brother picked you up. You're in the car. What's the first thing he starts telling you in the car with Roz present?"

Joel Kaplan was immediately on his feet. "Objection! Hearsay!" the defense lawyer shouted.

"Overruled," Judge Dresnick declared. The jurist commanded the lawyers to "come sidebar."

A lengthy conference out of earshot of the jury ensued. As the lawyers argued, the jurors fidgeted. In the end, the judge affirmed his ruling and allowed Von Zamft to continue his line of questioning.

"You're in the car with Neil and Roz. Neil starts to talk. What does he start telling you about what had just occurred?"

"He had just come from Frank Abbandando's club, Party Girls, and he just had a conversation with Junior. By Junior, I mean Frank Abbandando, and he had told Frank Abbandando that there was no need to feel uncomfortable about Roslyn Vargas, that she knew everything about the drug deal that they were involved in some months prior . . ."

Judge Dresnick interrupted him in midsentence. He addressed the jurors: "Let me make it clear that I am allowing this testimony in not for the truth of assertions made in the testimony, i.e., that she knew, but for the fact that this conversation occurred, and you can decide whether or not it's true, whether this conversation is true or not."

Rocco resumed his testimony: "There was no need to be upset, that she knew everything. At that time Frank Abbandando looked at my brother and says, 'I don't know what you're talking about' and walked away."

"Now Rocco, as your brother's telling you this, what was his attitude and demeanor when he's talking about getting out and Roz knowing all about him?"

"It was so blasé. It was if it was a joke, and Roslyn was turned to the side in the front seat sideways, so she could see me as well as talk to my brother, and was joking as well."

"Did you hear her say anything about, No, I don't know anything; No, I'm not involved; No, I don't want to be here? Anything like that during that part of the conversation?"

"No."

The conversation turned to Neil and Roz's Orlando sojourn. Roz, Rocco testified, never said that she did not want to go there. He never heard her complain about having gone. And she never said anything that led Rocco to believe that she had not enjoyed herself.

"Let's talk about what happened when you arrived at Angelo Ali's law office. What happened?"

"Roslyn Vargas and my brother sat on the couch. . . . They were very affectionate. They were lying on the couch, kissing. Angelo just thought she was one of my brother's girlfriends."

"You say they were kissing. Was it one-sided? Was your brother doing all the hugging and kissing?"

"No, no, no, it was mutual. They acted as if they were newlyweds on a honeymoon. They were bubbly, giggly, very affectionate."

The hugging and kissing went on for ten minutes, Rocco said, after which Roz and Neil left the lawyer's office while he remained there. Rocco met up with them later at the Seybold Building, where he saw Neil and Roz holding hands.

From there they drove to Velma Byrne's apartment in North Miami. His brother dropped him there and drove away with Roz. Choking back tears, Rocco recalled Neil's last words to him: "'I'll see you later." He explained: "Being that I had just come down from New York, we'd go to dinner together that evening, or I'd just meet him later on, and that's the last time I saw my brother, Wednesday the thirteenth, 1995, the last time I saw him."

Rocco testified that in the following days, he searched for his brother and he phoned Roz.

"Did you speak to her?" Von Zamft asked. Rocco said he did, "but she was a completely different person. She didn't want to speak to me. At first, she hung up the phone." On one occasion, Rocco recalled, Roz told him to speak to her attorney.

When Roz wouldn't answer his calls or return his pages, Rocco dialed her pager number and put in his brother's code, 007. He explained: "I had already suspected foul play, and I had a very strong feeling that something had happened to my brother, so being that Roslyn was the last person seen with my brother, I had suspected her, and so I thought this was a great opportunity to find out if Roslyn really didn't know where my brother was."

"Did you page her?"

"Yes, I did."

"Did you get a call back?"

"Immediately."

━━━━━━

The Everglades may have been burning, but sparks would fly across Judge Dresnick's third floor courtroom during Joel Kaplan's cross-examination of Rocco Napolitano.

The defense attorney questioned him about his feelings about Roz. Rocco admitted that he disliked her, and that he believed that his brother's relationship with the organized crime detective brought about his death. The defense attorney elicited testimony about Neil's personality, his affinity for crime, and Rocco's role in his brother's drug-trafficking ring. Neil, Rocco said, supplied him with illegal steroids, which he sold in New York City. And Rocco admitted that his brother was a braggart and a liar.

Q. *As far back as the early nineties your brother was involved in criminal activity, correct?*

A. *Yes.*

Q. *He was not someone who kept his business to himself, right?*

A. *He kept his criminal business to himself.*

Q. *He had a way of showing off, right?*

A. *My brother was a very flashy individual . . . in the way he dressed, very flashy jewelry, [and he] flashed money around a lot.*

Q. *Making himself appear something that he might not be, right?*

A. *Basically, some criminals are very quiet about their behavior, and they . . . conduct themselves in a way not to bring attention to them. My brother didn't do that. He attracted attention.*

Q. *And he also exaggerated his activities, right?*

A. *Sure.*

Q. *Would he ever lie?*

A. *Sure, my brother has lied before.*

Q. *Did he lie about things he had done?*

A. *It's possible, yes.*

Q. *Generally speaking, your testimony is that your brother lied?*

A. *Sure.*

*Q. And is it also fair to say that your brother tended to
     exaggerate and embellish things and events, correct?*
A. Sure.

Kaplan questioned Rocco's motive for testifying.

Q. You're here voluntarily, right?
A. That's correct.
*Q. Has anybody associated with the State, be it a pros-
     ecutor or a police officer, promised you anything for
     your testimony here today?*
A. No. I am receiving nothing.
*Q. Has anybody connected with any government, state
     or federal, offered you enrollment in the Witness Pro-
     tection Program for your testimony in this case or any
     other case?*
A. No.
*Q. You testified on direct that you hope to get a benefit
     for your testimony.*
A. Yes.
Q. How do you hope to get this benefit?
*A. By my testifying against Roslyn Vargas, I have an
     opportunity to shed light on everything that happened
     during that time, and that will help clarify what hap-
     pened in my situation.*
*Q. You're charged with killing Frank Abbandando Jr.,
     correct?*
A. Yes.
*Q. Am I correct in understanding that your hope is that
     in exchange for your testimony against Roz Vargas,
     you're hoping that the first-degree murder charge
     against you shall be reduced or will be reduced?*
A. No, no, nothing was promised to me.
Q. But your hope is that it will be reduced, right?
A. Yes.

Before concluding his cross-examination, Kaplan asked Rocco about Neil's hopes. "Did your brother aspire to be a member of La Cosa Nostra?"

"My brother was interested in making money."

"Did he aspire to associate with people like Nicky and Joseph Corozzo?"

"He didn't aspire, he did."

Minutes later detectives led Rocco from the courtroom. Judge Dresnick declared a recess.

"If there's no deal in place, he must be desperate," Joel Kaplan told the *Herald* reporter covering the trial. Kaplan was referring to Rocco's admission that he hoped prosecutors would reduce his first-degree murder charge. Neil's younger brother, the defense attorney opined, "was putting on an act to please prosecutors so they will reduce his first-degree murder charge."

When court reconvened, prosecutors called Miami Beach detective Tommy Moran. Questioned by Mary Cagle, the veteran lawman testified that he began investigating Neil Napolitano in 1993, when narcotics detectives informed him that they suspected that Neil was dealing drugs in Miami Beach. The following year, Moran said, the FBI contacted him about the Napolitano brothers and Joe Stracci.

"They told us that they were moving up in the ranks and had become associates of some pretty significant organized crime figures from the Gambino family, Anthony Trentacosta, Fred Massaro, and Frank Abbandando Jr.," he said.

He recalled meeting with Detective Roz Vargas prior to her going undercover to brief her "on who all the players were and what we suspected they were involved in." The lawman testified that he was present when Roz Vargas gave her sworn statement on February 22, 1996. The prosecutor handed him State's Exhibit 1-D.

"Do you recognize that?" she asked.

"Yes, that's Roslyn Vargas's sworn statement."

"Is there a date on the front of that statement?"

"Yes, February 22, 1996."

"Why was the truthful testimony of Detective Vargas so important to the people who were there?"

"The investigation revealed that at least in the last couple of weeks of Neil Napolitano's life, Detective Vargas had been in close company with him . . . and these were critical weeks that we felt might have caused him to get killed."

During cross-examination Moran testified that he believed Neil Napolitano's bringing Roz Vargas to the dinner at the Villa Perrone "was the motive for his murder."

Prosecutors would call eleven more witnesses to bolster their contention that Roz's meetings with Neil Napolitano were not work-related and that she was with him voluntarily.

Reynaldo Gispert testified that in the summer of 1995, he learned that Neil and Carmen Sanchez had broken up and that there was a new woman in Neil's life. Two weeks before the Miami bad boy went missing, Gispert had a telephone conversation during which Neil put a woman on the line who identified herself as Roz or Roslyn.

MDPD Sergeant Barbara Gentile testified that she supervised the organized crime squad that Roslyn Vargas joined on October 31, 1994. Her squad had already targeted Napolitano for investigation. Sergeant Gentile described Detective Vargas as "a very good detective," "an experienced investigator," who "came to my squad with high credentials," "somebody I could rely on, depend on."

"Did she turn her police reports in on time?" Mary Cagle asked.

"Yes."

"During the time period that Roslyn Vargas was assigned and she was writing reports, did you ever have a problem with the completeness of those reports?"

"No. Roz, up until the last report that was written, which

was June 1 of 1995, every report, every detail was documented. She'd keep notes, and then she would put everything into a detailed report."

Under further questioning, Sergeant Gentile testified that Neil's reputed connections to Gambino gangsters Junior Abbandando and Fred Massaro led her to believe that he could provide investigators with a window into their activities, but months of surveillance yielded very little, so Detective Vargas, the lead detective, volunteered to go undercover. After just two meetings, Gentile said, their confidential informant Joe Stracci revealed to Neil that Roz was a cop. As a result, the squad's investigation of Neil Napolitano was suspended, but the Miami bad boy continued to contact Roz. He told her he had information about the disappearances of Alvino Reyes and John Davidson, claiming that Joe Stracci had murdered the missing men.

"He kept telling us that he had a tape recording of our confidential informant admitting to these murders that we really believed Neil had committed," the sergeant said.

On two occasions in late May 1995, Neil appeared at the SIB office for an interview, but he provided "absolutely no information." Instead, Gentile said, "He was just talking in circles and not giving us any information worthy of anything." On June 1, Sergeant Gentile instructed Detective Vargas to tell Napolitano "that if he's got any information to give the police, he can call between 9:00 and 5:00." Sometime later, after learning that Neil had been paging Roz "at all hours of the day and night," she ordered the organized crime detective to have contact with Napolitano during regular business hours only. "That," Sergeant Gentile declared, "was a direct order to her."

Q. Did she ever document in a police report again after June 1, 1995, her activities, any activities, regarding Neil Napolitano?
A. No.

Q. *If Roslyn Vargas had had any contact whatsoever
with Neil Napolitano that was work related after June
1, 1995, would she have been required to tell you
about that?*

A. *She would have been required to tell me about it. She
would have been required to document it. She would
have written a report, and it would have been documented in her work sheets also.*

Q. *Subsequent to June 1, 1995, are you aware of any
telephone contact that Roslyn Vargas had with Neil
Napolitano outside normal business hours?*

A. *No, I am not aware of any phone calls, and if there
were any phone calls that were work related, she
would have had to notify me and document it in a
police report, like she has previously documented
every phone call, every beep, in reports prior to
June 1.*

Q. *So during the time period of June 1 up until the time
she's relieved of duty, you are not aware of any after-
hours telephone contact that she was having with Neil
Napolitano?*

A. *That's correct. I was unaware of her contact
with him.*

About the evening of September 13, 1995, when Sergeant Gentile went to Detective Vargas's home to relieve
her of duty, Cagle asked, "Did she ever indicate to you that
Neil Napolitano had held her against her will?"

A. *No, she never said anything like that. The only thing
she said was she was really sorry she let us down.*

Q. *Would it have made a difference to you if she had?*

A. *Of course it would have made a tremendous difference if she had told us that, and we would have finally
had the case we all wanted against Neil. We would
have had a kidnapping case of a police officer, would*

*have gone out hunting him down and put him in jail
if she had told us at that time that something like that
occurred.*

In the days after she relieved Roz Vargas of duty, Gentile said she stopped by the Vargas home "just to say hello and see how she was doing."

Q. Did she say anything to you about the case?
*A. It was hard to talk, since we couldn't talk about [the
case] at all, so we would just talk about family or
different things. She walked me out to my car when I
was leaving one day and she says to me, "You know,
somebody could be like two different people." Another
thing, one day, when we were outside and I just made
a comment. She was wearing a T-shirt and brand new,
I think they were either Nikes or Reeboks, real expensive looking sneakers, and I said, "This is really nice.
Your shirt and sneakers match." And she says, "Yeah,
I got that up in Orlando."*

After a recess for lunch, Joel Kaplan began his cross-examination of Barbara Gentile. He elicited testimony that, despite thousands of hours of investigation, her squad had not brought any criminal charges against Neil Napolitano.

*Q. Is it fair to say that by [May 31, 1995] the cat was out
of the bag? Napolitano knew he had been investigated
by police officers who posed in an undercover role?*
A. That's correct.
*Q. And you had decided that this investigation was going
nowhere, correct?*
A. That's correct.
*Q. As of May 31, 1995, how long had this investigation
been running?*
A. About a year.

Q. And how many hours did you and your squad members devote to that investigation over that year? Would thousands be fair to say?

A. Possibly. A lot of time was spent on it.

Q. How about a lot of money? Was a lot of money spent?

A. Yes.

Q. And you came up with nothing, right?

A. We came up with intelligence information.

Q. Well, nothing prosecutable, right?

A. That's correct.

Gentile testified that she and others in law enforcement believed that Neil Napolitano was a very dangerous individual. She explained: "We believed he was responsible for two murders. I would consider that dangerous. He was involved in steroid deals and possibly burglaries, home invasions. That's the basic information we had on him."

And she acknowledged that the MDPD required its police officers to have their pagers turned on at all times and to return all pages even while off duty; that she knew that Detective Vargas had contact with Neil Napolitano at a gas station on Biscayne Boulevard after June 1, 1995; and that she recalled another contact Roz told her about. She also conceded that not every work-related activity was written up.

Q. Everything one of your officers did was documented, correct?

A. When it was work related, yes, it was documented.

Q. Every phone call that officers made was documented?

A. If it was related to work, yes.

Q. Every phone call?

A. If it was substantially important. I mean, not every phone call to every officer. If they gain nothing, it wouldn't be documented.

Later, in a series of rapid-fire questions and answers, Joel Kaplan asked Sergeant Gentile about the night she relieved Roz Vargas of duty

Q. Did you question her?
A. No, I didn't question her.
Q. Did you ask her what happened?
A. No, I didn't.
Q. Did you ask her why it happened?
A. I figured this was a domestic between her and her husband.
Q. Did you ask her why she was with [Neil Napolitano]?
A. She told me she was in a relationship with him.
Q. Did you ask her if it was a voluntary relationship or an involuntary relationship?
A. No, I didn't ask.
Q. But in terms of the question of whether or not it was voluntary, involuntary, if she was happy, depressed, you didn't ask those questions, right?
A. She would have told me if something was criminally done, or she would have done something about it. My God, she's a police officer!

On redirect, Mary Cagle elicited testimony from Sergeant Gentile that Roz Vargas would have known when Neil was calling because "she was aware of certain [phone] numbers he'd use, and she was also aware that he used the code 007." Then the prosecutor asked, "If the defendant Roslyn Vargas had a telephone conversation with another police officer or any kind of conversation with another police officer just in general, while they were working the case, is that something that you would document?"

A. Not unless it was significant to an investigation. If it was just a general phone call, no, it wouldn't be documented.

Q. *What about telephone calls from sources, or like in this case, an individual who had been a target in the investigation?*

A. *Telephone calls or meetings with a confidential informant and a target of an investigation are much more serious, and are required to be documented.*

Q. *If it was work related, it had to be documented?*

A. *If it was work related, it would be documented. It would have to be.*

———————

The final witness of the day was Margie Johnson, the court reporter who recorded and transcribed Roz Vargas's 128-page sworn statement of February 22, 1996. She testified to the authenticity of the transcript. Afterward, Judge Dresnick declared a recess for the long Memorial Day weekend. The trial would resume, he said, on Tuesday, June 1.

16

"THAT KID ARIEL, HE'S NO GOOD. HE'S GOT TO GO."

GAMBINO CRIME FAMILY ASSOCIATE FRED MASSARO

The Memorial Day weekend provided no respite for prosecutors or defense attorneys. Both sides worked feverishly through the weekend, taking advantage of the breather to prepare for the trial's finale. Prosecutors planned to call ten more witnesses, while the defense prepared a motion for a directed judgment of acquittal and weighed the pros and cons of putting Roz Vargas on the witness stand. Moreover, both prosecution and defense prepared their closing arguments.

There was no holiday respite for the FBI's organized crime squad in Miami either. The agents were closing in on the Beachside Mario's crew. Ariel Hernandez's telephone conversation with Fred Massaro on March 20—the one heard by the BSO deputy Roble—linked Fred Massaro to the murder of Jeanette Smith. FBI agents Terry Feisthammel and Howe Grover interviewed Hernandez. On April 8, while waiting in a monitored interview room for the G-men to show up, Hernandez began massaging his groin while lawmen in another room watched on closed circuit TV.

"You're not going to believe what this guy just did," an astounded BSO lieutenant told the G-men when they arrived.

"What?" they asked.

"He jerked off, and he wiped his hands on a trash can."

Lawmen sent the trash can to a lab for DNA analysis. No one was surprised when the report came back: it was a match for the semen the medical examiner took from Jeanette Smith's mouth.

One week earlier, on April Fool's Day, the FBI intercepted a midmorning phone call Hernandez made from the jail to Fred Massaro. Hernandez vowed to shield the Gambino gangster from murder charges. He told Massaro that he fabricated the story of paying Smith for rough sex and promised to "take the whole rap" for Smith's murder so that Massaro would not be implicated.

At least that's what he told the Gambino gangster. According to Hernandez's lawyer, Jeffrey D. Weinkle, the ex-marine named names and gave lawmen information about the crew members' criminal activities. His statements to police, the criminal defense attorney declared, were "full and complete," and his client "answered virtually all questions and detailed his own involvement."

Hernandez's change of heart came after he learned that Massaro had taken out a contract on him. The plot was hatched in the back room of Beachside Mario's on Saturday, March 27. The plotters were Fred Massaro and his designated hit men, Carlos Garcia and Francisco "Frankie Goldtooth" Valdes. According to an FBI informant, Massaro told Garcia: "That kid Ariel, he's no good. He's got to go." Their plan was to lure the ex-marine to a local bar and inject him with a fatal overdose of cocaine. According to lawmen, Massaro, an insulin-dependent diabetic, supplied

Garcia and Valdes with syringes. Luckily for Hernandez, the police got to him before Garcia did. Later that month, on April 15, a grand jury in Broward County indicted the ex-marine for first-degree murder and sexual battery.

COUNT I
MURDER IN THE FIRST DEGREE

ARIEL HERNANDEZ on or about the 20th day of March in the year of Our Lord 1999, in the counties of Broward and Dade, State of Florida, did then and there unlawfully and feloniously and from a premeditated design to affect the death of human being JEANETTE SMITH and/or while the said ARIEL HERNANDEZ was engaged in the perpetration of or in the attempt to perpetrate a sexual battery did kill and murder the said JEANETTE SMITH by strangulation against the form of the statute in such case pursuant to Section 782.04 Florida Statute, and,

COUNT II
SEXUAL BATTERY

ARIEL HERNANDEZ on or about the 20th day of March in the year of our lord Lord 1999, in the counties of Broward and Dade, State of Florida, did commit a sexual battery upon JEANETTE SMITH, a person 12 years of age or older without her consent by causing a blunt object to penetrate . . . the anus of JEANETTE SMITH, and in the process thereof ARIEL HERNAN-DEZ used actual physical force which caused injury to JEANETTE SMITH, against the form of the statute in such case pursuant to Section 794.011(3) Florida Statutes, made and provided to the evil example of all others in the like case offending and against the peace and dignity of the State of Florida, a true bill.

At his arraignment Hernandez was ordered held without bail.

———————

The investigation into the murder of Jeanette Smith became part of the FBI's Operation Gemstone. Through wiretaps, surveillance, and a half-dozen informants, agents tied Ariel Hernandez to Fred Massaro, and Massaro to Gambino crime family members Anthony "Tony Pep" Trentacosta and Anthony "Fat Andy" Ruggiano, who was paroled from prison in 1997 after serving ten years behind bars. Fat Andy died two years later, on March 19, 1999, two days before Jeanette Smith's body was found in a canal in the Everglades.

At the time of her death, lawmen were closing in on the Beachside Mario's crew. Through wiretaps, surveillance, and a half-dozen Mob informants, they linked Fred Massaro to the Gambino crime family and to soldier Anthony "Tony Pep" Trentacosta and capo Anthony "Fat Andy" Ruggiano, who was paroled from prison in 1997 after serving ten years behind bars. He died two years later, on March 19, 1999, two days before Jeanette Smith's body was found in an Everglades canal.

Gemstone produced evidence that Massaro and his crew were involved in racketeering, murder, loan-sharking, extortion, drug trafficking, and mail and wire fraud in connection with the Trump Financial Group, the bogus currency-trading firm that Massaro took over when Gambino associate John Porcaro disappeared the year before.

An informant told agents that he ran into Fred Massaro after Porcaro had been missing for a week. At that time, Massaro told him that Porcaro was "gone." When the informant—a low-level mobster with hopes of getting a lighter sentence after pleading guilty to credit card fraud—suggested that Porcaro was probably on a fishing trip in the Bahamas, the Gambino gangster shook his head and said, "No, he is gone, gone."

Lawmen also developed evidence that Fred Massaro was the mastermind behind a phony check-cashing scheme. Calling Ariel Hernandez Massaro's "do boy," another informant revealed that the ex-marine "handles the fraudulent identification and [counterfeit] checks for Massaro."

The phony check scheme couldn't have happened without the help of an accomplice at the Checking Exchange, a check-cashing store in the Broward County city of Wilton Manors. The accomplice supplied Hernandez with a steady stream of photocopies of legitimate corporate payroll checks. Using a computer and a laser printer installed in the back room of Beachside Mario's, Hernandez churned out phony IDs and duplicated the legitimate checks, which he and others took to national retailers, where they were used to buy merchandise. They would return the items for cash refunds or sell them for 50 percent of the retail prices. Lawmen also learned that one of the participants in the counterfeit-check scheme was Jeanette Smith.

Employees of at least one store identified her as having been with Ariel Hernandez on at least one occasion when he passed a bogus check. Investigators believed there were more and that Smith had gone to stores on her own, purchased items with the counterfeits, and returned the goods for cash refunds.

Lawmen do not know why she became involved, whether she was coerced, or whether she was an eager participant in the scam. Smith didn't need the money. She was earning as much as two thousand dollars in cash per night from appreciative men who generously stuffed her G-string with twenties and fifties. But Smith, lawmen learned, had expensive tastes, and she shared her earnings with her parents, sisters, and longtime boyfriend.

Although investigators did not know why she became involved with Fred Massaro's crew, a Mob informant provided the FBI with the likely motive for her murder: "An order came down from up north to take care of some girl, a dancer, who was an informant for the FBI." Lawmen believed that the order was sanctioned by Fat Andy Ruggiano before he died. Smith had been recruited by Hernandez, who had been brought into the crew by Fred Massaro, which meant that it was their joint responsibility "to take care of" her.

More than a year would pass before Operation Gemstone would wrap up with the indictment and arrest of Fred Massaro and others. Meanwhile, as the 1999 Memorial Day weekend ended, the Roslyn Vargas perjury trial was about to get underway again.

17

STATE OF FLORIDA
V. ROSLYN VARGAS

DAY THREE

It had been one of the soggiest Memorial Day weekends on record, but the heavy rains didn't reach the Rotenberger Wildlife Management Area in southwest Palm Beach County, where ten thousand acres of dried-out marshland still smoldered. A change in wind direction, however, carried the smoke away from South Florida, and the choking haze that had enveloped Miami for the first two days of the Vargas perjury trial had given way to clear skies by the time court reconvened on the morning of June 1. At 9:15 Judge Dresnick banged his gavel, and prosecutors called one of their own to the witness stand—Assistant State Attorney Flora Seff.

The prosecutor testified that she had been assigned to prosecute Rocco Napolitano for the first-degree murder of Frank Abbandando Jr. and that she had also been involved in the investigation into Neil Napolitano's death. In response to Mary Cagle's questions, Seff testified that in January 1996, she and Cagle met with detectives from the North Miami Police Department, the Miami Beach Police

Department, and the MDPD to share information about the Abbandando slaying and the death of Neil Napolitano. It was at that meeting, Seff said, that homicide investigators identified Roz Vargas as someone to be questioned because of her relationship with Neil Napolitano.

Seff also was present for Roz's sworn statement of February 22, 1996. In response to a question from Cagle, Seff opined that Detective Vargas "had crossed the line over what she should have been doing as a law enforcement officer in this case." Joel Kaplan objected, but he was overruled. Under cross-examination, Seff acknowledged that investigators believed that Neil was killed because he brought Roz Vargas—Detective Roz Vargas—to the Mob dinner at Villa Perrone.

MDPD Sergeant Cynthia Truncale followed Flora Seff to the witness stand. Questioned by Mary Cagle, Truncale testified that she conducted an internal affairs investigation into Roz Vargas's relationship with Neil Napolitano. She said that on September 19, 1995, she took an administrative statement from the relieved-of-duty detective. Roz never mentioned that she was with Neil involuntarily in September of 1995. Nor did she mention it during a second administrative statement on November 3, 1996, when, Truncale said, she gave Detective Vargas "an opportunity to tell why she had been with [Neil Napolitano] in Orlando."

Joel Kaplan objected to Truncale's testimony about what Roz Vargas said and did not say in her statements to the internal affairs investigator, arguing that it was inadmissible under the Garrity Rule, the landmark 1967 U.S. Supreme Court ruling that protects police officers and other public employees who are compelled to give statements under threat of discharge or discipline. Under Garrity, compelled statements may not be used in a criminal proceeding against the officers or employees who gave them.

The rule stemmed from *Garrity v. State of New Jersey*, a case that involved the questioning of police officers during an investigation into a ticket-fixing scheme. Before they were questioned, investigators warned the officers that anything they said could be used against them in court and that they had the right to remain silent if an answer would incriminate them. They were also warned that they would be fired if they refused to respond to even one question. Rather than lose their jobs, the cops answered the questions. Their answers were used against them when they were subsequently prosecuted for conspiracy to obstruct the administration of traffic laws. Found guilty, the officers appealed.

They argued that their answers were inadmissible because they were compelled to give them under threat of losing their jobs. In an 8 to 1 ruling, the U.S. Supreme Court agreed. The high court declared that the choice given the officers—protecting their livelihood or paying the penalty of incriminating themselves—violated their constitutional rights against self-incrimination. Reversing the convictions, the justices held that "the protection of the individual under the Fourteenth Amendment against coerced statements prohibits use in subsequent criminal proceedings of statements obtained under threat of removal from office and that it extends to all, whether the police or other members of our body politic."

Despite Kaplan's spirited argument, Judge Dresnick overruled his objection. Not only did he allow Sergeant Truncale's testimony, he also allowed prosecutors to introduce Roz Vargas's actual statements to Internal Affairs into evidence.

Next, prosecutors called Bermuda Triangle bouncer Joe Defuria. Questioned by Michael Von Zamft, Defuria recalled that Roz and Neil came to the Fort Lauderdale nightspot "approximately a couple of months" before Neil disappeared. They were "hand in hand," Defuria recalled, and Neil introduced her by saying "this is Roz." Once seated at a table, Defuria said, they ordered drinks—Neil asked for orange juice—and [they] took a few turns on the dance floor. Said Defuria: They "were pretty cozy together, rubbing hands, pecking, kissing." Although that was the only time he laid eyes on Roz, Defuria testified that Neil told him that he was in love with the MDPD detective a month or so before they appeared at the club. Under cross-examination, Defuria admitted that his testimony was motivated by his belief that Rocco Napolitano wanted him "to do the right thing for his brother to show she is a liar."

Rosemary Miranda, the fiancée of Neil's deceased friend Richie Ferrara, testified that Neil brought Roz Vargas to her home for dinner in June or July or August of 1995. Questioned by Mary Cagle, Miranda testified that she met the organized detective once or twice, and that Neil introduced her as his "girlfriend." Under cross-examination Miranda said she believed that Carmen was the name of the woman who visited her home with Neil, and she revealed that she heard the name Roslyn Vargas for the first time from prosecutors. Under redirect, Miranda testified that she had been suffering memory lapses ever since her fiancé was killed in a work-related accident in 1998.

The next witness was Monica Byrne-Henry, the Napolitano brothers' sister. The U.S. Navy veteran testified about phone calls she received in August and September 1995. Questioned by Michael Von Zamft, Byrne-Henry claimed that in late August, a woman Neil identified as Roz cried, professed her love for Neil, and told her "that she was going to leave her husband, that she was going to leave her children, and she was going to leave her job" to be with him. Henry claimed she spoke to Roz again after Labor Day. The conversation consisted of nothing more than "Hi, hello, how are you?" She spoke to Roz Vargas again in September. Roz, she said, boasted that she and Neil had not been out of their hotel room "in a couple of days."

Joann Walter, the Party Girls bartender Neil confided in, testified that Neil told her he was having a relationship

with Roz Vargas. Questioned by Mary Cagle, Walter
recalled that in the summer of 1995 she came face-to-face
with Vargas outside Party Girls, after which Neil sought
her opinion of Roz. Neil, Walter said, told her that Roz was
an undercover detective who was investigating him. Walter
claimed she saw Roz and Neil again at Nick's at Night,
where they danced and behaved romantically.

Next, jurors heard from Glen Corbitt. Questioned by
Michael Von Zamft, Corbitt testified that in September
1995 he was employed as a sales clerk at the Sergio Tacchini
retail clothing store in Orlando, Florida. Corbitt identified
Roz Vargas as the woman who entered the store with Neil
Napolitano on or about September 10, 1995. He recalled
being interviewed by Miami Beach police in October 1995,
telling detectives that Neil and Roz were very affectionate
with each other the entire time they were in the store, "hugging and kissing" and "playing grab ass." Corbitt recalled
that Neil purchased four hundred and fifty dollars worth of
clothing, including a pair of jeans that bore a Sergio Tacchini label and a small Italian flag. Roz, he said, did not
appear to be having any problem with Napolitano.

The State's final witness was MDPD Detective Joe
Gross. The veteran lawman testified that he spent hundreds
of hours poring over telephone records for pagers and tele-
phones used by Roz Vargas and Neil Napolitano. Prosecutors had prepared large charts that listed the calls between
them and to others, matching calls to events Roz testified
about in her sworn statement of February 22, 1996, as well
as to events others testified about. Prosecutors hoped that
Gross's testimony would bring everything together for the
jurors, and they would conclude that in her sworn statement of February 22, 1996, Roslyn Vargas committed
perjury when she said she was not with Neil voluntarily
from September 5, 1995, to September 11, 1995; that she
committed perjury when she declared she did not go with
Neil Napolitano voluntarily on September 12, 1995; and

that she committed perjury when she denied that she had a personal relationship with Neil Napolitano before Labor Day of 1995. Joe Gross put it this way: "Off the payroll. No reports. All by yourself in contravention of standard operating procedures. Dancing and making out with a man after midnight while lying to your husband about it—is [that] a work-related relationship?"

Among the calls Gross linked to Roz Vargas's personal cell phone were calls to Neil's sister Monica in San Diego on August 30. The first was dialed at 7: 12 P.M. The second, at 7:15 P.M., lasted for nineteen minutes. Was this the call Monica testified about? The one during which the woman Neil introduced as Roz proclaimed her love for Neil and vowed that she was ready to leave her job and her family to be with him? There was no way to know, but prosecutors believed jurors would conclude that it was.

Gross's chart showed another call at 7:33 P.M from Roz's cell phone to Monica's phone in San Diego. A fourth call to Monica on September 5 was dialed from a cell phone Neil was using while he and Roz were in Orlando. The implication was that this was the call Monica was talking about when she testified that Roz bragged that she and Neil had not been out of their hotel room "in a couple of days."

The phone records also showed that in the wee hours of September 3, long before Roz Vargas walked away from her family in a huff, she tried to contact Neil. She began paging him at 3:17 A.M. She dialed him again at 3:18 A.M., and again at 1:18 P.M., 2:54 P.M. and 3:13 P.M. Neil attempted to call her on her cell phone at 10:21 P.M. Unable to contact her, Neil dialed Roz's home phone number at 10:51 P.M. Six minutes later he reached her on her cell phone. That phone call lasted for eighteen minutes. At 11:19, Roz paged Neil from a pay phone inside the Denny's that she had walked to in the aftermath of her spat with her husband. Three hours later, Neil appeared. They ate breakfast at a nearby Waffle House, then checked into the

Holiday Inn. Under cross-examination, Detective Gross testified that he read Roz Vargas's February 22, 1996, statement many times. He conceded that she never uttered the word *voluntarily.*

At the conclusion of Detective Gross's testimony, the State rested. Prosecutors hoped that the pattern of phone calls and the testimony from witnesses who had seen Roz and Neil behaving romantically would convince jurors that Detective Roslyn Vargas had become romantically involved with Neil Napolitano, that her contacts with him after June 1 were not work-related but personal, and that she was with him of her own free will from September 3 to September 12, 1995.

Joel Kaplan moved for a judgment of acquittal because, he argued, the prosecutors failed to prove the four essential elements of the crime—perjury in an official proceeding—for which his client was tried. Those elements, he argued, are (1) making a false statement that (2) one does not believe to be true, (3) under oath in an official proceeding (4) in regard to any material matter.

"Motion denied," Judge Dresnick declared.

"The defense rests," Kaplan announced.

It was a stunning legal maneuver. It meant that no one would take the stand to defend or vouch for Roslyn Vargas. Nor would they hear the former organized crime detective speak for herself. Prosecutors were stunned. Michael Von Zamft, an unrelenting cross-examiner, had spent most of the Memorial Day weekend preparing to question her. But the defense decision did not surprise some of the lawmen who were involved in the case. They didn't think Roz would make a very good witness in her own behalf. "Too cocky," said one. "Arrogant," declared another. Closing arguments were set for Thursday morning June 3, after which Judge Dresnick would instruct the jury on the law. If all went according to his plans, jurors would begin deliberating that afternoon.

The perjury trial of Roslyn Vargas began dramatically, with Assistant State Attorney Michael Von Zamft displaying two poster-sized photographs of Roz Vargas enjoying herself at Disney World with Neil Napolitano. The photos were meant to discredit Vargas's sworn statement that she spent September 5, 1995, through September 11, 1995, with Napolitano against her will because she feared him. Prosecutors called nine witnesses who had seen them together or spoken to them in the weeks before, during, and after September 11. They testified to the romantic nature of their relationship, while Barbara Gentile testified that Roz told her, "I'm involved in a relationship with a much younger man. He's not a cop. I might have to resign." The parade of witnesses was meant to discredit Roz's statement that she was with Neil for work-related purposes in August 1995, as were the phone records.

Prosecutors may have had the facts on their side, but defense attorney Joel Kaplan believed he had the law on his, so in his closing argument the defense attorney pounded on the law. He pulled no punches.

"Monica-gate two," he thundered indignantly, referring to allegations that President Bill Clinton lied about his sexual relationship with White House intern Monica Lewinsky. Kaplan said prosecutors charged Roz Vargas because they and the MDPD "didn't like her conduct," so they decided to punish her "with the words she used."

As to count 1, which covered her assertion that she met Neil Napolitano in August of 1995 "for work-related purposes," Kaplan said that the State failed to prove it was false. He conceded that Roz Vargas did not document her work-related encounters with Neil during that period of time, but "the evidence did not show that all her encounters in August of 1995 with Napolitano were not work-related."

For that reason her statement in count 1 was not shown to be false beyond a reasonable doubt.

As to counts 2 and 3, Kaplan declared that Roz never said the things prosecutors accused her of saying in her sworn statement of February 22, 1996. To be guilty of perjury, he argued, Florida law required unambiguous questions and clear, factual answers, not opinions or statements of belief. He reminded jurors that Detective Gross acknowledged that Roz never uttered the word *voluntarily*; nevertheless, count 2 alleged that Vargas's statement "that she was not with Neil Napolitano voluntarily from September 5, 1995, to September 11, 1995" was perjurious. Also untrue was the allegation in count 3—her statement "that she did not go with Neil Napolitano voluntarily on September 12, 1995."

Moreover, under Florida law, perjury required materiality, which means for a statement to be perjurious, it has to be material to the stated purpose of the proceeding, which was to find out who killed Neil Napolitano. Said Kaplan: "Long before February 22, 1996, lawmen knew why and who likely killed Napolitano. [Detective Joseph] MacMahon, [Detective Tommy] Moran, and [Assistant State Attorney Flora] Seff all acknowledged as much. So whether Roz Vargas's meetings in August of 1995 with Neil were work-related or personal, and whether she was with him voluntarily from September 5 through 11, 1995, or on September 12, 1995, did not affect the focus of the inquiry about which she was questioned—the homicide of Neil Napolitano." The defense attorney implored jurors to return a verdict of not guilty.

In her closing statement, Assistant State Attorney Mary Cagle characterized Roz Vargas as desperate to save her career. She was "in a jam," the prosecutor explained, faced with an Internal Affairs investigation and "worried about her job." Said Cagle: "The truth would have been so simple: I fell in love with Neil Napolitano." But that wasn't

what Roslyn Vargas did. Instead, "she concocted a lie."
Cagle pointed to photographs taken at Disney World. She
reviewed phone records, and she reminded jurors about the
testimony they heard from witnesses that Roz was with
Neil Napolitano by choice; that she deliberately hid the
relationship from her MDPD supervisors and her family;
and that she had many chances to leave Neil. The prosecutor prepared a chronology. It was printed on poster-sized
flash cards, which Cagle mounted on an easel and read to
the jurors one by one.

FROM JUNE 2, 1995, THROUGH JULY 27, 1995

- The defendant's county issued cellular telephone called
  numbers linked to Neil Napolitano nine (9) times, and
  no more than once on any specific day.

BETWEEN JULY 28, 1995, AND AUGUST 30, 1995

- There are more than seventy calls from the defendant's county issued cellular telephone to numbers
  linked to Neil Napolitano. There are as many as six
  (6) in one day.

DURING AUGUST OF 1995

The defendant's county issued cellular telephone records
show more than twenty (20) calls with numbers linked
to Neil Napolitano during her "*off duty*" hours.

The defendant *did not*:

- document these calls on her worksheets.
- document these calls in police reports.
- inform her supervisors of the calls.

When asked during her sworn statement why she did not document these meetings and contacts, the defendant stated that the reason was that *everybody was afraid of Neil Napolitano.* When asked the same questions by Internal Affairs Investigators, the defendant stated there was *no reason* she did not document these meetings and contacts.

ON WEDNESDAY, AUGUST 30, 1995

- Monica Byrne, Neil Napolitano's sister, spoke to Neil Napolitano, and then to Roslyn Vargas by telephone.
- Roslyn was very upset and told Monica Byrne she was in love with Neil Napolitano and that she was going to leave her family for him.
- When interviewed by investigators, Monica Byrne knew details of the defendant's personal life she could only have gotten from Neil Napolitano.

ON FRIDAY, SEPTEMBER 1, 1995

- The defendant went to Orlando with her family.

ON SUNDAY, SEPTEMBER 3, 1995

- During the evening, the defendant had an argument with her husband and walked away.
- At midnight she contacted Neil Napolitano (who was in Miami) from a telephone in an Orlando Denny's.
- Neil Napolitano drove to Orlando and picked her up.
- They spent the night in a hotel together.

ON MONDAY, SEPTEMBER 4, 1995

- The defendant called her supervisor, Sergeant Barbara Gentile, and asked for Tuesday off.

ON TUESDAY, SEPTEMBER 5, 1995

- The defendant and Neil Napolitano went to a mall where she purchased some clothes.
- After returning to the Holiday Inn with Neil Napolitano, the defendant picked up her purse during a conversation with him about leaving. Neil Napolitano grabbed the purse from her and took her gun out of it. There was a brief struggle after which Neil Napolitano returned the gun to her unloaded.
- In the evening, the defendant called her supervisor, Sergeant Barbara Gentile, and asked for the rest of the week off.

ON WEDNESDAY, SEPTEMBER 6, 1995

The defendant and Neil Napolitano:

- return to Broward County in his car.
- go to Neil Napolitano's apartment.
- go to Neil Napolitano's mother's apartment where Roslyn Vargas is introduced to Neil's mother.

They call Ray Gispert. Mr. Gispert says Neil and Roslyn sound happy. They

- go to dinner at the Villa Perrone Restaurant in Hallandale with a group of people including Dr. and Mrs. Jeffery Kamlet.
- go to the Bermuda Triangle nightclub in Broward County.
- go to Bajas nightclub in Coconut Grove.
- go to Denny's in Hallandale.

- return to Neil Napolitano's apartment and spend the night.
- According to some of their dinner companions, the defendant and Neil Napolitano were very affectionate to one another during the dinner at the Villa Perrone Restaurant.
- Joanne Walters sees Neil Napolitano and the defendant in a nightclub together. They are very affectionate to one another.

ON THURSDAY, SEPTEMBER 7, 1995

The defendant and Neil Napolitano

- awake in the afternoon.
- eat at the Roadhouse Grill in Broward County. En route, Neil got out of the car to get the address from a phone book.
- go to see a romantic movie, *A Walk in the Clouds.*
- returned to Neil's apartment and spent the night there.

ON FRIDAY, SEPTEMBER 8, 1995

The defendant and Neil Napolitano:

- eat at Burger King.
- go to Dadeland Mall, where the defendant bought a black pants suit.
- return to Neil's apartment to pick up clothes.
- eat at Pollo Tropical.
- drive to Orlando.

- check into the Holiday Inn. The defendant sat in the lobby while Neil Napolitano checked in under the alias of "Cam Jackson."
- go to a nightclub at Paradise Island.
- go to a nightclub named Mannequins.
- eat at the Waffle House.
- spend the night at the hotel.

ON SATURDAY, SEPTEMBER 9, 1995

The defendant and Neil Napolitano:

- go to Disney world.
- eat at McDonalds.
- return to the hotel and change clothes.
- go to Old Town, where they drove the go-carts.
- go to the nightclub Mannequins.
- return to the Holiday Inn and spend the night together and have sex together for the first time.

ON SUNDAY, SEPTEMBER 10, 1995

The defendant and Neil Napolitano:

- go to the outlet mall, where Neil Napolitano purchased clothing at the Sergio Tacchini store.
- call her supervisor, Sergeant Barbara Gentile, from the hotel and discussed possibly resigning.
- spend the night together at the hotel.

The salesperson at the Sergio Tacchini store, Glenn Corbitt, states that the defendant and Neil Napolitano were affectionate to one another while they were in the store. He also states that the defendant was left alone in the store while Neil Napolitano was in the changing room trying on clothes.

IN THE EVENING OF SUNDAY, SEPTEMBER 10, 1995

The defendant called her supervisor, Sergeant Barbara Gentile, and stated she was alone.

She also stated that she was in a relationship with a younger man and may be resigning from the police department.

ON MONDAY, SEPTEMBER 11, 1995

The defendant and Neil Napolitano:

- checked out of the Holiday Inn at about 2:00 A.M.
- drove back to Neil Napolitano's apartment in Broward County.
- dined at an Italian restaurant.
- the defendant talked with a fellow detective about a police case.
- drove to the Miami Subs Restaurant at US 1 and Sheridan Street, where the defendant had arranged for her son to pick her up.

ON TUESDAY, SEPTEMBER 12, 1995

- Neil Napolitano paged the defendant, and she called him back.
- Neil Napolitano told the defendant she had some things at his apartment and suggested she come pick them up.

- The defendant went to Neil's Napolitano's apartment. The defendant was not afraid of him and was not worried he would not let her go.
- The defendant and Neil Napolitano spent the day in the apartment talking. The defendant missed a doctor's appointment to do this.
- The defendant left without taking her belongings.
- The defendant went to Blockbuster Video, where her son Julio worked.
- On his own, Neil Napolitano went to the Blockbuster Video.
- The defendant called her son Nick at home and had him come to the Blockbuster Video store.
- While waiting for Julio Jr. to get off of work, they played some video games.
- They all went to Applebee's Restaurant and had dinner together.
- The defendant and Neil Napolitano left Applebee's together.
- The defendant spent the night with Neil Napolitano at his apartment.

ON WEDNESDAY, SEPTEMBER 13, 1995

The defendant and Neil Napolitano:

- go to her doctor's office.
- go to Hialeah, where they picked up Neil's brother, Rocco Napolitano.
- go to attorney Angelo Ali's office in downtown Miami. After a brief meeting with the attorney, they departed, leaving Rocco behind. While at the office,

Neil introduced the defendant to the secretary as his *girlfriend*.

- Rocco Napolitano gave Neil Napolitano a Rolex watch. Neil gave the watch to the defendant to hold for him.

ON SATURDAY, SEPTEMBER 16, 1995

- The defendant admits in her sworn statement that she beeped Neil Napolitano in the morning.
- The defendant's cellular telephone billing records show calls to Neil Napolitano's beeper at

  - *8:18 A.M.*
  - *8:19 A.M.*
  - *8:31 A.M.*
  - *10:50 A.M.*
  - *2:13 P.M.*
  - *2:17 P.M.*

ON SUNDAY, SEPTEMBER 17, 1995

- The defendant's cellular telephone called Neil Napolitano's beeper at 8:43 A.M. and 10:37 A.M.
- The defendant went to Neil Napolitano's mother's apartment and gave her the Rolex watch that she was holding for Neil.
- Neil's mother states that the defendant was very upset because she had not been able to locate the defendant Neil Napolitano and he had not returned her beeps.

ON TUESDAY, SEPTEMBER 19, 1995

The defendant gives a sworn statement to Miami-Dade Police Internal Affairs investigators and makes *no*

mention or report of having been held against her will
by Neil Napolitano.

ON FRIDAY, NOVEMBER 3, 1995

The defendant gives another sworn statement to Miami-
Dade Police Internal Affairs investigators and again
makes *no mention or report* of having been held against
her will by Neil Napolitano.

To conclude her closing statement, Mary Cagle read
aloud the sign above the judge's bench: "We who labor
here seek only truth." Roslyn Vargas, Cagle said, failed to
follow that maxim. The prosecutor implored the jury to
find Roslyn Vargas guilty on all three counts.

Jurors didn't spend a lot of time deliberating. Armed
with copies of Vargas's sworn statement, they needed just
two hours before announcing that they had reached a verdict, which the clerk read: guilty on all three counts. Roz
Vargas didn't flinch. Judge Dresnick set sentencing for
August 20. The former organized crime detective showed
no emotion and declined comment as she bolted from the
courthouse accompanied by her husband, children, and
parents. Judge Dresnick set sentencing for September 3 at
9:00 A.M.

The next day's *Miami Herald* reported that Roz Vargas
had turned down a pretrial deal that would have allowed
her to "walk away from police work in lieu of facing criminal charges." Instead, the paper said, Roz Vargas "gam-
bled on her chances with a jury." She lost that gamble, but
there would be other surprising turns in the bizarre case
of the undercover detective who went under the covers
with the man she was investigating.

18

A SWEEPING INDICTMENT

Fred Massaro followed the Vargas perjury trial in the *Miami Herald*. What he thought about the verdict is not known. What is known is that even though his "do boy" Ariel Hernandez was behind bars, the Gambino gangster tried to conduct business as usual, but he was under mounting pressure. Without Hernandez, the counterfeit check scheme that netted five hundred thousand dollars had come to an abrupt end. It put a big dent in Massaro's wallet, and he worried about being able to pay his Gambino boss. Massaro was also worried that Ariel Hernandez would flip and reveal his role in the Jeanette Smith murder.

The situation wasn't good for the fifty-nine-year-old Gambino gangster's health. It was rapidly deteriorating. His diabetes was barely under control, and he was having difficulty breathing. His arteries were clogging up, and doctors urged him to undergo a heart bypass operation. Adding to his woes were the death of his Mob friend and former boss Anthony "Fat Andy" Ruggiano and his breakup with his longtime girlfriend, Carol.

While Fred Massaro grappled with his troubles, Vargas's defense attorney Joel Kaplan spent most of the summer preparing for his client's sentencing. In the weeks after the verdict, he filed a motion for acquittal and, if denied, a motion for a new trial. If Judge Dresnick denied the motion for a new trial, he would appeal Vargas's conviction to the Third District Court of Appeal.

The Operation Gemstone lawmen were busy that summer, too. The investigation that had been initiated by FBI Special Agent Terry Feisthammel was making slow but steady headway. As the lead case agent, Feisthammel, the father of two small children, put in long hours. A tireless and intrepid crime fighter, he was on call around the clock. He oversaw the wiretaps, the surveillance and the undercover activities, the investigation into the crew members' financial transactions, as well as the execution of warrants and analysis of documents. No one worked harder than the forty-two-year-old Feisthammel, who was named Law Enforcement Officer of the Year in 1995 by the U.S. attorney's office in Miami. "The most dedicated and conscientious agent that I've had the opportunity of working with in over ten years," declared Special Agent Mike Welch, his supervisor.

"Terry was the sparkplug behind the case, a no-nonsense agent and seasoned investigator who loved what he did—building cases against organized crime figures and putting them behind bars," said Lawrence LaVecchio, an assistant United States Attorney in Miami who worked closely with the G-man.

Feisthammel and his team routinely shadowed Fred Massaro, while a surveillance camera installed high atop a pole directly across from Beachside Mario's recorded who went in and out of the pizza joint. And they cultivated informants and cooperating witnesses, among them Louis Maione, the Gambino insider whose information helped put Nicholas Corozzo behind bars. As they accumulated evidence, investigators considered charges ranging from racketeering conspiracy to murder against Massaro, his crew, and Gambino capo Anthony "Tony Pep" Trentacosta.

The Gambino crime family didn't formally anoint Tony Pep boss of the crew until after Fat Andy died, but lawmen believed that Trentacosta had been his "de facto boss," and that Tony Pep "directed the affairs of the enterprise from Fat Andy's incarceration [from 1984 through 1997] and throughout the time period from Fat Andy's release from prison, up to and including his death," said agent Howe Grover, Feisthammel's partner. Trentacosta, investigators learned, received his share of the crew's profits in tribute from Massaro and passed part of his share to Peter Gotti, John Gotti's brother. Lawmen were making steady progress when the investigation suffered a setback on July 10, 1999, when Terry Feisthammel was hospitalized. He died three days later. Doctors said the lawman had suffered a stroke.

A strapping six-foot-two, Feisthammel kept himself in top shape, jogging and working out in the FBI's gym daily. The sudden loss stunned the agents in the bureau's Miami office. It derailed the investigation and forced lawmen to regroup. Howe Grover became the lead case agent, while the bureau added more agents to the case. Nevertheless, it would take months to bring everyone up to speed and get the investigation back on track.

On September 3, Roslyn Vargas and Joel Kaplan were back in Judge Dresnick's third floor courtroom. After denying Kaplan's motions for acquittal or a new trial, the jurist sentenced the former organized crime detective to sixty days in jail. The judge agreed to stay the sentence pending the appeal, which Kaplan filed on September 22.

Two weeks later, on Thursday, October 7, FBI agents and other lawmen, friends, and colleagues gathered at the U.S. attorney's office to honor Terry Feisthammel. His family was out in force, too: his children, Griselle, five, and

Justin, two, and his wife of six years, Grisel; Feisthammel's mother, Charlotte; brothers and sisters and their spouses; and other relatives. The FBI presented Grisel Feisthammel with a plaque bearing her husband's badge and a framed letter from U.S. Attorney General Janet Reno praising Feisthammel for his dedication, intelligence, and innovation. There would be tributes from others who praised the crime fighting G-man, too. "We consider Terry to be the standard by which other law enforcement agents should be judged," wrote Assistant U.S. Attorney J. Brian McCormick, the chief of the organized crime section in Miami.

Another year would pass before prosecutors brought Operation Gemstone, the case Terry Feisthammel had worked so hard on, to a federal grand jury in Miami. When it was finally presented on September 19, 2000, the jurors handed down a sweeping twenty-five-count RICO indictment. It was immediately sealed pending the release of Fred Massaro from a hospital, where he was recuperating from a heart bypass operation. The indictment identified its target as "the South Florida crew of the Gambino Crime Family." The crew, it said, was "supervised and controlled by the hierarchy of the Gambino Crime Family located in New York." It "generated profits from criminal activities for the benefit of the Gambino Crime Family." Nine men were named in the indictment.

- Count 1 charged Trentacosta, Massaro, Hernandez, Francis "Little Frankie" Ruggiero, Julius Bruce Chiusano, Adam "Sonny" Silverman, Carlos Garcia, Charles Patrick Monico, and Anthony Raymond Banks with racketeering conspiracy. Maximum penalty: life.
- Counts 2–16 charged Massaro, Hernandez, and Chiusano with bank fraud. Maximum penalty: thirty years.
- Count 17 charged Massaro and Hernandez with conspiracy to murder Jeanette Smith. Maximum penalty: ten years.

- Count 18 charged Massaro and Hernandez with the murder of Jeanette Smith. Maximum penalty: death.

- Count 19 charged Silverman, Monico, and Banks with being accessories after the fact to the murder of Jeanette Smith. Maximum penalty: fifteen years.

- Count 20 charged Massaro and Garcia with conspiracy to murder Ariel Hernandez. Maximum penalty: fifteen years.

- Count 21 charged Massaro, Hernandez, and Chiusano with making, uttering, and possessing counterfeit checks. Maximum penalty: ten years.

- Count 22 charged Massaro and Ruggiero with loan-sharking. Maximum penalty: twenty years.

- Count 23 charged Massaro, Ruggiero, Silverman, and Garcia with extortion in connection with loan-sharking. Maximum penalty: twenty years.

- Count 24 charged Massaro with theft of goods "stolen and unlawfully taken from ABC Distributing Inc., while they were moving as part of an interstate shipping property." Maximum penalty: ten years.

- Count 25 charged Massaro, a previously convicted felon, with illegal possession of firearms: a Raven MP-25 semiautomatic pistol, a Colt MK Trooper III .357 Magnum, a Marlin 60 semiautomatic rifle, a Smith and Wesson revolver, and a silencer. Maximum penalty: ten years.

On September 26, with arrest warrants in hand, FBI agents rounded up Massaro and the rest of the crew before sunrise. By nine o'clock that morning, all had been booked, fingerprinted, and photographed. Lawmen arrested Tony Pep at his home in Georgia. Ariel Hernandez was already behind bars. The others were rounded up in the Miami area: Chiusano, who allegedly supplied Hernandez with copies of legitimate corporate payroll checks; Silverman, who allegedly collected loan-sharking debts and helped dispose of Jeanette Smith's body; Ruggiero, who lawmen alleged was a loan shark working under Massaro; Monico and Banks, who allegedly passed counterfeit checks to South Florida retailers; and Garcia, who allegedly worked as an enforcer for Massaro's loan-sharking operation and plotted with him to murder Ariel Hernandez.

Declaring Massaro, who was charged in twenty-four of the twenty-five counts of the indictment, a danger to the community, U.S. Magistrate Judge Barry Garber ordered him held without bail until trial even though he was still on the mend from heart bypass surgery. At a hearing in Atlanta, a federal magistrate at first agreed to release Trentacosta on bond, but the Gambino capo remained in custody after prosecutors in Florida successfully appealed the ruling to the presiding judge in Miami, arguing that Trentacosta "is a lifelong criminal" who had numerous convictions, including assault with a gun, and had sworn "lifelong allegiance to one of the most powerful criminal organizations in the United States." Eventually, however, Trentacosta was able to bond out of jail, but he was placed under house arrest and FBI agents were permitted to tap his phones and monitor his conversations.

On December 7, less than three months after he was indicted in the Gemstone case, Fred Massaro found himself facing even more legal trouble—he was indicted again, this time for extortion. Federal prosecutors charged that in May 2000, the Gambino gangster and an accomplice demanded four hundred thousand dollars from the owner of an Internet pornography website. They threatened to harm the man and his family if he did not come up with the money. Moreover, prosecutors also pondered whether to seek the death penalty for him and Hernandez. Two days after his client was arrested, Massaro's lawyer announced that he was preparing for the worst. "We have to take that threat as a real possibility," declared Fort Lauderdale criminal defense attorney Fred Haddad. He characterized the grand jury's action as little more than a "typical fed indictment."

But lawmen didn't see it that way. Prosecutors Lawrence LaVecchio and Jeffrey Sloman believed they had overwhelming evidence to prove that Fred Massaro orchestrated the murder of Jeanette Smith because he believed she had become an FBI informant. Massaro even ordered and supervised the cleanup of the motel room where Smith died, as well as the dumping of the slain stripper's body in the Everglades. When that was done, he ordered the execution of Ariel Hernandez.

The death penalty remained on the table for Jeanette Smith's alleged killers until May 17, 2001. That's when federal prosecutors announced they had decided not to seek it. The decision, which was approved by U.S. Attorney General John Ashcroft in Washington, meant that Fred Massaro faced life behind bars if convicted on the federal murder charge. Although Hernandez would be spared execution by U.S. authorities, the ex-marine still faced a state trial for the murder of Jeanette Smith, and Florida prosecutors had not taken the death penalty off the table. As for Tony Pep, lawmen didn't think they had sufficient evidence to link him to the murder, and he was charged with one count of racketeering.

Meanwhile, the case had been assigned to U.S. District Judge Paul C. Huck. The Kentucky-born jurist studied law at the University of Florida, graduated in 1965, and practiced in Miami until President Bill Clinton appointed him to the bench in May 2000. In the months leading up to the trial, six of the nine defendants decided to plead guilty to various charges.

- Julius Bruce Chiusano, fifty-two, described in the indictment as a member of the crew who "controlled and operated Check Cashing Unlimited II . . . Wilton Manors, Broward County, Florida, which business was utilized by the crew of the Gambino crime family in obtaining financial information of the customers of Check Cashing Unlimited II and transmitting that information to Frederick J. Massaro and Ariel Hernandez for their use in creating and negotiating counterfeit checks for the benefit of the Gambino crime family," pled guilty to racketeering conspiracy.

- Francis Ruggiero, sixty-two, described in the indictment as a member of the crew who "assisted Frederick J. Massaro by making and financing extortionate extensions of credit and by conspiring to collect extensions of credit by extortionate means," pled guilty to racketeering conspiracy.

- Charles Patrick Monico, forty-three, described in the indictment as a member of the crew "who primarily assisted defendants Frederick J. Massaro and Ariel Hernandez by negotiating counterfeit checks at businesses located within the Southern District of Florida," pled guilty to racketeering conspiracy.

- Anthony Raymond Banks, twenty-seven, described in the indictment as a member of the crew "who primarily assisted defendants Frederick J. Massaro and Ariel Hernandez by negotiating counterfeit checks at businesses located within the Southern District of Florida," pled guilty to racketeering conspiracy.

- Adam Silverman, twenty-five, described in the indictment as a member of the crew "who primarily assisted defendant Frederick J. Massaro in the use of extortionate means to collect and attempt to collect extensions of credit," pled guilty to being an accessory after the fact to the murder of Jeannette Smith.

- Carlos Garcia, thirty-three, described in the indictment as a member of the crew "who primarily assisted defendant Frederick J. Massaro in collecting extensions of credit by extortionate means," pled guilty to conspiracy to engage in violent crimes in aid of racketeering.

Sentencing was withheld. All agreed to cooperate with the government and, if requested, to testify at the trial of Trentacosta, Massaro, and Hernandez. More than a year would pass before that case would come to trial. Meanwhile, on October 3, 2001, the Third District Court of Appeal handed down its decision in the Roslyn Vargas perjury case. Writing the unanimous opinion for the three-judge panel, Judge John Fletcher said:

> *Vargas's answers in all three counts were immaterial to the underlying investigation into Napolitano's murder, and merely reflect her state of mind at the time these events occurred. In the context of the record, Vargas's statements can only be characterized as statements of opinion or belief, and not of fact. For this reason, the statements forming the basis for all three counts of perjury are outside the reach of that crime under Florida statutory and common law. We therefore reverse Vargas's convictions and sentences for perjury.*

The state decided not to appeal the decision, which meant that Roslyn Vargas was eligible to return to duty with the MDPD. But the case of the undercover detective who went under the covers with Neil Napolitano would take yet another unexpected turn.

19

UNITED STATES OF AMERICA V. ANTHONY TRENTACOSTA, FREDERICK J. MASSARO, AND ARIEL HERNANDEZ

On Tuesday November 20, 2001, after more than a year of legal squabbling and maneuvering, the Gemstone trial got under way at the Federal Courthouse in Miami amid heightened security in the aftermath of 9/11. America was on terror alert, still in a state of shock from the terrorist attacks in New York and Washington, D.C., and the crash of hijacked Flight 93 in Pennsylvania. Closer to home, Floridians were reeling from a deadly anthrax attack in October on the Boca Raton headquarters of tabloid publisher American Media, the parent company of the *National Enquirer*, the *Globe*, the *Star*, and other supermarket weeklies. One employee died, and several others nearly died from exposure to the deadly spores.

As for the trial of Anthony Trentacosta, Frederick J. Massaro, and Ariel Hernandez, a jury of twelve plus three alternates had been impanelled the day before. The government was represented by Assistant U.S. Attorneys Lawrence LaVecchio and Jeffrey Sloman. They were joined at the prosecution table by the lead case agent, FBI Special

Agent Howe Grover. Had Terry Feisthammel not died, he would have been there instead.

U.S. Marshalls escorted Massaro and Hernandez into the courtroom. Unshackled and wearing jackets and ties instead of jailhouse jumpsuits, they took seats at a long table with their lawyers: Jeffrey Weinkle for Hernandez, and Fred Haddad for Massaro. Still free on bond but under house arrest, Trentacosta strolled into court with his attorney, Stephen Rosen. Tony Pep appeared confident and cocky, smiling at onlookers and looking more like a nightclub singer about to take the stage than a gangster on trial. A sketch artist was in the courtroom, too, illustrating the unfolding legal drama for the *Miami Herald*.

Judge Huck began by addressing the jurors. He told them that they could take notes if they wished but urged them to pay careful attention to the testimony. The judge cautioned jurors to "not give your notes any precedence over your independent recollection of the evidence or the lack of evidence, and neither should you be unduly influenced by the notes of the other jurors." Next, the jurist read the indictment. When that was done, he called on prosecutors for their opening argument.

Assistant U.S. Attorney Lawrence LaVecchio rose to address the jury. The forty-six-year-old Rhode Island native studied law at the University of Miami. He graduated in 1980 and began his career as an assistant state attorney in Dade County in 1980 under Janet Reno, eventually becoming chief of the Organized Crime/Public Corruption Prosecution Unit. He joined the U.S. attorney's office in 1995.

LaVecchio reviewed the grand jury's indictment, telling jurors that the state would prove all of the counts. He declared that "human life became absolutely irrelevant" to the defendants. He promised the men and women of the jury that they would get a crash course on organized crime, and then proceeded to review the history and structure of the Mafia, describing it as a pyramid sending money up. He told jurors about loan-sharking, extortion, and the "vigorish"—the illegal interest rates the mobsters charged. "On the street," the federal prosecutor said, "interest is known as vigorish or vig or juice." He explained that South Florida is open territory for the Mafia, meaning that any of the five New York crime families can have crews operating there. And he told them about the Gambinos, its notorious former boss John Gotti, and the crime family's penchant for violence.

The prosecutor reviewed counts 2 through 16, the bank fraud counts. Said LaVecchio: "Massaro and Hernandez bought big and small ticket items and would either sell them on the street for fifty cents on the dollar or return them for cash refunds." About the murder of Jeanette Smith, the prosecutor said, "The evidence will show that another person who participated in the scheme was a young woman by the name of Jeanette Smith. . . . The evidence will show that she assisted Ariel Hernandez by returning merchandise to at least two different places, like Home Depot and Office Depot."

Said LaVecchio: "The evidence will show that on March 20, 1999, Jeanette Smith was brutally beaten and strangled by Ariel Hernandez. The body was bound and stuffed in a stereo box, and it was dumped in the Everglades by Ariel Hernandez, Frederick J. Massaro, and a third individual. It was part of a plan, part of a scheme to eliminate Jeanette Smith as a potential problem. The evidence is going to show that Frederick J. Massaro and Ariel Hernandez committed the murder of this young girl because they feared that she was cooperating with law enforcement agents."

This was not true, LaVecchio declared. He promised the jurors that they would hear wiretaps in which Ariel Hernandez vowed to take the rap for Massaro.

About count 20, which charged Fred Massaro with plotting the murder of Hernandez, LaVecchio told jurors that they would hear testimony that Massaro put out a contract on the ex-marine, ordering two hit men to inject him with a lethal dose of cocaine because he feared Hernandez would implicate him in Smith's murder. When it was time for the defense lawyers to deliver their opening statements, Trentacosta's attorney went first, stunning the courtroom with an unprecedented admission—his client, he said, was indeed a "made member" of La Cosa Nostra.

"We acknowledge the existence of the Gambino crime family" and "we acknowledge his membership in the Gambino family," declared Stephen H. Rosen. Trentacosta had signed a stipulation in which he admitted to membership in the Mob family.

It was the first time that a capo admitted his Mafia membership at his own trial, and court watchers noted that Trentacosta didn't seem uncomfortable as Rosen revealed his ties to organized crime. Instead, the Gambino gangster smiled proudly. The stunning admission made strategic sense. The government had FBI videos and still photos of Trentacosta with John Gotti and Sammy Gravano outside Gambino headquarters, the Ravenite in Little Italy. Trentacosta risked losing all credibility with the jury if he denied his Mafia membership, so Rosen conceded his client's ties but claimed that Trentacosta had long ago retired from organized crime.

The bearded defense attorney challenged the prosecution to prove the allegations in the indictment—that Trentacosta was responsible "for the day-to-day control of the [South Florida crew] of the Gambino crime family"; that he "maintained authority and control" over the crew; or that he received "a portion of the proceeds derived from criminal acts committed by and through its members."

"Let's see the proof," Rosen demanded. "Tell me the amount of money, the percentage of tribute that my client received from Freddie Massaro or anyone else." Mafia members, he said, deny their membership in the

Mob, and they refuse to even admit that Italian organized crime exists, but his client had adopted a different strategy to spare the jurors from having to endure listening to two decades' worth of wiretaps or thousands of pages of printed transcripts proving that Trentacosta was indeed a member of the Gambino crime family. And he cautioned jurors not to permit "the sensationality of murder" to cloud their judgment. Smith's murder, the defense attorney said, had nothing to do with the Gambino crime family.

Massaro attorney Fred Haddad declared that there was no evidence that his client was "the point man" for the South Florida Gambino crew, describing the mobsters who hung out at Beachside Mario's as "the gang that couldn't shoot straight." As for the murder of Jeannette Smith, he asked, "If this were Gambino, why didn't they bring in a professional killer?"

And attorney Jeffrey Weinkle said that his client, Ariel Hernandez, accidentally strangled Smith, who was a willing participant in a session of rough sex in his client's motel room, adding that it was a tryst for which she was paid. "I guess you feed them before you take a hit," the defense attorney declared. Then he implored the jurors to "use your common sense—does that sound like a Mob hit to you?"

The trial was expected to last for six weeks, but it ended in little more than three. Prosecutors presented evidence that Massaro and the crew engaged in a pattern of racketeering activity under the supervision of Trentacosta, linking the Gambino capo to the Beachside Mario's crew with testimony and voice recordings demonstrating that he controlled and profited from its criminal activities.

Among the first to so testify was Gambino crime family turncoat Louis Maione. Under questioning Maione recalled a 1992 conversation he had with Trentacosta during which the Gambino capo asked him, "Don't they [other mobsters] know that he [Massaro] is with me?"

Robert Engel, identified in an another 1996 indictment as a Gambino crime family associate, took the stand and testified to a conversation he overheard in 1995 or 1996 between Trentacosta and acting Gambino boss Nicholas Corozzo during which Trentacosta, referring to Massaro, told Corozzo, "He's with me." Engel also testified about two other conversations he had with Massaro during which Massaro told him that he was with Trentacosta.

Steven Horowitz testified that in 1992 he and Fred Massaro opened Father and Son Moving of Jacksonville Inc., and that Massaro told him to pay Trentacosta's wife five hundred dollars per truck per month as a consulting fee even though there was no "credible explanation justifying these payments." Horowitz said the payments totaled $4,000 per month. The moving company, he said, also paid for Trentacosta's use of leased cars, a Miami apartment, cell phones, pagers, and food whenever the Gambino capo visited South Florida.

Prosecutors called FBI Special Agent George Gabriel. No one in the FBI knew more about the Gambino crime family than Gabriel.

———————

George Gabriel was thirty years old in 1986 when the bureau chose him as the case agent for John Gotti and the Gambino crime family. His assignment: gather evidence against the boss of the Gambinos. For six years, Gabriel and his team used long-lens cameras and high-tech video equipment to photograph the comings and goings of the Gambino boss and his soldiers and capos from a nearby observation post. Gotti required his underlings to meet with him at least once a week at the Ravenite, the social club in the Little Italy section of Manhattan where Gotti held court. From their perch two blocks away, the agents' cameras recorded the Gambino made men walking and talking with their boss, even hugging and kissing him. Among them was Anthony "Tony Pep" Trentacosta.

Along with sworn statements from informants, the images enabled Agent Gabriel to take the investigation to the next phase—court-authorized electronic surveillance of the Ravenite on grounds that the social club was where the Gambino mobsters plotted their criminal activities. Through an informant, Gabriel learned that Gotti used a tiny apartment three floors above the Ravenite for secret meetings. With court approval, the FBI planted a bug in the apartment and recorded John Gotti discussing prior murders and plotting future hits, bragging about the tribute he was receiving from the Gambino crime family's rackets, and describing himself as the family's boss.

In one recorded conversation, Gotti's own words revealed his powerful position: "Tomorrow I wanna call all our [capos] in. I'm gonna tell them: I'm the *represente* till I say different. Soon as anything happens to me, I'm off the streets, Sammy ["The Bull" Gravano] is the acting boss. . . . This is my wishes, that if I'm in the fucking can, this family is gonna be run by Sammy. I'm still the boss . . . but when I'm in the can, Sammy's in charge."

In the early evening hours of December 11, 1990, Gabriel led a team of FBI agents into the Ravenite, where they arrested the top leaders of the Gambino crime family—Gotti, Gravano, and consigliere Frankie Locascio. Neither Gotti nor Locascio went home again. As for Gravano, he turned on Gotti, agreeing to testify against his boss after prosecutors let him listen to tapes in which Gotti could be heard talking about whacking him.

———

Eleven years after he slapped handcuffs on John Gotti's wrists, read him his rights, and hauled him off to a federal lockup, George Gabriel was in Judge Huck's Miami courtroom to testify as an expert on the Gambino crime family. He was an impressive witness: six feet, four inches tall, knowledgeable, and not easily rattled by defense attorneys no matter how withering their cross-examination. Responding to the prosecutor's questions, Gabriel described the hierarchical structure of the family. He testified that Trentacosta's admission that he was a member of organized crime was without precedent—a violation of omertà that could get a made man killed. Jurors also heard Gabriel say that the Gambino family required nonmember associates like Fred Massaro to disclose their criminal activities to their capos and to share their proceeds with those above them in the family. The lawman also testified that when a nonmember associate had reason to believe that his crew had been infiltrated by an informant, it was the associate's responsibility to "eliminate" the informant.

Buttressing Steven Horowitz's testimony regarding payments to Trentacosta's wife from their moving company, Gabriel stated that "tribute payments can take the form of cash or paying the expenses on behalf of an organized crime member through the transfer of funds between businesses controlled by organized crime members."

Jurors also heard testimony from Roseann Pontorno. She worked with John Porcaro at Trump Financial. A week after Porcaro disappeared, in June 1998, Pontorno recalled, "Freddie came in and told me that he was taking over now that John's gone." Later that month, Pontorno had a falling out with Massaro over money and asked Trentacosta to intercede on her behalf. Trentacosta did, and the dispute was settled in her favor.

The government introduced dozens of hours of recorded conversations that demonstrated Trentacosta's supervision and control of Massaro's loan-sharking operation. In one, a conversation recorded on November 12, 1998, between Massaro and another Gambino family associate who wore a wire, the associate asked Massaro to arrange a loan for a nephew of John Gotti. Massaro could be heard saying that he was attempting to reach Trentacosta to get his approval for the loan. In a subsequent conversation recorded four days later, Massaro informed the associate that Trentacosta did not approve the loan.

In another conversation, recorded on April 30, 1999, Fred Massaro could be heard talking to a loan-shark victim, explaining that he had to answer to a higher Mob authority, presumably Trentacosta. Said Massaro: "Whatever I do, I record. You understand I put it on record. . . . You first have to go get permission to do what you want to do. And then when you get the permission, you can operate."

The jury also heard wiretapped conversations between the raspy-voiced Trentacosta and Massaro that corroborated prosecutors' contention that Fred Massaro worked for Trentacosta.

- Government Exhibit 544, recorded March 25, 1999: Steve Horowitz called Massaro at home to set up a conference call with Trentacosta. During the conversation, Trentacosta ordered Massaro to collect one hundred dollars from "Frankie from F-Troop," and he ordered him to send flowers or candy to a mobster's mother.

- Government Exhibit 574, recorded April 2, 1999: Trentacosta phoned Massaro, who responded to him by saying "Yes, sir" when reminded that Trentacosta expected him to drive him to the airport.

Testimony regarding the murder of Jeanette Smith was particularly gruesome. Broward County Associate Medical Examiner Dr. Lisa Flannagan testified to the brutality of the murder. She gave a detailed explanation of the twenty-two-year-old dancer's injuries, her words eliciting gasps and moans from the dead woman's family. Jurors were shown the horrific autopsy photos, which were entered into evidence. They also heard wiretapped conversations related to the murder.

- Government Exhibit 514, recorded on March 20, 1999: Ariel Hernandez could be heard telling Massaro, "I tied up the loose end and I got a package I gotta get rid of. . . . What should I do?" Jurors heard Massaro's response: "I don't know. I'll talk to you in person. Let me shower and shave and I'll be out there." The jury heard evidence that Massaro placed the call in response to a page from the ex-marine.

- Government Exhibit 517, recorded on March 20, 1999: Massaro could be heard ordering Adam Silverman to help Hernandez remove Smith's body from room 121 at the Olympia.

- Government Exhibit 529, recorded at noon on March 21, 1999: Adam Silverman told Fred Massaro that the experience of moving the young dancer's body was a "shockeroo" and that he would never reveal what he saw to anyone. In another phone call later that day, Silverman was heard telling Hernandez that Massaro wanted him to get rid of the items Hernandez took from Smith's car and that Massaro said he was going to give Hernandez a "slap" for not getting rid of that stuff.

- Government Exhibit 571, recorded April 1, 1999: Four days after Ariel Hernandez was charged with the murder of Jeanette Smith, Trentacosta called Steve Horowitz. They talked about Massaro's impending appointment with detectives from the Broward Sheriff's Office, scheduled for later that afternoon.

On the witness stand, Adam Silverman testified that he drove a borrowed SUV to the Olympia Motel and stood by watching as Ariel Hernandez carried the Sony stereo carton holding Jeanette Smith's body to the SUV and loaded it into the rear of the vehicle. Then, he said, he followed as Hernandez drove the dead woman's car to Surfside, where he abandoned it. Hernandez then climbed into the SUV, and the two men drove to Beachside Mario's, where they picked up Massaro and another man, Dominick Marchese, a Massaro acquaintance who happened to have been at the pizza joint having a slice of pizza. The four men then drove to a boat ramp at Mile Marker 31 on Alligator Alley, where Hernandez removed the stereo box and put it into the Everglades canal. They then headed back to Miami, scattering the dead stripper's belongings along the way as they drove. Prosecutors introduced cell phone records that backed up the route.

Called to testify, Marchese corroborated Silverman's testimony. Jurors heard him say that he watched Massaro and Hernandez remove the stereo box from the rear of the SUV and drop it into the canal. On the drive back to Miami, Marchese recalled, Massaro and Hernandez were in high spirits, joking and laughing about what they had just done. Marchese claimed that he had no idea what Massaro and the others were planning to do when he was invited along for the ride, and he said that he was afraid he would be next if he went to the cops.

In Government Exhibit 548, a phone conversation that began at 2:09 A.M. on March 27, 1999, Massaro could be heard telling Hernandez to "take my word that Frankie is not the problem. Put your attention on the other place, what she said in the car. That's where your problems are coming from." According to prosecutors, the "she" Massaro referred to was Jeanette Smith, the only woman involved in the counterfeit check-cashing scheme, and the gangster's words indicated his belief that Smith had alerted investigators to Hernandez's involvement in it.

The jury heard testimony about Ariel Hernandez's arrest on the morning of March 28, 1999, and his subsequent statements to investigators. Among the lawmen who took

the stand was BSO Detective Frank Ilarazza. He testified
that Hernandez admitted that he killed Smith during rough
sex, but claimed that it was an accident and the sex was
consensual. The ex-marine's signed confession was read
aloud and admitted into evidence, as was a sworn statement Fred Massaro gave to Broward sheriff's detectives
on April 1. In it, Massaro claimed that Hernandez didn't
work for him, that he never spoke to Hernandez about the
death of Jeanette Smith, and that he only knew the former marine because he frequently stopped into Beachside
Mario's for pizza.

But in the days after his arrest, Hernandez was recorded
speaking on the phone with Massaro from the county jail.
In one, Government Exhibit 559, recorded on March 29,
1999, Ariel Hernandez could be heard advising Massaro
that he was "taking everything," to which Massaro gave an
affirmative reply. Hernandez informed the Gambino gangster that he told police that Smith's death was the result
of rough sex and that he, Massaro, "did not have to worry
about anything." In another phone call on April 1, Government Exhibit 567, Hernandez could be heard telling
the Gambino gangster that he "was taking the whole rap"
and that he fabricated the story about rough sex "so that
nobody else will get incriminated."

Jurors also heard testimony from Francisco Valdes and
Carlos Garcia. They testified that Massaro hired them to
kill Hernandez to prevent the ex-marine from linking him
to the Smith murder. Valdes testified that he owed Massaro
money. As payment for the murder, Massaro promised to
forgive his debt and pay Garcia in cash. He said that Massaro, a diabetic, provided them with syringes so they could
inject Hernandez with a lethal overdose of cocaine.

Jurors also heard from Dr. Jeffrey Kamlet, the medical
doctor who was a witness at the Roslyn Vargas perjury trial
in 1999. In that trial, Dr. Kamlet testified about the dinner

Vargas attended with Neil Napolitano on September 6, 1995, at the Villa Perrone with Fred Massaro and Anthony Trentacosta. This time his testimony linked Massaro and Beachside Mario's to the phony check-cashing scheme and to stolen merchandise.

Questioned by Larry LaVecchio, the medic revealed that Massaro had been his patient from 1992 up until he was jailed on September 26, 1999, and that he had also treated the Gambino gangster's friends and associates, including Junior Abbandando, Trentacosta, Adam Silverman, and John Porcaro.

"When did you first meet Frederick Massaro?" LaVecchio asked.

> A. *Originally, I met Mr. Massaro through other friends*
> *or associates of his who came into the emergency*
> *room as patients.*
> Q. *Who specifically?*
> A. *Junior Abbandando.*

Massaro referred Trentacosta, and it wasn't long before Kamlet was socializing with the mobsters and stopping at Beachside Mario's for a slice of pizza "once or twice a week."

> Q. *Did you ever see a computer in Beachside Mario's?*
> A. *Yes, there was a computer.*
> Q. *Where was it within the pizza parlor?*
> A. *It was kind of on a table, sitting in the back room in*
> *plain view of anybody who would walk in there.*
> Q. *Did there ever come a time when you purchased a*
> *computer from Frederick Massaro?*
> A. *Yes. . . . At another time when going to the pizza par-*
> *lor to get a slice of pizza, Mr. Massaro mentioned to*
> *me he had a brand new laptop someone he knew had*

> *purchased . . . and was unable to return, but he [the purchaser] needed money, he needed some cash, and he was looking to sell it.*
>
> *Q. And did Mr. Massaro tell you how much money he wanted for it?*
> *A. Yes. I believe it was approximately $800 or so.*
> *Q. Did you ever see a receipt for the computer?*
> *A. Yes. . . . He readily showed me a receipt.*

The prosecutor showed the physician Government Exhibit 63, a copy of the original receipt, noting that the computer's original cost was $1,483.99 and that it was paid for on March 27, 1999, with a check from Fairline Intermedia.

"Can you identify this document?"

"Yes," the doctor answered. "This is a Xerox copy of the receipt for the computer."

"Is that a true and accurate copy of the receipt that you received from Mr. Massaro?

"That's correct, sir."

Next, prosecutor LaVecchio directed the physician's attention to Government Exhibit 121, a Compaq Presario laptop computer.

"Are you able to identify that item?" the prosecutor asked. Kamlet said he could and proceeded to examine it. He compared the serial number on the receipt with the one on the laptop and declared that it was the one that he purchased from Fred Massaro. Kamlet said that he last saw the computer on August 9, 2000, when Howe Grover came to his medical office and impounded it.

To corroborate testimony from Garcia and Valdes that Massaro had syringes, the federal prosecutor asked Dr. Kamlet about Fred Massaro's diabetes. The medic confirmed that the mobster was insulin dependent, that he self-injected "several times a day" using "small insulin syringes." LaVecchio thanked Dr. Kamlet for his testimony. "No further questions," he declared.

"No questions, your honor," announced Steven H. Rosen, Trentacosta's lawyer,

"I don't have any questions," said Fred Haddad, Massaro's defender.

"No questions, your honor," declared Jeffrey Weinkle, the attorney for Ariel Hernandez.

Turning to the witness, Judge Huck thanked him and excused him. As Dr. Kamlet walked from the witness stand to the exit, he nodded to the two men who had been his patients and pals. Trentacosta avoided eye contact with the physician, while Massaro smiled and nodded, too.

Under RICO, to prove count 1, racketeering conspiracy, prosecutors had to convince the jury that Trentacosta, Massaro, and Hernandez agreed to participate in a pattern of racketeering activity or in the collection of an unlawful debt. That could be done by proving an agreement, explicit or implicit, on an overall objective, or by showing that the defendants agreed personally to commit two predicate acts for the benefit of the conspiracy. When they rested their case on December 12, the prosecutors were confident they had succeeded. They were also confident that they had proved Fred Massaro and Ariel Hernandez guilty beyond a reasonable doubt of all the other counts they had been charged with. If jurors hoped they would hear from the defendants, they were disappointed. Not Trentacosta, or Massaro, or Hernandez took the stand on his own behalf.

20

BEYOND A REASONABLE DOUBT

9:00 A.M.
December 14, 2001

Three months had passed since the attacks of September 11. At the site of the World Trade Center in New York, workers sifted through the mountains of rubble that once were the Twin Towers. They were looking for human remains before loading the debris onto dump trucks. The evening newscasts the night before broadcast a videotape in which terror mastermind Osama Bin Laden gloated over the death and destruction the hijacked planes had wrought.

Meanwhile, in a federal courtroom in Virginia, a defiant Zacarias Moussaoui—who, it was alleged, would have been aboard one of the planes as a hijacker had he not been arrested by the FBI just weeks before 9/11—was in a federal courtroom in Virginia for a hearing. In Judge Huck's Miami courtroom that morning, jurors were getting ready to deliberate the guilt or innocence of Anthony Trentacosta, Frederick J. Massaro, and Ariel Hernandez, who, prosecutors alleged, conducted a reign of terror of their own as a result of their links to the Gambino crime family. As soon as all the lawyers and the defendants were in place, the judge ordered bailiffs to bring the jury into the courtroom.

It was a complicated case: three defendants, a twenty-five-count indictment, and RICO. The jurist began by instructing the jurors on the presumption of innocence: "Every defendant is presumed by the law to be innocent," he said. "The law does not require a defendant to prove innocence or to produce evidence at all, and if a defendant elects not to testify, you should not consider that in any way during your deliberations."

And he defined reasonable doubt: "Real doubt based upon reason and common sense after careful and impartial consideration of all the evidence in the case." Proof beyond a reasonable doubt, the judge said, "is proof of such a convincing character that you would be willing to rely and act upon it without hesitation in the most important of your own affairs." The prosecution, the judge said, "has the burden of proving a defendant guilty beyond a reasonable doubt, and if it fails to do so you must find that defendant not guilty."

Judge Huck told the jurors to consider only the evidence that he admitted. He explained: "The term *evidence* includes the testimony of the witnesses and the exhibits admitted in the record. Anything the lawyers say is not evidence in the case. It is your own recollection and interpretation of the evidence that controls your decision. What the lawyers say is not binding upon you."

And he explained the difference between direct and circumstantial evidence: "Direct evidence is the testimony of one who asserts actual knowledge of a fact, such as an eyewitness," while "circumstantial evidence is proof of a chain of facts and circumstances tending to prove, or disprove, any fact in dispute." The jurors need not concern themselves with whether the evidence is direct or circumstantial, the judge said, because "the law makes no distinction."

The judge noted that many of the government's witnesses were criminals. Six had even been named codefendants in the indictment but struck deals, plea bargains, with prosecutors. In their closing statements, defense attorneys went to great lengths to discredit their testimony and impugn their motives. Judge Huck told the jurors that plea bargains were permissible. "Such plea bargaining, as it's called, has been approved as lawful and proper, and is expressly provided for in the rules of this court," he said. But he cautioned the jurors to carefully consider the testimony of witnesses who plea-bargained because "a witness who hopes to gain more favorable treatment may have a reason to make a false statement because the witness wants to strike a good bargain with the government." Although a witness who testifies as part of a plea bargain may very well be telling the truth, the judge urged the jurors to "consider such testimony with more caution than the testimony of other witnesses."

After reviewing the counts of the indictment and the fine points of the law for each count, Judge Huck explained racketeering conspiracy as "a kind of partnership in criminal purposes." To find a defendant guilty of racketeering conspiracy, the evidence, Judge Huck declared, must show beyond a reasonable doubt that two or more persons "came to a mutual understanding to try to . . . engage in a pattern of racketeering activity . . . or to collect an unlawful debt."

And he defined *enterprise*: "A group of individuals associated in fact, although not a legal entity." He explained *unlawful debt*: "A debt which is unenforceable under state or federal law . . . because of the laws relating to usury."

As for racketeering activity, the judge offered concrete examples: acts or threats involving murder, extortion, loan-sharking, bank fraud, theft from interstate shipments, and obstruction of justice, when done as part of an illegal enterprise.

To find Massaro and Hernandez guilty of count 17, conspiracy to murder Jeanette Smith, and count 18, the murder of Jeanette Smith, the jurors had to first find that the evidence proved they were part of a racketeering enterprise and that the murder was for the purpose of "maintaining or increasing their position in the [racketeering] enterprise."

Before sending the jurors to the jury room to begin deliberations, Judge Huck said: "It is your duty as jurors to discuss the case with one another in an effort to reach agreement, if you can do so." Each juror, he said, must decide the case for him or herself "after full consideration of the evidence with the other members of the jury." And he urged them to not abandon their beliefs "solely because the others think differently or merely to get the case over with."

Finally, Judge Huck told the jurors that "in a very real way you are the judges, judges of the facts. Your only interest is to seek the truth from the evidence in the case." A few minutes later, five men and seven women filed out of the courtroom to deliberate the guilt or innocence of Anthony Trentacosta, Frederick J. Massaro, and Ariel Hernandez. Toward evening, jury foreman Rolando Delgado passed a note to a U.S. Marshall, who immediately brought it to Judge Huck. It said, "We have reached a verdict." The judge summoned the lawyers, and he ordered marshalls to return the defendants to court. Considering the length of the trial and the complexity of the case, the jury wasn't out long. When everyone was back in the courtroom, the verdicts were read:

Anthony Trentacosta: count 1, racketeering conspiracy, guilty.

Frederick J. Massaro: count 1, guilty; counts 2 through 16, bank fraud, guilty; count 17, conspiracy to murder Jeanette Smith, guilty; count 18, the murder of Jeannette Smith, guilty; count 20, conspiracy to murder Ariel Hernandez, guilty; count 21, passing or possessing counterfeit checks, guilty; count 22, loan-sharking, guilty; count 23, extortion, guilty; count 24, receiving or possessing stolen goods, guilty; count 25, a convicted felon in possession of firearms, not guilty.

Ariel Hernandez: guilty on all nineteen counts for which he was charged, including murder, conspiracy to murder, bank fraud, counterfeiting, and racketeering.

The defendants' reactions to the verdicts varied. At first Trentacosta seemed stunned, in a state of disbelief. He had been mostly cheerful and confident throughout the trial; now his shoulders drooped noticeably. Judge Huck ordered his bail revoked. Massaro showed no emotion, while Hernandez became unruly and had to be restrained by marshalls, who escorted him from the courtroom. Judge Huck set sentencing for the following April.

Long before then, all six members of the crew who plea-bargained had been sentenced. Judge Huck gave Adam Silverman forty-two months in prison; Julius Bruce Chiusano was given twenty-four months; Francis "Little Frankie" Ruggiero, eighteen months; Carlos Garcia was sentenced to twenty-five months; Anthony Raymond Banks got twenty-one months; and Charles Patrick Monico was sentenced to time served. All six would be on three years of probation following their release from federal custody.

On April 23, Trentacosta, Massaro, and Hernandez and their lawyers were back in court. Before their sentences were pronounced, Judge Huck permitted family members of the victim and the convicted mobsters to address the court. Krissy Smith, Jeanette's still-grieving sister, wanted the judge to impose maximum sentences, but life in prison would not be justice, she said. "The highest sentence this court can give is life. That isn't enough. My sister didn't get life. She received death."

She choked back tears when she remembered her slain younger sibling as "a daughter, a granddaughter, sister, niece, cousin, aunt, and a real friend to so many." The mobsters, she said, "destroyed not only her life but the lives of those who love her." Her family, she said, had not had a day without tears since her sister died. "Our Jeanette as been taken from us. They thought she was an FBI informant. Their mistake was deadly. They call themselves the Mafia, or the family. They have no idea what family is truly about."

Through tears, too, Massaro's daughter Erica, a lawyer, asked the jurist to consider her father's frail health: "I beg the court to assign my dad to a medical facility so that he can see his appeal through."

When it came time to pronounce sentence, Judge Huck threw the book at the three mobsters. Eight years and four months for Trentacosta, a sentence that exceeded the federal guidelines by more than a year. "When you look at his history and his involvement with organized crime," the judge explained, "it justified an upward departure."

Massaro was next. Found guilty of count 1, racketeering conspiracy, the Gambino gangster was sentenced to life; for counts 2 through 16, the bank fraud counts, thirty years each count; for count 17, conspiracy to murder Jeanette Smith, ten years; for count 18, the murder of Jeanette Smith, life; for count 20, conspiracy to murder Ariel Hernandez, ten years; for count 21, possession of counterfeit checks, ten years; for count 22, loan-sharking, 10 years. For count 23, extortion, ten years; and for count 24, possession of stolen goods, ten years. All sentences to run concurrently.

Hernandez heard his fate, too: count 1, life. Counts 2 through 16, thirty years per count. Count 17, ten years. Count 18, life. Count 21, ten years. All sentences to run concurrently.

Once again the ex-marine became unruly. He began cursing and yelling the most vile obscenities about Jeanette Smith. Marshalls restrained him and removed him from the courtroom. As Trentacosta was led away, he turned to his wife, Denise, and said, "I love you." Marshalls came between the couple when they tried to embrace.

Trentacosta and Massaro were remanded to the custody of the Federal Bureau of Prisons to serve their sentences in the federal system, while Ariel Hernandez went back to Broward County, where his state trial was pending and where the death penalty was still very much on the table.

"He's earned it," says Miami-Dade Assistant State Attorney Michael Von Zamft, who took on the case in July 2004, after the venue was changed from Broward County to Miami-Dade, where, investigators determined, Jeanette Smith died. A Miami-Dade grand jury reindicted the former marine on August 18, 2004. Two days later, Von Zamft filed notice of the state's intention to seek the death penalty. As of this writing, the state trial is still pending, but prosecutor Von Zamft needed no introduction to Hernandez or the Gambino crew. Having prosecuted Roz Vargas for perjury, he knew them all too well.

MDPD detective Roslyn Vargas returned to duty on December 12, 2001, after her conviction was overturned by the Third District Court of Appeal. Six months later, the department held a three-day inquiry into her conduct as a police officer. Everyone agreed that she had been an outstanding police officer until she went undercover and met Neil Napolitano. It was a costly relationship, one that he paid for with his life, while she would now pay for it with her career. On June 26, 2002, Roslyn Vargas was officially terminated by the MDPD. The remarks section of the department's personnel change document was stamped, "Would Not Rehire."

AFTERWORD

At first it looked like a simple story about the death of an aspiring young mobster named Neil Napolitano. He should have slept with the fishes forever, but when his bones washed up on Miami Beach in September 1995, three police agencies—the MDPD, the Miami Beach police, and the FBI—went to work to try to figure out what had happened.

The investigations uncovered a trail of murder and mayhem that left nine people known or presumed dead, ended the once-promising career of Detective Roslyn Vargas, ended the criminal activities of the Gambino crime family's South Florida crew, and sent nine men to prison.

Among them was Anthony "Tony Pep" Trentacosta, described at his trial as "a real-life Tony Soprano." The Gambino capo died at the Federal Bureau of Prisons Medical Center in Butner, North Carolina, on Christmas Day 2005. The cause of death: pancreatic cancer.

Fred Massaro died in prison, too. The man prosecutors called "the direct nexus between the activities of the crew and the members of the Gambino family" succumbed to kidney failure on August 17, 2003. Five months before he died, a federal judge sentenced Massaro to eighteen months for conspiracy to receive the proceeds of extortion from the owner of an Internet porn site, a charge to which Massaro pled guilty.

As of this writing, Ariel Hernandez is in the custody of the Miami-Dade Department of Corrections, awaiting trial on state charges for the murder of Jeanette Smith. In an interview with a reporter from the *Miami New Times*, Hernandez denied he knew Smith before she died: "I didn't know the bitch. I just went to the club to get lucky."

And he proclaimed his innocence. Someone else killed her after he left the motel room to buy cocaine, he said. Hernandez didn't report the murder when he returned because his room was filled with stolen electronic equipment and he was carrying a bag of cocaine. Besides, there was nothing more anyone could do for her. "When a body's dead, it's dead," the former marine told the reporter. As for the phone call in which he informed Massaro that he had a package he needed to dispose of, Hernandez claimed that he was referring to a package of counterfeit checks.

Five members of the crew, Adam Silverman, Julius Bruce Chiusano, Francis Ruggiero, Charles Patrick Monico, and Anthony Raymond Banks, served their time and completed their probations. Carlos Garcia tested positive for cocaine while on probation in January 2005 and went back to jail. He was released on December 21, 2005.

Rocco Napolitano pled guilty and was sentenced to eighteen years in state prison for the murder of Frank Abbandando Jr. I interviewed him at the Moore Haven Correctional Facility in Moore Haven, Florida. I expected a thug but found him articulate, introspective, and remorseful. For more than two hours we talked about his brother, Neil; Neil's relationship with Roz Vargas; and the Gambino crew. Rocco believes that in the last weeks of his life, Neil was sincere when he said that he wanted nothing more to do with the Mob, that he had come to see his gangster pals as "piranhas." Neil, he said, had become disgusted with the life of crime he had been leading and desperately wanted to turn over a new leaf.

As for Roz Vargas, Rocco believes that as far as his brother was concerned, their relationship "began as a game" because "Neil liked to show that he could outsmart the cops" and that the organized crime detective had been providing his brother with information about her squad's investigations. Rocco scoffed when I told him that lawmen found no evidence of that. Roz, he said, must have known that their relationship would have marked Neil for death. "She should have protected him," Rocco declared.

Rocco told me that he gunned down Abbandando not for revenge, but for survival. He believes that Junior was gunning for him because he, like Neil, knew too much and could link the South Florida crew to higher-ups in the Gambino crime family, like the Corozzo brothers.

As for the lawmen, Gary Schiaffo, Tommy Moran, Joe MacMahon, Jerry Brown, Barbara Gentile, and Cynthia Truncale have retired from their respective departments, as has Howe Grover of the FBI. As of this writing, Joe Gross has one more year until he retires. Prosecutor Mary Cagle left the state attorney's office and is currently the director of Children's Legal Services for the Florida Department of Children and Families. Michael Von Zamft is still a prosecutor, a senior trial counsel in the Miami-Dade state attorney's office. He is preparing to prosecute Ariel Hernandez for the murder of Jeanette Smith. Assistant U.S. Attorney Lawrence LaVecchio is still prosecuting gangsters. He is regarded as one of America's foremost Mob busters.

In June 2009, Assistant U.S. Attorney Jeffrey Sloman was named Acting U.S. Attorney for the Southern District of Florida. From his office in downtown Miami, he supervises more than five hundred federal prosecutors and support personnel. A framed photo montage of the gangsters, the lawmen, and the attorneys who were involved in the Gemstone case hangs on the wall of his office. "It was the most interesting case I ever worked on," he says.

The judges—Florida Circuit Court Judge Ronald Dresnick and U.S. District Court Judge Paul C. Huck—are still on the bench, while defense lawyers Joel Kaplan, Steven H. Rosen, Fred Haddad, and Jeffrey Weinkle are still practicing law in South Florida.

As for Roslyn Vargas, the ex-detective still lives in Davie, Florida, with her husband, Julio. I reached out to her twice via letters that I mailed to her home requesting an interview, but Roz didn't respond. I even knocked on her front door, but no one answered. If she had, I would have asked her to reflect on all that had happened since October 1994, when she joined Barbara Gentile's organized crime squad, volunteered to go undercover to gather evidence against the Gambino gangsters, but wound up under the covers with Neil Napolitano instead.

GLOSSARY

ASSOCIATE—Someone affiliated with a Mafia family but not an official member.

BORGATA—Mob slang for crime family.

BUTTON MAN—A Mafia soldier who carries out a murder.

CAPO—The head of a Cosa Nostra crew. Synonyms include captain, skipper, *caporegime*.

CAPO DI FAMIGLIA—The head of a family.

CAPO DI TUTTI CAPO—The boss of all bosses.

COMMISSION—The Mafia's ruling body that was created in 1931 to oversee La Cosa Nostra activities in the United States and Canada.

CONSIGLIERE—An advisor to the boss.

CREW—A group of soldiers and nonmember associates under a capo.

LA COSA NOSTRA—Italian for "our thing" or "this thing of ours."

MADE MAN—A member of La Cosa Nostra who has sworn allegiance to the Mob in an elaborate initiation ceremony.

OMERTÀ—The oath of silence. It forbids divulging information about Mob activities.

RICO—Racketeer Influenced and Corrupt Organizations Act.

SOLDIER—A "made man" member of La Cosa Nostra. Synonyms include friend of ours, goodfella.

STRAIGHTENED OUT—Initiated into La Cosa Nostra.

TRIBUTE—Compensation that mobsters pay to their boss for protection and guidance.

UNDERBOSS—The second in command of a Mafia family.

VIGORISH (VIG)—The interest charged by a loan shark.

WHACK—To murder.

WISEGUYS—Members and nonmember associates of La Cosa Nostra.